THE LIFE AND WRITINGS OF
HUGH HENRY
BRACKENRIDGE

THE LIFE AND WRITINGS OF HUGH HENRY BRACKENRIDGE

By CLAUDE MILTON NEWLIN, Ph.D.

PAUL P. APPEL, *Publisher*

MAMARONECK, N.Y.

1971

Originally Published 1932
Reprinted 1971

Published by Paul P. Appel
by Arrangement With
Princeton University Press

Library of Congress Catalog Card Number 73-162498
SBN 911858-20-2

PREFACE

IN THIS book I have attempted to present an account of the life and writings of our first back-country writer—a man whose experience covered a unique combination of phases of American life during the last years of the colonial period and the first decade of the Republic. His writings give us glimpses of colonial Pennsylvania, of Princeton College, of the Revolution, of frontier society, of Pennsylvania politics, of the Whiskey Insurrection, and of undisciplined democracy. Imbued with a love of Horace when he was a farm boy in a Scotch-Irish settlement, he acquired a further bent toward the classical and satirical literary modes in college. During the Revolution he expressed an ardent and somewhat naïve faith in democracy. Then, having his way to make, he was forced to migrate to the West. Inevitably there was a clash between the individualistic scholar and the levelling frontier. He was a friend of the radical Freneau, an admirer of the French Revolution, and an organizer of Jeffersonian democracy; but he had a critical intelligence and could not permanently follow a party into enthusiastic vagaries. Hence his writings and his personality were deeply marked by his conflict with his environment.

It has seemed to me that an account of Brackenridge's career might throw certain sidelights on areas of American history that have not elsewhere been fully presented in the same combination.

In preparing this study I have been able to use sources that have been only slightly exploited; in some cases they have not previously been used at all. Hence I have used a large number of quotations from this material. I have felt particularly free to use this method with Brackenridge's writings because they are inaccessible and will probably never be reprinted in a collected edition.

The rare books, newspapers, and manuscripts on which this biography is based have been found in a large number of libraries of American universities and historical societies. To the officials of these institutions I am indebted for privileges. Especially I am *grateful to librarians of the Historical Society of Pennsylvania and of the Library of Congress for freely granted permission to quote from manuscripts.* ·

It is pleasant to acknowledge assistance from other workers in American literature and history. I owe especial thanks to Professor Kenneth B. Murdock for encouragement, advice, and criticism given at the time when my study of Brackenridge was in the stage of a doctoral thesis, and to the late Vernon L. Parrington for encouragement at a time when I needed reassurance. My greatest debt is to my wife, Dorothy Hull Newlin, who has brought a trained historical and literary sense to her cooperation in every phase of my task.

C.M.N.

EAST LANSING, MICHIGAN

CONTENTS

CHAPTER I

BOYHOOD—SCOTLAND AND PENNSYLVANIA

IN THE heart of the eighteenth century—that century when the lusty infant Democracy was already beginning to upset the time-honored industrial and social habits of the world— there was born in western Scotland a child who, in time, and on a far frontier, was to prove himself one of Democracy's sanest and wittiest champions. Hugh Henry Brackenridge,[1] the son of William Brackenridge, first opened his eyes on the world in Kintyre near Campbellstown, Scotland, in 1748.

The bracken was green in old Kintyre, and blue heather and yellow gowan covered the hills and dales of Bellivolan Farm. But the land was more fruitful in beauty than in productivity, and life was a stern business there; made sterner, too, by the political and social troubles which racked Scotland during this period, troubles of which the Brackenridge family had borne their share. Hugh's great-grandfather, a M'Donald, a "dead-doing" man, had done valiant service with his claymore at the battle of Killicrankey, under Dundee, and his grandfather, called out in a conscription of feudalists under Argyle, had fallen at the battle of Culloden Moor.[2] Impoverished by the civil wars, and despairing of improving his condition at home, William Brackenridge turned to the New World to rehabilitate his fortunes, and in 1753,[3] when Hugh Henry was five years old, the family embarked for Pennsylvania, a microcosm in that great Celtic migration of the eighteenth century

[1] He was apparently christened "Hugh Montgomery," a name which he retained until 1781 when he substituted "Henry" as his middle name.

[2] H. H. Brackenridge, *Modern Chivalry* (edition of 1819), Vol. II, p. 358.

[3] H. M. Brackenridge, *Biographical Notice of H. H. Brackenridge*, in *Modern Chivalry* (edition of 1856), p. 159; and *Southern Literary Messenger*, Vol. VIII, p. 1.

which gave to the American colonies their first real frontiersmen.[4]
The journey, in that day, was costly, even when the strictest
economies were practised, and when the Brackenridges reached
Philadelphia they were obliged to sell even their surplus clothing
before they could continue on their way to the West.[5] A thrifty,
staunch-hearted folk, whose sturdy individualism was sustained
by the ideal of religious and political democracy fostered by the
Scottish Church, they faced their new life, penniless and empty-
handed, perhaps, but little the worse for that.

Like most others of their race and class they had to pass beyond
the older settlements in order to find cheap land. They leased a
farm in the southern end of York County—a district which came
to be known by the suggestive name of "The Barrens."[6] York
County, which had been established in 1749, was a frontier community. The Susquehanna River, the eastern boundary of the
county, had until recently been the officially recognized limit of settlement.[7] By the time the Brackenridges arrived, a Scotch-Irish
settlement had already been formed on the Barrens—a settlement
of the type that was growing up in scores of back-country districts
from New York to South Carolina. Among the pioneers, hardy
axemen inured to rocky soil, hard labor, and Calvinistic doctrine,
the Scottish farmer and his family no doubt found themselves
quite at home.

Life in the settlement was a stubborn fight with hardwood trees
and a soil of short-lived fertility, with the constant dread of Indian
attack to add a seasoning of danger. Possibly Hugh's lifelong
hatred of the Indians was generated during the months of terror
that followed General Braddock's defeat in 1755.[8]

The frontier environment offered much to interest a growing
boy of Hugh's quick intelligence and keen curiosity. There were
strange birds and beasts to amaze the child from another land;
the streams invited the construction of waterwheels and dams;

[4] These memories of Brackenridge's early boyhood he embodied in an *Epistle
to Walter Scott*. This poem, written in 1811, is the only source of information
for this period of his life.

[5] *Biographical Notice*, p. 151.   [6] *ibid.*

[7] John Gibson, *History of York County*, p. 23.   [8] *ibid.*, pp. 101-2.

playhouses could be built of the chips that fell from the blows of
the axe as the forest gave way before the steady advance of the
clearing.[9] But the struggle with soil and forest must be a family
affair with the Brackenridges as with other pioneers,[10] and Hugh,
however reluctant, was soon called from his childish dreams and
pastimes to take his place behind the plough. Years later he described with zest a serio-comic memory of these boyhood days.

> When of an age to ca' the pleugh,
> My father used to say "Gae Huoch,
> And louse the horses frae the tether,
> It's time to yoke." Without a swither,
> I bided biding, but mayhap,
> Just leke a man that's ta'en a cap,
> I doiter'd, minding what I saw,
> More than the orders; ah, fou' fau'!
> A bird's nest or a beastie's bed,
> Aft turn'd me frae the gate I gaed;
> Mare, when I saw the thing itsel,
> And ran to catch it by the tail,
> As ance a thing just leke a cat,
> I saw, and what wa'd I be at,
> But try to grip it, a wild pousie
> And bring it hame to catch a mousie.
> Before I knew what I was doing,
> Or mischief that the thing was brewing,
> A spout o' water frae its tail
> Came on me: O the smell, the smell.
>
> As fast as I could lift a heel,
> Ran hame, and said the muckle deel,
> Or some war thing, alang the fence,
> Had drain'd its bags at my expence,
> And rais'd a funk, and made me wet—
> They ca'd it something, I forget
> That strones upon a man and dog,
> That tries to take it by the lug,

9 H. H. Brackenridge, *Law Miscellanies*, p. iii.
10 *Biographical Notice*, p. 151.

And leaves a scent about the place:
That it behoved to change my claes;
Sae stripp'd me o' my sark and trouse,
And hung them out to get the dews,
And bade me tak' mare care again,
And keep frae things I did na ken.[11]

This verse shows certainly that Hugh's heart was not in the work of reclaiming the soil. Luckily for this boy whose nature was already urging him toward the intellectual rather than the active life, opportunities for education were not lacking even on this far frontier. In spite of their hard and narrow life, the settlers clung tenaciously to their religious and intellectual ideals. Before 1750 a school was maintained in the First Presbyterian Church, a log building at the confluence of Scott's Run and Muddy Creek.[12] Other elementary schools were established as other churches were organized, and eventually a classical school was opened in the Slate Ridge church in Peach Bottom Township, where the Bracken-ridges lived.[13]

For all his poverty, William Brackenridge "neglected no opportunity in his power of giving his children the best education."[14] And Hugh, on his part, took full advantage of every opportunity offered him. In the country school he soon attracted attention by his zeal and aptitude for learning; indeed, the teacher complained that his unusual progress discouraged the other pupils. In the Slate Ridge school he first discovered and learned to love the classics,[15] and this love bore immediate fruit in a vigorous effort to master the ancient languages. A friendly clergyman of the neighborhood offered lessons in exchange for help with chores, and by the time Hugh was thirteen he was well grounded in Latin and had acquired some knowledge of Greek. So we may picture the growing boy, still in the first fervor of his classical enthusiasm, chanting the Odes of Horace in the fragrant dusk of the cattle-shed, while the

[11] *Tree of Liberty,* June 20, 1801.
[12] John Gibson, *History of York County,* p. 360.
[13] *ibid.,* pp. 360, 402.   [14] *Biographical Notice,* p. 152.
[15] John Gibson, *History of York County,* p. 360.

milk drummed into the pail; and we may feel, too, his grief and despair when the precious volume of Horace, left on a nearby stump while its owner labored in the fields, was "chewed up" by an all too "literary cow"—a loss so great that its hurt was never forgotten.[16] So deep, indeed, was the impression which the classics made upon Hugh that, from his boyhood to the end of his life, they formed the pattern for much of his thinking. They colored at once his attitude toward the homely necessary toil involved in turning forest into farm. Always repugnant, no doubt, it now took on almost the semblance of sacrilege to one who dreamed of dryads in every tree, and nymphs and fauns in stream and thicket.

> Soon after this I gaed to Latin:
> And read a buke, I kenna what in,
> That talk'd o' things that whir in bushes,
> Dryads, Hamadryads, Muses,
> On tops o' hills wad sing leke Mavies,
> And in the shady woods, and cavies,
> Thought I, it maun be this vile clearing,
> And grubbing up the trees, and bleering,
> And burning brush and making fences,
> That scares these things out o' their senses;
> And drives them frae our fields and patches;
> For who sees any, now or catches,
> A moor-land deity or Nymphy,
> That roosts in trees, or wades in lymphy?
> Or hears a musy in the thicket,
> Just as you wad hear a cricket?
> May be in places farther back,
> The vestige may na be sae slack;
> Where woods are green and country new,
> The breed may yet remain, a few,
> May sing to mak' our spirits glow.[17]

Hugh's attitude toward the daily tasks in which his help was so sorely needed might well have caused friction in a less understanding family, and certainly there must have been times when William

16 *Biographical Notice*, p. 152.
17 *Tree of Liberty*, June 20, 1801.

Brackenridge's patience wore thin. But Hugh had a staunch supporter in his mother, whose pride in her brilliant son knew no bounds, and to both these simple pioneers, love of learning spelled a vocation for the ministry; they already looked forward to the attainment of the supreme Scottish joy of having a son in the Church.[18]

Hugh's quest for learning soon exhausted the resources of the Barrens settlement. Fortunately there was, at Fagg's Manor in Chester County, thirty miles to the east, a classical school of some note. The master was the Rev. John Blair, who was soon to be appointed Professor of Divinity and Moral Philosophy at Princeton College.[19] On Saturday nights Hugh walked the thirty miles to Fagg's Manor to borrow books and newspapers, returning to his farm work on Monday morning. He no doubt received some instruction also on these visits, and there is a vague reference to his having been a pupil at Fagg's Manor school.[20] To perfect his work in mathematics, a subject which was and always remained troublesome and uninteresting to him, he made a bargain with another youth of the community to exchange lessons in the classics for mathematical instruction.[21]

One who had shown so little taste for farm labor and such a vigorous appetite for knowledge could not, of course, be satisfied to remain one of the great host of Scotch and Scotch-Irish farmers. Hugh's first move for a better environment was to apply for a place as teacher in a free school at Gunpowder Falls, Maryland, just across the southern boundary line of Pennsylvania. Since he was only fifteen years old, "the trustees were not less surprised at the application than by the qualifications of the applicant; and after some hesitation gave him the place."[22]

[18] *Biographical Notice*, p. 152.
[19] John Maclean, *History of the College of New Jersey*, Vol. I, p. 292.
[20] In the course of a newspaper controversy in Pittsburgh in 1787 the Rev. S. Barr wrote: "If I am not mistaken I heard one of them say the letter was from Fagg's Manor, the place where Lawyer Brackenridge received the first rudiments of his education." *Pittsburgh Gazette*, June 30, 1787. See also H. M. Brackenridge, *Biographical Notice*, p. 152.
[21] *Biographical Notice*, p. 152.   [22] *ibid.*, p. 152

Confronted in this typical district school with the unruly sons of the frontier, many of them older and brawnier than he, Hugh had the chance—was, indeed, faced with the necessity—of proving his mettle. No doubt the fifteen-year-old schoolmaster was a joke to these thick-headed, tough-muscled rustics, to be boisterously laughed at for a few days, and then to be laughed out. But, as it turned out, the laugh was on them, for at the first attempt to defy his authority, the teacher seized "a brand from the fire, knocked the rebel down, and spread terror around him." The bullies appealed to authority, as bullies will. "An investigation was the consequence; and Hugh was confirmed in his office with honour."[23]

It was during this period at Gunpowder Falls that, "on one occasion, he shut up his school for a few days to attend a celebrated trial for murder at Annapolis." When he heard the eloquence of the lawyer, Jenning, he determined that he too would be an orator. It may well be that there was born at this time the first uneasy doubt, whether, after all, the bar might not offer a better chance for glory than the pulpit.

Hugh remained at Gunpowder Falls "until he had exhausted the sources of learning near him; and his thirst for knowledge urged him to seek more copious streams."[24] The search led him to Princeton College.

[23] *ibid.*, p. 152.
[24] *ibid.*, p. 153.

CHAPTER II

PRINCETON COLLEGE

PRINCETON College was founded in 1746 to perpetuate sound learning and Presbyterianism in the middle colonies. When Brackenridge presented himself at the school in 1768, a new president, Dr. John Witherspoon, had just arrived from Scotland. Under his vigorous administration the small provincial institution soon became one of the most important intellectual forces in the colonies.

To the colonial youth of the day, especially to those from the rural districts, the college must have seemed delightfully cosmopolitan. One of Brackenridge's fellow students wrote of it in 1772:

I have an Oppertunity in some small Degree of acquainting myself with Mankind, by observing the Conduct & Temper of the Students in this Seminary: Which is filled with Young-Men not only from almost every Province, in this Continent; But we have also many from the West-Indies, & some few from *Europe*. So that from the Difference in their early Education, their Manner is extremely different, which makes our Observations on them both agreeable & profitable.[1]

Upon this heterogeneous student body there was imposed the usual strict discipline of the time. From morning prayers to half-past five there was a steady routine of religious services, recitations, declamations, and study periods.[2] Tutors, and even the august president himself, were accustomed to swoop down unexpectedly on the students' quarters during study hours. But youthful spirits could not be wholly repressed, and occasionally such naïve amusements as stealing chickens and rolling cannon balls in the college halls demanded faculty action.[3]

The course of study was largely classical, but far from being narrow. The subjects were thus outlined by Dr. Witherspoon in 1772:

[1] P. V. Fithian, *Journal and Letters*, p. 16.   [2] *ibid.*, pp. 7-9.   [3] *ibid.*, p. 18.

In the first year they read Latin and Greek, with Roman and Grecian antiquities, and Rhetoric. In the second, continuing the study of the languages, they learn a complete system of geography, with the use of the globes, the first principles of philosophy, and the elements of mathematical knowledge. The third, though the languages are not wholly omitted, is chiefly employed in mathematics and natural philosophy. And the senior year is employed in reading the higher classics, proceeding in the mathematics and natural philosophy. In addition to these, the President gives lectures to the juniors and seniors, which consequently, every student hears twice over in his course,—first upon chronology and history, and afterwards upon composition and criticism. He also taught the French language last winter, and it will continue to be taught to those who desire to learn it.

During the whole course of their studies, the three younger classes, two every evening formerly, and now three, because of their increased number, pronounce an oration, on the stage erected for that purpose in the hall, immediately after prayers; that they may learn, by early habit, presence of mind and proper pronunciation and gesture in public speaking. This excellent practice, which has been kept up almost from the first foundation of the College, has had the most admirable effects. The senior scholars, every five or six weeks, pronounce orations of their own composition, to which all persons of any note in the neighborhood are invited or admitted.[4]

This curriculum was, in general, admirably suited to the taste of the boy who had searched for dryads in the shady woods and had read Horace on winter nights by the light of the blazing embers, and in the open fields under the summer sun. Mathematics continued to give him trouble, but he excelled in "belles lettres and general literature; in languages, philosophy, moral science, and ethics."[5] The oratorical exercises in the college hall were to him glorious occasions. "In wit and eloquence he stood unequalled. He could reason well, had a fine voice, a fine person, and an eagle eye."[6] His skill in the composition of speeches soon came to be so well known as to be often in demand when fellow-students wished to shine with the lustre of borrowed oratory. No doubt it proved a most valuable talent to a boy whose pockets must have had scant

4 John Maclean, *History of the College of New Jersey*, Vol. I, p. 362.
5 *Biographical Notice*, p. 153.   6 *ibid.*

lining of cash. It is recorded that on one occasion when he had produced a particularly eloquent address for vicarious delivery, he was rewarded by the grateful orator with a handsome suit of clothes and a smart cocked hat.[7]

The formative influences to which Brackenridge was being subjected at college were rapidly stamping their imprint on his thought and diction. The lectures on political science at once made a deep impression on his receptive mind. Dr. Witherspoon, holding Locke's "compact" theory of government, taught that the purpose of the social union "should be the protection of liberty, as far as it is a blessing."[8] Brackenridge, drinking in these words, was absorbing the doctrine that was to dominate his own political thinking.

In his lectures on rhetoric Dr. Witherspoon pointed to the Queen Anne men as models.

Of modern authors in our own language, Mr. Addison is a noble pattern of elegance, dignity and simplicity. Swift in his political pieces, writes with great strength and force, and is perhaps a pattern of stile, which has scarcely been exceeded since his time. . . . I cannot help here cautioning you against one modern author of some eminence, Johnson, the author of the Rambler. He is so stiff and abstracted in his manner and such a lover of hard words, that he is the worst pattern for young persons that can be named.[9]

A score of years later, Brackenridge echoed these ideas in his own best work.[10]

Of the classical authors whom he studied during his Princeton days, he acknowledged having been especially influenced by the Greek satirist Lucian. As he read the difficult language slowly, the turn of Lucian's thought became firmly fixed in his mind and eventually induced a satirical taste and habit.[11]

The two literary clubs, the Whig and Cliosophic, which were organized while Brackenridge was at Princeton, offered a decided

[7] *Biographical Notice*, p. 153.
[8] John Witherspoon, *Lectures on Moral Philosophy*, in *Works* (Philadelphia, 1802), Vol. III, p. 419.
[9] *ibid.*, Vol. IV, p. 193.
[10] *Modern Chivalry* (edition of 1926), pp. 97,202.
[11] *ibid.*, p. 97.

stimulus to his literary development. The Whig society was formed on June 24, 1769, under the leadership of Brackenridge, Philip Freneau, James Madison, and William Bradford.[12] The Whigs and the Cliosophians, or Tories, were of course rivals, and their disputes sometimes took the form of "paper wars" in which wits were matched in satires and squibs. The contributions of Brackenridge, Freneau, Madison, and Bradford[13] to the "paper war" of 1770 form a series of crude poems entitled *Satires against the Tories. Written in the last War between the Whigs and Cliosophians in which the former obtained a compleat Victory.*[14]

Brackenridge found this battle of wits a glorious occasion for exercising his satirical talent. His ten poems no doubt contributed materially to the "compleat victory" of the Whigs even if they did not add notably to the enrichment of American literature. He thus addressed the penmen of the rival society:

> What madness, friends, has seiz'd your minds
> To write like fools of various kinds?
> The Muse, I fear, that med'ling jade,
> Has tempted each to leave his trade
> And bellows forth to our surprize
> The tempest of a thousand lies.
> Ye Gods! What pitiful pretence!
> What vile unheard of impudence!
> What Daemon from the realms of night
> Has bid your glowing poets write?
> Bards that could lately weild a goose[15]
> Or make a coat sit tight and spruce
> Or skil'd in each mechanic art
> To geld a sow or drive a cart.
> And is it not a pretty story

[12] C. R. Williams, *The Cliosophic Society*, p. 4; and F. L. Pattee, *The Poems of Philip Freneau*, Introduction, Vol. I, pp. xvi-xvii.

[13] Bradford was Brackenridge's roommate. See *Incidents of the Western Insurrection*, Vol. III, p. 143.

[14] These poems are extant in a manuscript notebook which formerly belonged to William Bradford and is now in the possession of the Historical Society of Pennsylvania.

[15] "Phelps and Warford, both taylors and champions of the Tory cause." Brackenridge's note.

That these should strive to blast our Glory
Who ne'er before would dare to mention
Our names with any base intention.
A Whig was once their greatest dread,
When he approach'd they shriek'd and fled,
His very visage struck with awe,
And made them tremble when they saw.
Yes—late they carried such a face
And such again shall be the case
As.sure as rhime & verse can flow
Or Pluto waits for them below.
And by the stars that gild the skies
I'll lose my hands and ears & eyes
But what I'll stop this whining Cub
And timely knock down Belzebub.[16]

The butt of several of Brackenridge's satires was a luckless student named Spring, whose literary efforts seem especially to have called forth the biting sarcasm of the Whigs. In *Spring's Soliloquy* the unsuccessful author is made to say:

What is this College? 'Tis a den
Of wicked boys and scribbling men.
What shall I do? I cannot write,
Well then I'll challenge them to fight.
. . . I fail in sense,
But with my fists I'll make defence,
For if at this time I remember
'Twas on the middle of December
I put a stop to Whiggish writing
By roaring, snoring, swearing, fighting.
Perceiving on our side the failure
I sally'd forth and collar'd Taylor
And thus again I'll play the bully
With hands so hard & head so woolly.[17]

In *Spring's Adventures* we see a Princeton student striving to appear a man of the world:

[16] *Satires against the Tories*, p. 34 in Ms. Am. 0336, Historical Society of Pennsylvania.
[17] *ibid.*, p. 13.

To Philadelphia now we travel
T'expose the weakness of the Devil.
With his old coat and Sunday Jacket
And all his money in his pocket
He paid his Grog and out he sally'd,
With store of dumplins in his wallet.
He cleared his way thro' dogs and taylors
And fought with oisterwives & sailors,
And now in town at length arrived
The following tricks he there atchieved.
On state affairs with rapture bent
First to the coffee-house he went
And enter'd into learn'd discourses
In which his judgment's like a Horse's.
There, after many a wretched blunder,
He shut his mouth and so knocked under.
Some pity'd him and thought perchance
He was one of the bankrupt merchants
Who had obtain'd 'mongst ale-house critics
Some small smattering in Politicks.[18]

Brackenridge also made sport of Spring's political satires. In *Spring's Confession* the wretched youth is made to say:

I will declare, for all must know it,
I long have strove to be a poet.
Besides this sin, alas, God knows,
I've wrote some dirty things in prose.
Yes, I remember, 'twas in Boston
I put some tawdry rhimes a post-on
About the Stamp act they were written,
How we were by Europeans bitten.
I thought by this means to have glory
In annals of immortal story.
But every one of those past on
Rais'd up a shout, went off and laughed on.
That bard, said they, design'd to tickle us,
And makes himself appear ridiculous.
Nay, Boston's sons were much enrag'd
To find such vermin had engag'd

[18] *ibid.*, p. 20.

To vent their balderdash among 'em
And had they found 'em would have hung 'em,
Or plunge them in a puddle souse
Or stuff them in an office house.[19]

Beneath the roistering foolery of these juvenile satires the reader may already sense the looming shadow of stirring events to come. Spring, in the coffee houses of Philadelphia, joined in the heated discussions of affairs of state; in Boston he wrote "tawdry rhymes" against the Stamp Act. The time was coming, all too soon, when paper wars were to give way to the grim reality, but happily these carefree sons of Old Nassau could not know this as they penned their biting diatribes among the peaceful academic shades of the little college town.

Meanwhile it may be noted that Brackenridge has begun what is to be a lifelong habit of conducting the disputes in which we shall find him so constantly involved through the medium of satirical verse.

[19] *Satires against the Tories,* p. 17 in Ms. Am. 0336, Historical Society of Pennsylvania.

CHAPTER III

"FATHER BOMBO'S PILGRIMAGE"

I T WAS in September 1770, at the end of his Junior year in college, that Brackenridge first undertook the writing of prose fiction. In collaboration with Freneau, he wrote *Father Bombo's Pilgrimage to Mecca, wherein is given a true account of the innumerable and surprizing adventures which befell him in the course of that long and tedious journey. Till he once more returned safe to his native Land as related by his own mouth.* Whether or not this fantastic tale was ever completed is not known. Only a fragment, labelled "Volume II," has been preserved in the Bradford notebook.[1] Of this the first section, designated as "Book III, Chapter I" is from Brackenridge's pen. Ludicrous and exaggerated as the story is, it deserves attention since it is the earliest example of American prose fiction, and since, too, it foreshadows certain features of Brackenridge's later narrative writing. His contribution is as follows:

Dear and worthy brethren!

The name of the French Captain who took the Commodore was Monsieur de Pivot. He appeared to me to be a very brave and worthy Gentleman, and I began to promise myself some happy days in the sunshine of his favor. For, as he was an extravagant lover of the polite arts, I became a very acceptable prisoner to him, as he found me to be a great connoisseur in the various parts, branches, and systems of moral philosophy as it is taught in all the learned nations of Europe. He frequently applied to me for instructions whereby he might regulate his conduct in life.

But all my fine hopes were soon blasted by a surprizing instance of the ups and downs of Fortune. For as the Captain and I were walking on deck the same evening on which we left the Kommodore, one of the

---

[1] Ms. Am. 0336, Historical Society of Pennsylvania. The story has not hitherto appeared in print. In the manuscript the punctuation is primitive and there is no paragraphing. In order to make it readable I have "edited" the fragment to the extent of adding modern punctuation and paragraphing.

Sailors from the round Top called out to the Captain that he spied a sail on the Larboard bow making towards us.

"Zounds," said the Captain, "it is one of the Enemy," and immediately gave orders to clear the Decks, throw the hencoops overboard, and have the Guns in readiness.

By the Time this was performed, the Enemy, who proved to be an Irish privateer, gave us a broadside. Monsieur de Pivot, standing on the quarter Deck in ten or twelve coils of the Kable, gave orders with great alacrity and courage.

Here I found myself in a miserable plight, for should I seem to act the Coward on the present occasion, my fate would be unavoidably fixed if the Frenchman gained the Victory; but if I fought Gallantly and suffered myself to play the Hero, I would be treated as a prisoner if the privateer should conquer. I therefore resolved to steer a mean between both, for according to that wise Philosopher Ovid, "in medio tutissimus ibis," The midway is the best.

Accordingly, while the Privateer was at some distance, I thought proper to assume an air of Fortitude and valour, and after that shape my Fortune according to the day. Now, taking off my Wigg, I swang it round in the air and gave the men three cheers.

"Courage, my Boys," said I, "the day is ours !"

Monsieur de Pivot, beholding my courage and Bravery, commended me to the skies and promised me advancement in Life according to the Services I should perform that day. But now, the Kannon of the other ship beginning to rain a shower of winged messengers upon us, I thought it the most prudent method to withdraw, least my pious resolution should be nipt in the bud by an immature death. So [I went], whispering to the officer who stood next me that I would just run down into the Kabbin and drink a Glass of Rum & gunpowder and come up again as courageous and bold as a Lion. But, however, I was not the fool to return so suddenly as I pretended, but waited there till I could find how the play was going above.

In a short time the Irishman boarded us and began to carry all before them, and upon hearing Monsieur de Pivot call out, "Strike the Flag, the day is lost !" I made down through a Trap door into the hold, and there wrapping myself in an old Fishing Net, I so entangled myself in it that I seemed to have been fast bound like a prisoner. There I lay struggling and Groaning, and making the most piteous Lamentation, when the Privateer men came down to search the Vessel.

Upon seizing me, one of them called out to his Comrade, "Arrah, Dear Bryan, here is the Divil!"

"Oh No," replied I, speaking in a very hoarse and hollow voice, "I am an Irishman, a countryman of your own. My name is Reynold McDonald. I was taken by these accursed Frenchmen about seven days agoe, and here they have kept me in this vile Dungeon, from the Light of the Sun, Moon, and Stars, without a drop of Drink, or a bit of victuals to cross my troat, so that I am almost famished to death with Hunger."

"Ah, dear O'Donnel, then," said the Irishman, "rise up and come away and by Shaint Patrick you shall fare as well as any one of us, for we have taken da vessel."

"Arra, my Shewel," quoth I, "I might as well fly away with de ship tro' de air as to get out of dese Ropes wid which I am bound."

"Arra, my Honey, den," said the Irishman, "I will cut them open with my Gully!" Upon this, opening his knife, he cut the Net from around me and set me at Liberty.

Pretending to be worn out with Famine and ill usage, I clambered to deck with my hands and Feet. I saluted the Teagues as my deliverers and my Friends. They indeed treated me very kindly, and when the French vessel was ready to be dismissed—for Monsieur de Pivot had ransomed her with the very same money he received from the Commodore—I say, when this was done I was put on board the Irish privateer, which hoisted sail that evening and stood away for the North of Ireland.

For several days after the Battle I entertained them with a Relation of the cruel Usage I received from the Frenchman. "Not a day passed," said I, "but I was hauled up to the Halyards to recieve [sic] four and thirty Lashes with the Ropes End."

"Arra, but," said Nus McSwine, the fellow that found me, "did you not tell me you neither saw Sun, Moon, nor Stars the whole time you were prisoner? I tought by day you had never been out of de hold at all."

"Very true," replied I, "neither did I see de light of the blessed Day, for tho' I was hoisted up on deck, they took care to have my wig drawn over my face and braced round mine head wid a piece of a Tarpaulin, so that I could neither see nor hear, no more than if I had been at the bottom of the Sea."

By this time the Captain of the Privateer, whose name was Lachlin

MacSwooly, heard of me, and, coming to see me, asked where I was born.

I answered him, "In Canickfugus." For tho' this was far from being the truth, yet I found it the most probable method to curry Favour in the present situation of my affairs.

"Arra, then," said he, "you are a brave Irish Boy."

"In truth, I am," answered I, "and it is no wonder if I don't speak my own country Dialect as I left it when I was a boy, and have never been there since."

"Ah, h, h," said he, "that's a great pity. But you shall be kindly used by us, and if you go along wid us in the privateer way you shall share in our Fortune. And if you are anything of a Scholar you have a chance to be advanced to some office when we return from our cruise."

"Scholar!" said I, "I am a most profound Scholar. I have learned Navigation, Astronomy, Astrology, and all the occult Sciences with the greatest attention. I can tell you the names of the Seven Planets and count you all the stars from the Tropics to the Tartric Circles. I know the names of the Twelve Constellations of the Zodiac and the Times of the risings of Orion and the bear star."

The Kaptain by this time began to stare at me as a prodigy, for these sublime Sentences were the same as Latin to him. Upon this, all the sailors came crowding about me, and set themselves to Listen with their mouths and Ears wide open, for the word had gone out among them that I was a man of wonderful Scholarship.

"Yes, Gentlemen," continued I, "I have had opportunities of knowing a great deal. I was put to School when I was young to the best masters in the kingdom. I have since travelled thro' the whole world. I have conversed with the Mufti of the Persians, the Bramin of India, the Mandarines of China, The Musselman of Turkey, and the priests of Busiris in Egypt. Twas there I received this wigg which you now see me wear. Some of them told me it sprang from the mud of the River Nile, enlivened by the prolific heat of the Sun; others again told me that it was the Wigg which Noah wore in the ark and which Saint Patric consecrated on the head of Ptolemy Philopater Seventeen hundred years ago. This Staff which I carry in my hand I recieved [sic] when I was at Rome from Pope Urban, who told me it was the very Staff which the Patriarch had when he travelled to Padanaram. These books which you see in my Wallet are of a religious kind. These"—showing them my Dictionaries—"contain the History of St. Crosten. This,"—showing them my Lucian—"is the Life of St.

Patrick. This,"—pulling out my Xenophon—"contains a sett of Ave Marias wrote in Latin and a copy of indulgencies which I received from the Pope's own hand."

When I had finished my Harrangue, the Captain treated me with the greatest respect, invited me down into the Cabbin, and having furnished me with an Elegant Supper, then asking me very politely if I was for Bed, I answered in the Affirmative.

"Patrick O'Konnel," said he, "Conduct this Gentleman to your birth in the steerage and lay him down by your Messmate Carney McGuire, and do you shift for yourself a night."

The Fellow conducted me to the Birth, but went away Grumbling, very much displeased to be so turned out of his birth. And I confess it was something hard for him, for as I understood afterwards, he was obliged to lay all night in a coil of the Cable Rope. This circumstance, small and trifling as may seem at first, proved the source of my future disasters, for the fellow, beyond measure enraged, spared no pains to signify by nods and whispers to his Messmates that he did not like my appearance.

"I am much mistaken," said he, "if he is not a Wizzard conjurer or something worse. I was troubled all night long," continued he, "with something running up and down the Ropes and strange noises in the bow and stern of the Ship." Then, nodding his head, he seemed to signify that he knew more than he would discover at that time. Hereupon they all began to hint that they had likewise seen something, least they should seem behind hand in sagacity and penetration.

"By my Troth," says one, "when I got up very Early this morning I saw a crow on the Topmast as big as my head, though I did not care to speak of it before."

"Upon my Faath," said another, "I saw two Hares run through the scuttle holes of the Ship. I tought den dey were rats, but now I find dey were Hares."

"If that is the Case," says a third, "and I verily believe it is, we must take care what we do with him. Last night I saw something on the prow of the ship in the Shape of a woman, which I took to be Sheelah, the Wife of Neal Ogen, the Kook. Now, in Troth, I could take my oath it was a witch. But, as I say, let us take care what we do with him, for if we were to throw him overboard he would blow up a Storm which would sink us to the Bottom."

"Ay, Faith, and that's true," replied another. "For I remember when Sheelah Mochklonnikhan with two or three more Witches raised a whirlwind and carried away an Oat Stack of my Father's, and did much more mischief to the country by Elve shooting the cows, and bewitching the people of the Neighborhood till Tuccan O'Klarty shot her with a pair of silver buttons."

"Let Donnel O'Loyd, immediately, then," said they, "acquaint the Captain that the man who he took for a priest we have found to be a Wizzard."

The mate having told the Kaptain the report of the Sailors, and added a great deal more to it—that he had seen me all night long up among the shrouds, sometimes hauling and reefing the sails, & at other times dancing like a witch out on the waves with his Wigg in his hand —"Egad," says the captain, "if that is the case keep a good look out after him and order him not to stir out of the Steerage on peril of his Life."

When I received this command, I found it was most expedient to obey it, for it was in vain to persuade them to any thing else but that I was a Wizzard. I had unluckily forgot my Wallet above Deck, not daring to venture on, myself. They resolved to wreck their fury on it, thinking they should destroy as much of my power as was contained in the books. Accordingly they burnt them, to my unspeakable Grief and mortification.

Here I was obliged to lye in a miserable plight for some days, none daring to come near to fetch me victuals, nor durst I venture out myself. For the Captain had Sworn if I did he would shoot me with a silver Bullet. In the mean time by long Fasting a violent cholic came upon me. I wreathed myself to and fro and Groaned most wofully, for indeed I was in extreme misery. The Sailors, overhearing me, fancied that they heard me pronouncing strange and uncouth expressions, and were firmly persuaded that I was about to call up a Ghost or raise a Spirit.

About this Time a Gale happened to spring up. "Ay, Fa-ath," says one, "now it comes we'll go to the Bottom presently. Something must be done."

There happening to be an old French priest on board, it was agreed to call for him to put a stop to the impending destruction. The priest, coming with a piggin of holy water, threw the half of it down the Hatchway on my Face. I was in the mean time in the greatest misery, not much regarding them. But what even at that time gave me some concern was this, that one of the Sailors, putting down a Fish Gigg, drew up my Wigg and consumed it along with my books.

The Storm still increasing, they began to be terribly afraid. The Kaptain, sometimes threatening me, at other times with fair Words, strove to persuade me to call down the storm, but it was all in vain, for had I been never so inclined, 'twas not in my power to do it. Finding now, as they imagined, that I was deaf to all their intreaties, they thought proper to throw me overboard. Accordingly, hoisting me up with a Block and Tackle, they lowered me down into a Tobacco hogshead, and the Cooper immediately heading it up and clapping on three Iron hoops, they tossed me into the ocean. Here I rolled, as Martin says in his philosophy, obsequious to the Waves and swelling Tides.

After a long time I found myself at rest on some shore, and knocking out the bung, I saw two men coming down towards me. By their voices I knew them to be Irishmen.

"Arra, Dennis," says one of them, "I'll lay a Groat yonder is a hogshead of onions or potatoes coming from some wreck!"

"Arra, by my Troth," says the other, "I believe it is."

And now, being come up, they hoisted up the hogshead on one end, and concluded it was about half full. Then, knocking out the end, they made way for me, and taking me, I suppose, for a witch, took to the Hills. I followed them to some distance, endeavoring to persuade them that I was a man, but having got up into the mountains, they were lost to my view.

I now found myself, my dear brethren, in the North of Ireland without house or home, books to read, or a Wigg to my head. But the manner in which I behaved and the adventures which befel me among the Wild Irish shall be the Subject of the Ensuing Chapter.

This was the last chapter written by Brackenridge. But we shall find, twenty years later, in *Modern Chivalry,* the same preoccupation with Irish character and dialect, the same facile but undisciplined imagination, and the same boisterous humor that distinguished this early picaresque tale of Father Bombo.

CHAPTER IV

"THE RISING GLORY OF AMERICA"

THE writings preserved from Brackenridge's Junior year show only the humorous and satirical side of his nature. No doubt his college themes and orations were solemn pronouncements on weighty subjects. At any rate his commencement parts, recited at graduation on September 25, 1771, were sufficiently serious, and clearly show the influence of his devotion to classical literature and to politics. As salutatorian he greeted the audience with a Latin oration entitled *De Societate Hominum,* and near the end of the program he recited a poem on *The Rising Glory of America,* which was "received with great applause."[1]

This poem was written by Brackenridge and Freneau in collaboration. Brackenridge "confessed that on his part it was a task of labour, while the verse of his associate flowed spontaneously."[2] The piece, which was published in Philadelphia in 1772, is not without signs of promise for both its authors. In form, it is a dialogue in blank verse, but, as Professor Pattee has noted, it is epic in content and inspiration.[3] The young poets were seriously trying to find in their own American colonial world material fit for the grand style inspired by Virgil and Milton.

After naming Memphis, Alexandria, Greece, Athens, Macedonia, Rome, and Britain as standard epic themes, they rejected them as being antiquated. They then sketched briefly the discovery of America, the settlement and the French and Indian War, and celebrated the greatness of American agriculture, commerce, and science.

[1] The commencement program, as reported in a contemporary newspaper, is printed in John Maclean, *History of the College of New Jersey,* Vol. I, pp. 312-13.
[2] *Biographical Notice,* p. 153.
[3] *The Poems of Philip Freneau,* Introduction, Vol. I, pp. ci-ciii.

The last third of the poem is a prophecy, most of it written by Brackenridge.[4] The college seer, then twenty-two years old, was full of roseate hopes for the future of civilization in the American colonies.

> And here fair freedom shall forever reign.
> I see a train, a glorious train appear,
> Of patriots plac'd in equal fame with those
> Who nobly fell for Athens or for Rome.
> . . .   .
>
> 'Tis but the morning of the world with us
> And Science yet but sheds her orient rays.
> I see the age, the happy age roll on
> Bright with the splendours of her mid-day beams,
> I see a Homer and a Milton rise
> In all the pomp and majesty of song,
> Which gives immortal vigour to the deeds
> Atchiev'd by Heroes in the fields of fame.[5]
> . . .   .
>
> This is thy praise, America, thy pow'r
> Thou best of climes, by science visited,
> By freedom blest and richly stor'd with all
> The luxuries of life. Hail happy land,
> The seat of empire, the abode of kings,
> The final stage where time shall introduce
> Renowned characters, and glorious works
> Of high invention and of wond'rous art
> Which not the ravages of time shall waste
> Till he himself has run his long career.[6]

So, devoted to liberty and to learning, and imbued with patriotic ardor, Brackenridge proceeded Bachelor of Arts. After his graduation he remained at the college for another year as master of

---

[4] It is possible to identify with some degree of accuracy the parts composed by Brackenridge, since Freneau reprinted his own part separately, with some changes and additions, in 1786 and again in 1806.

[5] *Poems of Philip Freneau*, ed. by F. L. Pattee, Vol. I, p. 78.

[6] *ibid.*, Vol. I, pp. 82-3.

24   HUGH HENRY BRACKENRIDGE

Nassau Grammar School[7] and "engaged in the study of divinity, until he was licensed to preach, when he was invited to take charge of an academy on the Eastern shore of Maryland."[8]

[7] *Princeton University, General Catalogue,* 1746-1906, p. 95; and *Biographical Notice,* p. 154.

[8] *Biographical Notice,* p. 154.

CHAPTER V

SCHOOLMASTER

B Y THE autumn of 1772 Brackenridge was established as master of an academy at Back Creek, near Princess Anne, Somerset County, Maryland. Our chief description of the school at this time is a glowing one written by Brackenridge himself and obviously designed to advertise its virtues to the public. Situated near Chesapeake Bay where communication was easy, the academy had grown to "considerable eminence" in the few years since its founding, and since there were no other seminaries of reputation in the vicinity, it fulfilled a real need in the community where it was already recognized as the torch-bearer of "virtue and science." Brackenridge boldly stated, too, that the academy was being managed with a spirit which did honor to the province. Here, through economical management and vigilant inspection on the part of the fifteen trustees, all "gentlemen of the first reputation in the country," the youth of the colonies might obtain a liberal education for the negligible sum of eighteen pounds per annum—thirteen pounds for board, and five for tuition.[1]

Beside Brackenridge's panegyric we may, by way of contrast, place Freneau's brief comment. "I arrived at this Somerset Academy the 18th of October. . . . I am assistant to Mr. Brackenridge. . . . We have about 30 students in this Academy, who prey upon me like Leaches."[2]

Certainly Brackenridge was happier in the situation than was Freneau. He received a "handsome salary" and "in the midst of a wealthy and highly polished society" he was "greatly respected as a man of genius and scholarship; while his wit, and superior social and conversational powers, always rendered him a welcome

---

[1] *Poem on Divine Revelation*, pp. 15-16, note.
[2] Written November 22, 1772. Quoted from *Poems of Philip Freneau*, ed. by F. L. Pattee, Vol. I, pp. xxii-xxiii.

guest."[3] Also he was a successful teacher. "Into the minds of his pupils he infused a love of learning; and used to speak with the pride of a Porson, of the Winders, the Murrays, the Purnells, and others who were afterwards distinguished."[4]

Such details as we have of Brackenridge's private life at this time are revealed in the correspondence of his college friends. In 1773, Bradford wrote to Madison: "As to Brackenridge he is still in Maryland. I lately received a letter from him in which he expresses the tenderest concern for your ill state of Health which I acquainted him with the last time I wrote. He complains of never hearing from you tho' he has frequently written—and supposes you cannot find an opportunity."[5]

Madison replied: "As you have a communication with Mr. Brackenridge tell him I write to him by every opportunity and by no means to ascribe his not hearing from me to any want of affection or endeavours in me; for I often lament our unlucky situation."[6] Early in 1774, Madison said in a letter to Bradford: "When you have an opportunity and write to Mr. Brackenridge, pray tell him I often think of him, and long to see him, and am resolved to do so in the spring. George Luckey was with me at Christmas, and we talked so much about old affairs and old friends, that I have a most insatiable desire to see you all."[7]

Meanwhile Brackenridge had been pursuing his studies with such zeal that he brought on a nervous breakdown.[8] His affliction received due notice in the letters of his friends. Bradford wrote to Madison later in the winter: "I received a Letter a few days ago

---

[3] *Biographical Notice*, p. 154.

[4] *ibid.* As late as 1842, when H. M. Brackenridge wrote the *Biographical Notice*, there was still a "traditionary remembrance" of him in the neighborhood of the Academy. p. 154.

[5] *Bradford Papers*, in manuscript department of the Historical Society of Pennsylvania. Letter of May 27, 1773.

[6] *ibid.* Letter of June 10, 1773, written from Orange County, Virginia.

[7] *The Writings of James Madison*, ed. by Gaillard Hunt, Vol. I, p. 20.

[8] In 1796 Brackenridge wrote: "From a stroke that I received from a sedentary life twenty years ago, I am subject to a delinquency or failing of nerves, especially when anything affects my mind." *Incidents of the Western Insurrection*, Vol. I, p. 63. H. M. Brackenridge said that this disorder was caused by "over application to study." *Western Insurrection*, p. 301.

from Finley in which he tells me that Breckenridge is sick and the disorder he labours under a dangerous one. But the ludicrous manner in which he mentioned it inclines me to think it is not so bad as he would have me imagine."[9]

Madison replied: "Mr. Brackenridge's illness gives me great uneasiness; I think he would be a loss to America. His merit is rated so high by me that I confess, if he were gone, I could almost say with the poet, that his country could furnish such a pomp for death no more. But I solace myself from Finley's ludicrous descriptions as you do."[10]

However ill Brackenridge may have been in the winter of 1774, he was able to travel in the spring. In May he sailed up Chesapeake Bay and landed at Annapolis. There he saw Samuel Chase, with papers in his hand, haranguing the citizens on the Boston port bill.[11]

In the autumn of 1774 Brackenridge, now a graduate of three years' standing, returned to Princeton to receive his Master's degree. For this event he had composed a *Poem on Divine Revelation,* which he read at the commencement exercises of September 28.

Adapting his performance to the occasion he opened his versified address with a glorified description of graduation day in Nassau Hall:

> This is a day of happiness, sweet peace,
> And heavenly sunshine; upon which conven'd
> In full assembly fair, once more we view,
> And hail with voice expressive of the heart,
> Patrons and sons of this illustrious hall.
> This hall more worthy of its rising fame
> Than hall on mountain or romantic hill,
> Where Druid bards sang to the hero's praise,
> While round their woods and barren heaths was heard
> The shrill calm echo of th' enchanting shell.

[9] *Bradford Manuscript.* Letter of March 4, 1774.
[10] *The Writings of James Madison,* ed. by Gaillard Hunt, Vol. I, p. 22.
[11] *Modern Chivalry* (edition of 1804), Part II, Vol. I, p. 201. Samuel Chase was a few years later Brackenridge's instructor in law.

Than all those halls and lordly palaces
Where in the days of chivalry, each knight,
And baron brave in military pride
Shone in the brass and burning steel of war;
For in this hall more worthy of a strain
No envious sound forbidding peace is heard,
Fierce song of battle kindling martial rage,
And desperate purpose in heroic minds:
But sacred truth fair science and each grace
Of virtue born; health, elegance and ease
And temp'rate mirth in social intercourse
Convey rich pleasure to the mind; and oft
The sacred muse in heaven-breathing song
Doth wrap the soul in extasy divine,
Inspiring joy and sentiment which not
The tale of war or song of Druids gave.
The song of Druids or the tale of war
With martial vigour every breast inspir'd,
With valour fierce and love of deathless fame;
But here a rich and splendid throng conven'd
From many a distant city and fair town,
Or rural seat by shore or mountain-stream,
Breathe joy and blessing to the human race,
Give countenance to arts themselves have known,
Inspire the love of heights themselves have reach'd,
Of noble science to enlarge the mind,
Of truth and virtue to adorn the soul,
And make the human nature grow divine.[12]

Then he lamented his long absence from the college:

How shall the muse from this poetic bow'r
So long remov'd, and from this happy hill,
Where ev'ry grace and ev'ry virtue dwells,
And where the springs of knowledge and of thought
In riv'lets clear and gushing streams flow down
Attempt a strain? How sing in rapture high

---

[12] *Poem on Divine Revelation*, pp. 1-2. The Druidical matter in this poem seems
to indicate that Brackenridge had recently been reading Ossian.

Or touch in varied melody the lyre
The lyre so long neglected and each strain
Unmeditated, and long since forgot?[18]

The main theme of the poem is the spread of Christianity from
Palestine to the American colonies. The Puritan migration is
treated thus in the most interesting section of the piece:

Brittania next beholds the risen day
In reformation bright; cheerful she hails
It from her snow-white cliffs, and bids her sons,
Rise from the mists of popery obscure.
Her worthier sons, whom not Rome's pontiff high,
Nor king with arbitrary sway could move,
Those mightier who with constancy untam'd,
Did quench the violence of fire, at death
Did smile, and maugre ev'ry pain, of bond,
Cold dark imprisonment, and scourge severe,
By hell-born popery devis'd, held fast
The Christian hope firm anchor of the soul.
Or those who shunning that fell rage of war,
And persecution dire, when civil pow'r,
Leagu'd in with sacerdotal sway triumph'd,
O'er ev'ry conscience, and the lives of men,
Did brave th' Atlantic deep and through its storms
Sought these Americ shores: these happier shores
Where birds of calm delight to play, where not
Rome's pontiff high, nor arbitrary king,
Leagu'd in with sacerdotal sway are known.
But peace and freedom link'd together dwell,
And reformation in full glory shines.
Oh for a muse of more exalted wing,
To celebrate those men who planted first
The christian church in these remotest lands;
From those high plains where spreads a colony,
Gen'rous and free, from Massachusett-shores,
To the cold lakes margin'd with snow: from that
Long dreary tract of shady woods and hills,
Where Hudson's icy stream rolls his cold wave,
To those more sunny bowers where zephyrs breathe,

And round which flow in circling current swift
The Delaware and Susquehannah streams.
Thence to those smiling plains where Chesapeak
Spreads her maternal arms encompassing
In soft embrace, full many a settlement,
Where opulence, with hospitality,
And polish'd manners, and the living plant
Of science blooming, sets their glory high.[14]

Brackenridge closed the poem with a few lines forecasting his own future:

Far hence I go to some sequestered vale
By woody hill or shady mountain side,
Where far from converse and the social band,
My days shall pass inglorious away:
But this shall be my exultation still
My chiefest merit and my only joy,
That when the hunter on some western hill,
Or furzy glade shall see my grassy tomb,
And know the stream which mourns unheeded by,
He for a moment shall repress his step,
And say, There lies a Son of Nassau-Hall.[15]

Lest these prophetic verses might be misunderstood and resented by his Maryland neighbors, the poet added a prose comment in which he said: "In these lines the author has not the least reference to his present place of residence but to some western part of America, where in the course of his life he may possibly be thrown."[16]

The *Poem on Divine Revelation* was issued in Philadelphia soon after it was delivered, and on November 17 it was advertised for sale by Samuel Loudon in *Rivington's New York Gazette*. In placing his second published poem before the public, Brackenridge properly felt, or at least expressed, some doubt about its quality, and attempted to disarm criticism by a prefatory apology:

The Author of the following poem, or as it may be better styled Poetical Oration, may seem to have been rather unhappy in the choice

---

[14] *Poem on Divine Revelation*, pp. 14-15. The last six lines describe the region where Brackenridge's academy was situated.   [15] *ibid.*, pp. 21-2.   [16] *ibid.*, p. 22.

of his subject, which being a good deal historical, did not admit of much poetic dress or ornament, nor gave much scope to fancy or imagination to exert itself, that in which the great strength of a poet lies. With respect to this he would beg leave to observe, that the subject was chosen perhaps happily enough, as the foundation of an Exercise in an institution under the patronage of gentlemen distinguished as friends to Revelation, and on an occasion when the greater number of them were convened.

In the second place it may be objected, that an imitation of the Poet Milton may be traced through the whole performance, though the Author has not been able to attain to any thing of the spirit of that immortal bard. To this he has only to reply, that an imitation of great originals is placed by Longinus among the sources of good writing. He therefore conceives himself free from censure on account of any imitation of the poet Milton, which may be seen in his performance, though he is sensible of his unhappiness in not having been able to attain to any degree of his excellent spirit. This however is a misfortune common to him with many honest writers, and for which he throws himself on the candour of the Public.[17]

The candour of Brackenridge's classmates gives us our only record of the public reception of the poem. Bradford wrote to Madison:

I send you, now, a poem on divine revelation which Mr. Brackenridge spoke at Commencement & has published. He desired me to do so & requested you to recommend it to your friends if you think it has any merit in order to assist the sale that the printer may not be a loser by him. I am afraid he has published it at an improper time; the political storm is too high for the still soft voice of the muse to be listened to; & indeed this does not seem to be the proper time for poetry unless it be such as Tyrtaeus wrote. I am glad however that our friend seems determined that these blossoms of Genius shall not "waste their sweetness on the desert air." It will encourage him to make still greater attempts & tutor him to heights he would once have trembled at. If I may judge he appears to have rather a strong and masculine Genius than a just & delicate taste. Imagination is his province. The consequence of this will be that his writings tho' enriched with many original beauties will be obscured with faults which even

17 *ibid.,* Preface.

a moderate Genius would have avoided. Perhaps the word Tartarean in this poem will justify the latter part of this remark. But where is the man who ever bestrode Pegasus and did not get a fall.[18]

Bradford also sent Brackenridge's poem to William Linn. Linn expressed his candid opinion in his reply:

I have perused the poem & think it a good performance tho' I doubt whether it be much superior to the one on "The Rising Glory of America." In what can his imitation of Milton consist unless in the word *Erst*? Or did he imagine he came so near *his* Excellence that we could not distinguish the difference? . . . But this he disclaims, with what sincerity the world may judge. What does he mean by his pedantic note about the school in somersett?[19] I am afraid he has grown some feet higher by this performance or surely he would not think himself and his school worthy of so much notice. In the preface & in this note I see the *Man*; in the poem I see the great genius and strong imagination.[20]

At the beginning of 1775 Brackenridge was still solicitous about the fate of his poem. Writing to Madison on January 20, Bradford said:

I had a letter the other day from Mr. Breckenridge in which he gave me the disagreeable task of telling him what the public said of his piece. I have enquired, but can meet with nobody who has read it, & shall therefore plainly tell him so and lay the fault on the subject the times & the publisher. He says nothing about his Canto's, which I am impatient to see. They would serve to counterballance several satire[s] that have been published this way against the Congress and patriotic party.[21]

As the public indifference to his poem continued, Brackenridge himself must at length have come to realize that the "still soft voice of the Muse" would never be heard above the storm. With this *Poem on Divine Revelation* he seems to have abandoned the heroic

---

[18] October 17, 1774. *Bradford Papers.*
[19] See above, pp. 25, 30.   [20] November 7, 1774. *Bradford Papers.*
[21] *ibid.* The patriotic "Canto's" on which Brackenridge seems to have been working in January 1775 have not come to light in either manuscript or printed form.

style (save in two patriotic dramas composed for propaganda purposes), and when we find him next seriously turning to literature, it will be in the satiric vein that marked his early Princeton manner. Yet he did not abandon the grand style without a pang. Writing a few years later he said of this phase of his literary development:

Miss Urany Muse, you must know, was my flame: The same lady that Milton talks of when he says,

"Descend from heaven, Urania, by that name,
If rightly thou art called."

. . . I was in love, that is the truth of it, and everything said, was, to me, the speech of paradise. I shall not stop to tell you the many pleasant evening walks that I had on this hill, and the tender things that Miss Urany deigned to say to me; for I cannot yet be persuaded but that I possessed some share of her affection. Nevertheless, it has so come to pass, that the hope I had entertained of making her one day my own, has long since vanished. The circumstances of this small affair must remain a secret to the world: Perhaps when I die some hint of it may be found amongst my papers; and some friend may inscribe it on my tomb.[22]

[22] *United States Magazine*, pp. 311-13.

THE REVOLUTION

B RACKENRIDGE had grown up in a democratic Scotch-Irish back-country settlement, and he had been taught liberal Whig political doctrines at Princeton. His natural place was, therefore, with those who opposed the claims of King George III and the British Parliament to full authority over the American colonies. He was a man of thought rather than a man of action, however. All his instincts and interests were literary, and it was therefore a matter of course that when the War for Independence came, he should choose to serve the cause of the colonies as a penman rather than as a soldier. In dramatic poems, in sermons, and in editorial work he contributed materially to the literature of propaganda which expressed the prejudices, the hopes, and the ideals of the American Whigs.

During the first year of the war Brackenridge remained at his academy. When glorified accounts of the Battle of Bunker Hill spread south from Boston, he seized the opportunity to instill patriotic sentiments into the minds of his pupils, and wrote a play, *The Battle of Bunkers-Hill,* "to be performed by the youth of the seminary."[1] He interpreted the battle as a moral victory, a glorious display of American bravery, cleverly emphasizing his point by putting praise of American valor into the mouth of the enemy leader, Lord Howe.[2] Using the form of the neo-classical heroic drama, he achieved real although moderate success in handling the grand style. The sentiment and style of the play are well illustrated in the following speech by Gardiner to the colonial troops:

> Fear not, brave soldiers, tho' their infantry,
> In deep array, so far out-numbers us.

[1] *Gazette Publications,* p. 279. Brackenridge says that the play was written in 1775, but it was not published until 1776.

[2] A. H. Quinn, *History of the American Drama from the Beginning to the Civil War,* pp. 50-1.

The justness of our cause, will brace each arm,
And steel the soul, with fortitude; while they,
Whose guilt hangs trembling, on their consciences,
Must fail in battle, and receive that death,
Which, in high vengeance, we prepare for them.
Let then each spirit, to the height, wound up
Shew noble vigour, and full force this day.
For on the merit, of our swords, is plac'd
The virgin honour, and true character,
Of this whole Continent: and one short hour,
May give complexion, to the whole event,
Fixing the judgment whether as base slaves,
We serve these masters, or more nobly live,
Free as the breeze, that on the hill-top plays,
With these sweet fields, and tenements, our own.[3]

Thirty years later Brackenridge, in republishing *The Battle of Bunkers-Hill,* made a sufficiently modest estimate of its value: "This dramatic thing is extremely juvenile; but on account of having some connection with the revolution, and shewing the part taken by me in it, I have thought proper to collect it as a scrap of that period."[4]

The invasion of Canada by the colonists was the subject of his second play, *The Death of General Montgomery.* Since the campaign against Quebec ended in failure, Brackenridge again had to use a defeat as subject for a patriotic drama.

From survivors of the battle he had received lurid accounts of British atrocities. "I have," he said, "conversed with those who saw the scalps warm from the heads of our countrymen. I have had the relation from their mouth who beheld the fires lighted up, and heard, with a soul paining sympathy, the horrid shrieks and

---

[3] Act V, Scene 2. There is an indication of the influence of Shakespeare's *King Henry V* in the following lines of the play:
> Let then *each spirit, to the height, wound up,*
> Shew noble vigour and full force this day.

This is obviously an echo from *King Henry V,* Scene 1, 11.15-17:
> Now set the teeth and stretch the nostril wide,
> Hold hard the breath, and bend up *every spirit*
> *To his full height.*

[4] *Gazette Publications,* p. 281.

gloomy howlings of the savage tribes in the execution of the poor
captives, who according to the threat of Carleton, were burned on
an island in the river St. Lawrence, after our unfortunate surrender at the Cedars."[5] On the basis of such representations of
events at Quebec, Brackenridge made British atrocities the main
theme of his play, giving special attention to the savage exploits of
England's Indian allies.

Writing of the fall of Montgomery at Quebec, he naturally recalled the death of General Wolfe, whose memory was sacred to
the colonists. The pallid ghost of Wolfe stalks the scene, calling
woe upon King and Parliament, and blessing the American union:

> Yes, from your death shall amply vegetate,
> The grand idea of an empire new,
> Clear independence and self-ballanc'd power,
> In these fair provinces, United States,
> Each independent, yet rein'd in and brac'd,
> By one great council, buckling them to strength
> And lasting firmness of immortal date.
> O happy empire, 'stablished in truth,
> Of high wrought structure, from first principles:
> In golden commerce, and in literature,
> Of many a bard, and wisdom writing sage,
> High flourishing, and filling length of time,
> With peerless glory and immortal acts.[6]

In publishing the play Brackenridge added a preface in which
he acknowledged the amateurish and topical nature of the piece:

It is my request that the following Dramatic Composition may be
considered only as a school piece. . . . It is intended for the private
entertainment of Gentlemen of taste and martial enterprise, but by
no means for the exhibition of the stage.[7] The subject is not love but

---

[5] *The Death of General Montgomery*, Act. V, Scene 5, note.

[6] *ibid.*, Act IV, Scene 2.

[7] It seems likely that Brackenridge's plays were presented in at least one other
school besides his own academy. Claude C. Robin, a French observer who visited
Harvard in 1781, said: "Their pupils often act tragedies, the subject of which is
generally taken from their national events, such as the battle of Bunker's Hill, the
burning of Charlestown, the Death of General Montgomery, the capture of Burgoyne, the treason of Arnold, and the Fall of British tyranny." *New Travels in
North America*, p. 17.

valour. I meddle not with any of the effeminating passions, but consecrate my muse to the great themes of patriotic virtue, bravery and heroism.

Soon after the Declaration of Independence was signed—perhaps at the end of the school year—Brackenridge left the academy to become a chaplain in the army.[8] During the next two years he was to address rousing sermons to soldiers rather than to compose heroic dramas for schoolboys.

In his new capacity we first find him addressing the troops at Morristown, New Jersey, where Washington had gone into winter quarters after the battles of Trenton and Princeton.[9] He first made clear to his regiment what his own service was to be:

There are two ways in which a man may contribute-to the defence of his country: by the tongue to speak, or by the hand to act. To rouse with words and animate with the voice is the province of the orator. To execute with promptitude, and resolution is that of the soldier. These mutually subserve and assist each other. . . .

But my voice is weak, my powers are feeble; and I need the apology of there being none better that offers, to fill the place in which I officiate. But though an orator of no waking powers, it seems to me I dream a little of what has been possessed by others. The Druids were the *chaplains* of our ancestors among the Germans. These by their words incited to war, and inspired the valour of the combatants.

The Bards were the *chaplains* of the aborigines of Britain. O! Ossian bard of Fingal! Could I have heard thy voice in Selma, Hall of Shells, rousing to deeds by thy magic words, even I who am but a man of the gown, and do not mix in battle, must have caught the madness and rushed to war.

Those therefore may be useful, who though not martial themselves, may rouse that temper in others. . . .

Let it not therefore be thought useless that I address military men. The talent of speech is mine, and that alone is my province.[10]

Brackenridge was with Washington's army during the Pennsylvania campaign of 1777. A few days before the battle of Brandywine he delivered a sermon in which he pronounced a glow-

[8] *Biographical Notice*, p. 154.
[9] *Gazette Publications*, p. 265. [10] *ibid.*, pp. 265-7.

ing tribute to England's former grandeur, although prophesying disaster to the British empire on account of her sins:

Even though hostile, yet I feel myself interested in her fate. I travel in imagination to the banks of the Cam, the Isis, and the Avon, where the fair form of a Shakespeare rises to my view. I am touched with the magic sound of Milton's harp, and the lyre of a Gray modulating soft music to my ravished ear. I lift my thought to the noble strains of Pope, and feel the enthusiasm of the bard rushing on my soul. I walk with her philosophers,—the Lockes, the Bacons, and the Newtons that she boasts. I mingle with her statesmen and patriots of every name—her Thomas Mores—her William Temples—her Hampdens—her Sidneys—her Raleighs—her Harringtons—her Russels, and all the illustrious throng that adorns her chronology in every age. I feel a momentary impulse of concern for a country that gave these noble spirits birth. I could wish that, bounded in her empire, she were immortal in her date. But the will of Heaven has determined otherwise, that she is infatuated in her counsels. Her renown is declining from its summit: Her great names fade upon my sight: Her virtue, her patriotism disappears: Her glory in commerce and in war is wholly gone. She is lost from the *things that are,* and the cold shades of oblivion are gathering on her isle.[11]

His next sermon, preached after the battle of Brandywine, breathes only pure hate for the King of England, and expresses a patriot's exaggerated view of the enemy's political "tyranny" and military "atrocities." After naming Alexander, Caesar, Tamerlane, and Genghis Khan as the great murderers of history, Cain's kin, Brackenridge assigns George III to their fellowship.

I leave behind me, all that is related of the Hun, the Vandal, and the Goth, and all the cruel, persecuting, bloody princes, and people in more modern times, when Europe floated as one sea of blood. I pass them by, and hasten on, for I have an object of greater wickedness in view—an object of such accomplished fraud, perfidy, and murder, that everyone heretofore mentioned is lost and disappears. I mean him of England—the fierce, cruel, unrelenting, and bloody king of Britain. What has this tyrant done? What has he not done?

---

[11] *Gazette Publications,* p. 132; *United States Magazine,* January 1779, pp. 25-8.

He meditated with himself in cold blood, and before he had the least foundation of resentment, the enslaving of this rising country. He could view without a tear, & without one check of conscience, this early land, bound in the chains of servitude, which he forged for it. This was the prospect, which he had painted to his own imagination. It was this which he endeavoured to accomplish by the insidious, and as he hoped insensible gradation of a slow approach, in bribery, and flattering promises to vain persons, and then by distant acts of parliament, that did not seem immediately to involve the loss of freedom, but did by sure steps lead to it.[12]

Further along in the diatribe the chaplain gave his soldier audience a lurid account of the sufferings of the American troops who had been captured:

Let the prisoners of Fort Washington, relate the hunger, cold and every shape of misery to which they were consigned. Sick, emaciated dying, let them tell, if by their last breath, they can give some faint account of it, How for many days they tasted not food, until sharp famine began to prey upon their vitals and destroy the love of life. How for many months they were detained, in the wintry and inclement season of the year, comfortless, in cold rooms, and without fire, until the blood of the body lost its motion in the veins. Let them tell of the quality and pernicious taste of that unwholesome food, which was served to them, and intended for their death. This let those who suffered speak; but we can testify, what was the appearance and lamentable state, of the meagre, faint and heart-dejected few, who for the time survived the usage, and at length to save some pretence of an exchange, were dismissed from the fangs of such barbarity.[13]

In his next sermon, *The Nature and Artifice of Toryism,* he denounced the American Loyalists. Introducing a wholly secular irony into the homiletic discourse, he said:

What is the reward which they have in view as the ground of this pernicious conduct? The favour of the tyrant is, undoubtedly, the object which plays upon their fancy. They promise to themselves great felicity, in the gladsome rays of his royal countenance. In his proclamations from his generals, and in his speeches from the throne, he will vouchsave them the heart-cheering appelation of my loyal subjects.

[12] *Six Political Discourses,* p. 9.   [13] *ibid.,* p. 11.

When the war has ended, and each has acted faithfully his part, he will send for them, and hold them out his hand to kiss, at St. James's in Old England. He will give some of them commissions, and admit them to the honour of serving him, in some capacity about the park, or the palace yard. One more eminent than the rest, he may constitute his butler; and another, he may graciously advance to the office of chief baker. Those of them, whom he cannot stow away in this manner, he will provide for, in America. He will give them posts in government. He will reward them for their villainy, with a number of the best houses, in some of our chief cities. He shall satisfy their cravings, with two or three of the forfeited plantations. Some of the more active and leading men amongst them, he will present with ten or fifteen thousand acres; and constitute them lords of some little manour, on the banks of Delaware or Schuylkil. He will promote them dukes, and earls, and baronets. He will promote them to very great honour, and he will do whatsoever they say unto him. This is what they have in view, as the ground of their pernicious conduct.[14]

Toward the end of the year 1777 the Americans were disturbed by a rumor that the French officers who were employed for the colonial army were about to be recalled to France to take charge of their own regiments. Brackenridge offered them solace in the promise of aid from heavenly allies.[15]

Are the officers of France called home, to take their places in her armies? 'Tis said they are; but what is that to us, my countrymen? The officers of France, are noble, gallant, and experienced, but still inferior to the bright and shining captains of the host of heaven. The officers of France have seen the wars in Germany, in Poland, and in Russia. The captains of the host of God have seen the war, and combat with the dragon—have seen the wars before the flood, and since in every age and country. These have come down to help us, and these shall be continued with us. Had we our eyesight we should behold chariots of fire, and winged steeds encompassing our mountains. We are afraid perhaps that Britain will recruit from the European continent, and send in thousands to augment her forces. Let us be confident that God is for us, and the armies of the universe are not sufficient to resist his providence.[16]

[14] Six Political Discourses, pp. 28-9.
[15] In a sermon preached December 18, 1777, in Queen Anne County, Maryland.
[16] ibid., pp. 59-60.

In spite of this display of confidence, he confessed later in the sermon: "I do not by any means expect a sudden issue to the contest."[17]

Brackenridge published most of his army sermons in 1778 in a volume entitled *Six Political Discourses founded on the Scriptures,* prefacing them with a note in which he confessed their secular nature:

Let not the word *scripture,* in the title page, prevent that general attention to these discourses which they might otherwise receive. I know it is natural for us to be cautious in looking into any thing that borders on religion, lest we should meet with some sly insinuation *like a bayonet point to dart upon the conscience.*

For this reason in the very *patibulo,* or entrance, I am careful to assure my countrymen, that these discourses are what they pretend to be, *of a nature chiefly political. . . .*

If they shall now more generally serve the great cause in which we are engaged, it will be an ample recompense for the time spent in transcribing them for publication.[18]

Whether in writing these sermons, which must, with their emphasis on the bloody atrocities of the enemy, and their "Gott mit uns" philosophy, ring with unpleasant familiarity in the reader's ears, Brackenridge was sincerely a victim of war-time psychology, or whether he yielded to the orator's usual temptation to sway his hearers by the spread-eagle eloquence beloved of the crowd, it is difficult to say. At any rate, they seem slightly out of character as the utterances of a man who was seldom to be swayed to emotional extremes by popular sentiment. Their non-theological content, at least, is significant. Brackenridge had by this time given up the intention to become a clergyman which had been fostered by his parents and, probably, by the Princeton faculty. In a thinly veiled autobiographical passage inserted in a work of fiction which he wrote the next year he said, after confessing his romance with Miss Urany Muse:

The next fair young lady for whom I conceived an affection was *Miss Theology,* a young lady of indeed great merit, and who had been

[17] *ibid.,* p. 60. [18] *ibid.,* Preface.

sometimes mentioned to me by my friends. But whether it is, because we are apt to dislike those who are too much pressed upon us; or whether it is that the will of heaven gave a new current to the affections of my heart, I cannot tell; but I had until this hour set light by her, and could see nothing handsome in her person, or captivating in her air and manner. My affection for Miss Theology was a stream of love springing from a cold aversion.

I have loved Miss Theology, and for five years I paid her constant attention. But so it is, that though with much condescension and many marks of tenderness, she received my addresses, yet we both saw the necessity of ceasing to indulge any fond thought of a union.[19]

Further, he found it impossible to remain orthodox. The process of the disintegration of his faith, which must have occurred between the time when he left Princeton and the time when he gave up his chaplaincy, is best related in the words of his son:

Mr. Brackenridge, although licensed to preach, was never ordained, nor formally consecrated to the ministry. As he grew older, he became convinced that his natural temperament called him to the scenes of active life. Besides, he found himself unable to yield a full assent to all the tenets of the church in which he had been educated. He declared that for two whole years, he laboured most sincerely and assiduously to convince himself; but in vain; and he could not think of publicly maintaining doctrines, in which he did not privately believe. On one occasion, in conversation with a Scotch clergyman, he stated his difficulties. The other replied to him, that he was pretty much in the same predicament. "Then, how do you reconcile it to your conscience to preach doctrines of whose truth you are not fully convinced?" "Hut man," said he, "I dinna think much about it—I explain the doctrine, as I wud a system o' moral philosophy, or metaphysics: and if I dinna just understand it noo, the time may come when I shall; and in the mean time I put my faith in wiser men, who established the articles, and in those whose heads are sufficiently clear to understand them. And if we were tae question but ane o' these doctrines, it wud be like taking a stane out o' a biggin; the whole wa' might fa' doon." As this mode of reasoning did not satisfy Mr. Brackenridge, he resolved to turn his attention to the study of the law—a circumstance, to which may be ascribed the unfriendly feeling manifested towards him afterwards

[19] *United States Magazine*, p. 312.

by some of the clergy, who looked upon him as an apostate; denounced him as one of the wicked; and which led him on more than one occasion, to retaliate. His writings display a liberality on the subject of religion, which is thought by some to border on free thinking. It is true, he hated hypocrisy, but reverenced the Christian religion as taught by the Scriptures; he was only skeptical as to some of the tenets of different sects, and had a fixed aversion to *creeds*, which he said, "are hardly comprehended by the makers themselves, while the precepts of the Gospel are so plain that a child may understand them"; yet he did not pretend to call them directly in question, preferring to pass them in silence, from unwillingness to lessen that general respect for religion and its teachers, which he considered necessary to the well-being of society. Whatever satirical freedom may be discovered in his works, is aimed at certain professors of religion, and not at religion itself, of which he always speaks with respect—frequently referring to the Scriptures, of which he was a perfect master.[20]

As the possibility of his remaining in the church gradually receded, Brackenridge turned to an ambition probably long nourished in secret, that of embarking on a literary career. The failure of the *Poem on Divine Revelation* to attract public notice should have warned him that this time of social and economic unrest was ill-suited to his project, but with the proverbial blindness of the lover, he abandoned the army in 1778 and set off for Philadelphia with a thousand pounds in his pocket, to pay his court once more to the Muses.[21]

[20] *Biographical Notice*, pp. 155-6. [21] *ibid.*, p. 154.

CHAPTER VII

THE UNITED STATES MAGAZINE

PHILADELPHIA at the end of 1778 was in a state bordering on chaos. The British had evacuated the city in June and all the problems resultant on their nine months' military occupation remained to be solved. Whigs strove for vengeance against the Tories who had so recently given aid and encouragement to the enemy; Tories sought by every means at hand to save their lives, their property, and their political influence; radicals of the Constitutional Society struggled with the conservatives of the Republican Society to prevent a revision of the democratic State constitution; while the mob, long held in restraint, reverted joyously to violence wherever the opportunity offered. Belles who had but lately enslaved the gay British officers by their wit and charm, now, with a keen sense of anticlimax, set themselves to turn the heads of the less sophisticated Americans, and to keep alive as best they might the feverish gaiety that had for so long marked the routs and balls of the captive city. Reckless extravagance was the rule of the day; failing credit and increased issues of paper money went hand in hand; soaring prices, futile legislation, hoarding, and speculation all played their part in the economic, social, and spiritual breakdown. Even great reputations were not safe: Benedict Arnold and Charles Lee were soon to be proven traitors; Robert Morris, John Jay, Henry Drayton, and Silas Deane were to be accused of attempted commercial monopoly. Weariness and depression were settling like a pall not only over Philadelphia, but over the whole colonial world.

These, then, were the uneasy times, and this the distracted audience on which Brackenridge chose to launch his new literary venture, *The United States Magazine*. That there was offered here material in plenty for the *jeux d'esprit* of a patriotic and democratic satirist is as obvious as is the fact that the times were utterly unsuited to the success of such a venture.

Brackenridge's statement of the purpose of the publication showed his full comprehension of the social revolution which was involved in the War of Independence.

We regard it as our great happiness in these United States, that the path to office and preferment, lies open to every individual. The mechanic of the city, or the husbandman who ploughs his farm by the river's bank, has it in his power to become, one day, the first magistrate of his respective commonwealth, or to fill a seat in the Continental Congress. This happy circumstance lays an obligation upon every individual to exert a double industry to qualify himself for the great trust which may, one day, be reposed in him. It becomes him to obtain some knowledge of the history and principles of government, or at least to understand the policy and commerce of his own country. Now it may not be the lot of every individual to be able to obtain this knowledge from the first source, that is from the best writers, or the conversation of men of reading and experience. In the one case it would require a larger library than most of us are able to procure, and in the other a greater opportunity of travelling than is consistent with our daily occupations.

The want of these advantages must therefore be supplied by some publication that will in itself contain a library, and be the literary coffee-house of public conversation. A work of this nature is *The United States Magazine*.[1]

In spite of this serious purpose, however, Brackenridge evidently did not feel safe in investing his thousand pounds of Continental currency in a purely educational organ. He continued:

Instruction will appear in every shape of essays, sketches, schemes, tracts and dissertations. Amusement will disport, in every form of letters, tales, dreams, scraps and anecdotes. The first of these will brace the mind, and make it capable to judge in matters of the highest moment. The last will pleasureably unbend it from what may border upon study and severer application.[2]

He also felt the need of a periodical which would afford a

---

[1] *United States Magazine*, p. 9.   [2] *ibid.*, p. 10.

medium of publication for such aspiring authors as himself and Freneau:

Magazines are greatly useful as the nurseries of genius. They put it in the power of young and rising authors to make trial of their strength without the risk of being checked in the first stages of their progress by ill natured critics, whose knowledge of their person generally excites their envy, and disposes them to censure what they themselves perhaps could not equal. Many men of great abilities have been prevented from venturing into literary life and reputation, from a want of some such means of making their first appearance to the public.[3]

Solicitous as he was for his own literary reputation, Brackenridge was concerned as well for the literary status of his country. He saw that American civilization needed something more than political autonomy and democratic government:

We are indeed happy to find a young and rising people so disposed to wish well to the labours of those men who make it their study to contribute to the entertainment, and to raise the credit of the age in which they live, by useful works of literature, that are the solace, and at the same time the ornament, of human nature. For what is man without taste, and the acquirement of genius? An Ouran Outan, with the human shape, and the soul of a beast.

It was the language of our enemies at the commencement of the debate between America and what is called the mother-country, that in righteous judgment for our wickedness, it would be well to leave us to that independency which we seemed to affect, and to suffer us to sink down to so many Ouran-Outans of the wood, lost to the light of science which, from the other side of the Atlantic, had just begun to break upon us. They have been made to see, and even to confess the vanity of this kind of *auguration*. The British officers who are, some of them, men of understanding, on perusal of our pamphlets in course of the debate, and the essays and dissertations in the newspapers, have been forced to acknowledge, not without chagrin, that the rebels, as they are pleased to call us, had some d——mn'd good writers on their side of the question, and that we had fought them no less successfully with the pen than with the sword. We hope to convince them yet more fully, that we are able to cultivate the *belles lettres,* even dis-

---

[3] *United States Magazine,* p. 11.

connected with Great-Britain; and that liberty is of so noble and energetic quality, as even from the bosom of a war to call forth the powers of human genius, in every course of literary fame and improvement.[4]

Behind all these high hopes for the service which the magazine might render to the country, there lurked fears as to the outcome of the venture. "It is our only doubt," Brackenridge said, "that in this undertaking, the public will not sufficiently attend to the expenses of the press."[5] However, suppressing his very legitimate anxiety, he addressed a gay birthday ode to *The United States Magazine*:

> Child of truth and fancy born,
> Rising like the beam of morn;
> From that shadowy silent place,
> Where the ideal shades embrace,
> Forms that yet in embryo lie;
> Forms of inactivity.
>
> Let me hail thee to the day,
> With thy natal honours gay.
> Thou art come to visit scenes
> Of Italian bowers and greens.
> Hear in wild wood notes with me
> What the world prepares for thee.
>
> Statesmen of assembly great;
> Soldiers that on danger wait;
> Farmers that subdue the plain;
> Merchants that attempt the main;
> Tradesmen who their labours ply:
> These shall court thy company;
> These shall say, with placid mien,
> *Have you read the Magazine?*
>
> Maids of virgin-beauty fair;
> Widows gay and debonnair;
> Matrons of a graver age;
> Wives whom household cares engage;
> These shall hear of thee and learn,

[4] *ibid.*, pp. 3-4.   [5] *ibid.*, p. 4.

To esteem thee more than Sterne;
These shall say when thou art seen,
Oh! enchanting Magazine.[6]

Brackenridge addressed himself intelligently to the task of pur-
veying instruction and entertainment to patriots, citizens, and
ladies. The first number of the magazine, published in January
1779, contained a pleasing variety of material. Current events
were presented in a "chronicle," in sections on foreign and domestic affairs, and in lists of members of Congress for 1779, and of
ships recently captured at sea. Patriotic sentiment found serious
expression in "An Oration on the Advantages of Independence,"
a Fourth of July address by Dr. David Ramsay, and in one of
Brackenridge's "Political Discourses founded on the Scriptures."

The British and the American Tories were treated ironically in
"The Cornwalliad," a mock heroic poem; and in "The Humble
Representation and Earnest Supplication of James Rivington"[7]
by President Witherspoon. American political problems were
vigorously handled in a "Letter to the Poets, Philosophers, Orators, Statesmen, and Heroes of Antiquity," in "The Representation
and Remonstrance of Hard Money," and in "Maxims for Republics." Belles and beaux were regaled with "General Lee's
Letter to Miss Franks." Belles lettres were represented by two
poems, by Freneau's "Account of the Island of Bermuda," and
by "The Cave of Vanhest," a story by Brackenridge.

The editor's own contributions show him to have been seriously
concerned with the political and financial issues of Pennsylvania
and the Union. The radical constitution of Pennsylvania, which
provided for a one-house assembly, unchecked by a senate, was
being vigorously attacked. Brackenridge was frankly puzzled
about this constitutional problem of the State and in the "Letter
to the Poets, Philosophers, Orators, Statesmen, and Heroes of
Antiquity" he appealed to the classic worthies for advice.

We often hear from you, and you appear to be well acquainted with
all affairs in which we are engaged. Almost every day we receive from

[6] *United States Magazine,* p. 43. Reprinted in *Gazette Publications,* pp. 177-8.
[7] Rivington was a Tory printer and bookseller of New York.

you some tract, dissertation, or essay in history, politics, or letters. The Gazettes and Magazines abound with lucubrations under the signatures of Nestor, Antenor, Trismegistus, Hermes, Mentor, Diogenes, Plato, Zeno, Dion, Hiero, Xenophon, Socrates, Aristotle, Euripides and others.

After urging the ancients to continue their contributions, he turned to his specific problem:

History and politics, however, will be more to the taste of the present times; and for that reason I am anxious to interest in our behalf those great legislators, Solon and Lycurgus, Numa Pompilius, Minos, Rhadamanthus, Eacus and others. The Sentiments of these great men, upon Government, will be of great service at the present day, as they will be able, from their own experience to inform us, whether a single or a double legislature, as we call it, be the most happy constitution of government. We are excessively puzzled on this head in Pennsylvania. For my own part I must confess that the arguments for and against, seem so perfectly to balance one another, that I can hardly tell to which I shall submit myself. When a single-legislature man takes me by the sleeve, and tells me of a house of Lords, and a King upon the back of them, I am greatly startled and in doubt what to say: When, on the other hand, a double legislature man asks me to dine with him and begins to push about the bottle pretty freely, I am almost brought to be of his opinion, that the multitude in all ages have been devils, and that no man, nor even they themselves can be safe in a commonwealth that is not checked by a variety of councils in the legislative body. If both of these meet me in the street, as is sometimes the case, I am held between them, and alternately shaken by their arguments. First, I nod to one and then to another, like a man that is half asleep, and recovers in the angle of a chimney.[8]

Thus, even before national independence was assured, Brackenridge was warily pondering one of the permanent issues of American democracy. His wavering between two extremes foreshadows the most important aspect of the later political satires which were to be his most important contributions to American literature.

[8] *United States Magazine*, pp. 11-12.

He also applied his canny and satirical mind to the problem of the depreciated Continental currency. In considering this question he was no doubt moved by anxiety as to the fate of his own savings, but he also saw clearly the general demoralization produced by the debased currency. In "The Representation and Remonstrance of Hard-Money" he made hard cash say of the paper money:

The Congress cannot greatly be pleased with him, on account of any regard he has paid to their determinations. It was early recommended by them to discontinue horse-races, cock-fights, and such unlawful sports and pastimes; and yet this fellow has been the cause of more irregularities of this kind, than any man I know of. There have been instances of many thousand dollars laying their wagers with each other, upon common scrub-horses; a conduct quite beneath the character of gentlemen.

The Congress cannot found their approbation of him on any marks of piety and virtue; for he is certainly a fellow of bad moral character. It is well known that he spends his time almost constantly in ordinaries, and beer-houses, calling for bowl after bowl, and pledging his hat and wig for the reckoning. I am well informed that he is also a frequenter of the bawdy-houses; several thirty dollar bills have been seen going to a certain *Charlotte,* a common prostitute of this city.

The Congress cannot but have heard that he is very generally accused not only of amours with women, but also of dishonesty in business. There are those who think him guilty of collusion with several in the different offices about the army,—sticking in their hands, and skulking, while it behoved him to have been upon the public service.[9]

The comments on the demoralized social life of Philadelphia contained in this passage are interesting in themselves. A further revelation of the frivolities of the time was attempted by Brackenridge through the publication of a letter from General Charles Lee to Miss Rebecca Franks, a society belle, who had laughed at Lee for wearing green breeches patched with leather. In a silly

[9] *United States Magazine,* pp. 28 *ff.* This satire on the paper currency was answered by Governor William Livingston of New Jersey in the February number of *The United States Magazine,* pp. 72-81.

letter of protest the gay general insisted that his breeches were of the smartest fashion.

T-o convict you therefore of the falsehood of this most diabolical slander, to put you to eternal silence . . . and to cover you with a much larger patch of infamy than you have wantonly endeavoured to fix on my breeches, I have thought proper . . . to send you said breeches, and, with the consciousness of truth on my side, to submit them to a most severe inspection and scrutiny of you and all those who have entered into this wicked cabal against my honour and reputation. I say, I dare you, and your whole junto, to your worst,—turn them, examine them inside and outside, and if you find them to be green breeches patched with leather, and not legitimate Sherryvallies, such as his Majesty of Poland wears . . . I will submit to all the scurrility, which I have no doubt you and your abettors are prepared to pour out against me, in the public papers, on this important and interesting occasion.

Brackenridge published this letter in full in the first number of *The United States Magazine.* The result was a letter of apology from General Lee to Miss Franks, which was published in *The Pennsylvania Advertiser.* Of Brackenridge, Lee said:

The impertinence and stupidity of the compiler of that wretched performance, with the pompous title of *The Magazine of the United States,* have, I find, been the means of my silly but certainly harmless letter to Miss Franks, being introduced into the New York papers, and I am told, of giving much uneasiness to that amiable young lady, for whose character, in every respect, I have the highest regard.[10]

In his reply, Brackenridge transferred the dispute to a new and dangerous topic—Lee's military conduct. In an open letter to Lee he said:

The name of *General Moultrie* in *The United States Magazine,* appears to be to you like holy water to a witch, it frightens you so effectually. Is it because he defended Fort Sullivan contrary to your judgement, which was to evacuate it?[11]

[10] *United States Magazine,* p. 163.   [11] *ibid.,* p. 169.

Lee, thoroughly alarmed by this question put to him, immediately addressed the following letter to John Jay, President of Congress:

Sir—

In a long and scurrilous libel against me which has, this morning, made its appearance, there is only one paragraph which can possibly give me uneasiness; of the rest I would rather be the subject than the author. The paragraph I allude to, Sir, is that respecting Gen. Moultrie's having defended Fort Sullivan against my judgment—This assertion throws me into the cruel alternative of either silently sitting down under a charge which may make an impression in the minds of the People unfavourable to my conduct and capacity or by justifying myself on these two points, expose to the world, at this critical juncture, a very dangerous truth with respect to that Post which has been held up as of such infinite importance—if Congress will condescend to appoint a Committee to hear what I have to say on this subject, I have no doubt of making my opinion and conduct appear well founded and satisfactory—but, if they think it descending from their dignity to make any inquiry in consequence of only what a scoundrel libellist such as this Brackenridge has thrown out, I entreat most earnestly that they will order to be republished the letter of thanks which they honored me with on the occasion but which ever measure They chuse to adopt, I earnestly request it may be immediately, as my affairs in Virginia are exceedingly distracted by my absence.[12]

Having indited this letter, Lee hastened to the editorial office with the intention of personally chastising "the scoundrelly libellist." He beat on the door, and Brackenridge, peering cautiously from an upper-story window, asked what was wanted.

"Come down," said Lee, "and I'll give you as good a horsewhipping as any rascal ever received."

"Excuse me, General," replied Brackenridge, who always preferred wit to bravery, "I would not go down for two such favors."[13] History remains discreetly silent as to the outcome of the dispute.

[12] *The Lee Papers,* Vol. III, p. 333. (In *Collections of the New York Historical Society for the Year 1873.*)
[13] *Biographical Notice,* p. 154.

It must be evident that Brackenridge had made a spirited effort in the first few numbers of *The United States Magazine* to excite and to hold the interest of the public, but apparently he soon lost hope and enthusiasm. The quality of the magazine deteriorated. Literary cleverness disappeared from its pages, giving place to prosaic military and political information. In the last few numbers Brackenridge filled much of his space by printing the State constitutions. His fears had been better founded than his hopes, and in the December issue he announced that the periodical would be discontinued:

This number which is for the last month of the year, will conclude the first volume of the Magazine: a publication undertaken at a time when it was hoped the war would be of short continuance, and the money, which had continued to depreciate, would become of proper value. But these evils having continued to exist through the whole year, it has been greatly difficult to carry on the publication; and we shall now be under the necessity of suspending it for some time, until an established peace, and a fixed value of the money, shall render it convenient or possible to take it up again.[14]

Brackenridge did not believe, however, that economic circumstances alone had determined the failure of his periodical. In caustic sentences he placed the responsibility upon the unpatriotic and the stupid.

There is one sort of people to whom the news of the suspension of this work will not be disagreeable; I mean those persons who are disaffected to the cause of America. These have been sorely pricked and buffeted with the sharp points of whiggism, which, like arrows from the great machines of Archimedes, have been darted out from it. They have been sorely injured by these points, and will be ready to believe, that in the suspension of the work is accomplished that prophesy of the Apocalypse, *And Satan shall be bound a thousand years.*

There is yet another class of men that will be sensible of some happiness, now that the mouth of this publication is in a fair way to be, at length, closed; I mean the people who inhabit the region of stupidity, and cannot bear to have the tranquillity of their repose disturbed by the villainous jargon of a book. Reading is to them the

14 *ibid.*, p. 483.

worst of all torments, and I remember very well that at the commencement of the work, it was their language, *Art thou come to tor-
ment us before the time.* We will now say to them, *Sleep on, and
take your rest.*

No man of common philanthropy would chuse to give pain to innocent though ignorant souls, when he has it in his power to help it.
It is but ceasing to blow our flutes for a while, and the beasts will
retire to their coverts, and be happy in the brown shades of their own
hills.[15]

Between the lines one may read a further reason for the failure
of the magazine. Brackenridge was already an adept in the gentle
art of making enemies. Almost every party and class had felt in
turn the sting of his biting wit, inspired in part by a concern for
the public good, and in part, it seems, by a spirit of sheer mischief.
The victims were naturally resentful. Charles Lee attempted re-
taliation with a horsewhip. Soberer citizens used saner means.
Henry Drayton, informed that Brackenridge had accused him
along with John Jay, Robert Morris, and Silas Deane of the
formation of a company to monopolize trade, wrote him an angry
letter of remonstrance. Brackenridge's reply, more conciliatory
than was usual with him, has been preserved. In it he reiterated
that there was a widespread belief in the existence of this profiteer-
ing organization:

If the Circumstances of your trading Connection is not true, you
and these Gentlemen have been greatly injured in the opinion of the
public, and you have been greatly injured in my opinion. For I assure
you that though I had thought it highly improbable, yet the frequent
relation had made such impression on my mind that I had appre-
hended there might be some truth in it, and this is the reason that
notwithstanding I have the honour to be introduced to yourself & to
these Gentlemen, yet I have cultivated your acquaintance with less
assiduity than I otherwise should have done. I had been led to believe
that not only you & these gentlemen were engaged in trade with Mr.
Deane, but that from that circumstance you were under biass to
screen him from an investigation into his affairs.[16]

[15] *Biographical Notice*, pp. 483-4.
[16] From manuscript copy of Brackenridge's letter in Ms. Department of the
Historical Society of Pennsylvania.

There was, of course, a brighter side to the picture. Bracken-ridge had made friends, many of them in influential quarters. His intellectual brilliance was well known, and he had achieved a repu-tation for oratory which secured for him the appointment to deliver "an Eulogium in memory of those brave men who have fallen in defence of our rights and privileges" at the elaborate ceremonies planned by the Constitutional Society of Philadelphia for the celebration of "the anniversary of our glorious Indepen-dence" in the year 1779.[17] The members of Congress and of the State Assembly had been invited to attend, under the escort of a company of militia and a military band,[18] and Brackenridge must have felt that he had been given an extraordinary opportunity for oratorical display when the ceremony began at the German Cal-vinist Church on Monday, July 5.

At twelve o'clock precisely the doors were thrown open, and the guards (with great politeness granted by General Hogan) were placed at the doors. The Ladies, an agreeable collection of whom honored the day with their presence, were handed through the guards, and in a radiant file adorned the front seats of the gallery.

The President of the State, the Minister Plenipotentiary and Consul of France, the Honorable the Members of Congress, the Council and Chief Justice of the State, the Clergy, the Magistrates, and Military Officers of the city, the Provosts, Professors and Students of the Col-lege, Gentlemen of the Law, Gentlemen of the neighboring States, and a respectable body of citizens, were present. Eighteen Gentlemen with white wands, were attentive to wait upon to proper seats, and to preserve order for the assembly.

A noble band of music favoured the occasion with marches, sym-phonies and overtures, and odes were sung at proper pauses in the delivery of the Eulogium.[19]

In this setting of officialdom and provincial pomp Brackenridge eloquently expounded his patriotic and democratic view of the Revolution:

[17] *United States Magazine,* p. 99.
[18] *Pennsylvania Archives, First Series,* Vol. X, p. 162.
[19] *United States Magazine,* p. 289.

I conceive it as the first honour of these men, that before they engaged in the war, they saw it to be just and necessary. They were not the vassals of a proud chieftain rousing them, in barbarous times, by the blind impulse of attachment to his family, or engaging them to espouse his quarrel, by the music and entertainment of his hall. They were themselves the chieftains of their own cause, highly instructed in the nature of it, and, from the best principles of patriotism, resolute in its defence. They had heard the declaration of the court and parliament of Great-Britain, claiming the authority of binding them in all cases whatsoever. They had examined this claim, and found it to be, as to its foundation, groundless, as to its nature, tyrannical, and in its consequences, ruinous to the peace and happiness of both countries. On this clear apprehension and decided judgment of the cause, ascertained by their own reason, and collected from the best writers, it was the noble purpose of their minds to stand forth and assert it, at the expence of fortune, and the hazard of their lives.[20]

While Brackenridge was editing *The United States Magazine* he was also prudently preparing himself for another profession. In *The Cave of Vanhest,* after telling of his abandonment of Miss Urany Muse and Miss Theology, he said:

The present object of my soft attentions is a *Miss Law,* a grave and comely young lady, a little pitted with the small pox.[21] Her steward, an old fellow of the name of Coke, is a dry queer genius, and with him I have almost every day a quarrel. However, upon the whole I am pleased with the old fellow, and tossing him about with a string of young fellows of a more chearful vein, and who are likewise attached to the family of Miss Law, I make myself merry with him. This young lady is of a prudent industrious turn, and, though she does not possess at present any very great fortune, yet what she has in expectancy is considerable.[22]

After the failure of *The United States Magazine,* Brackenridge evidently gave his attention wholly to the law. Of his further pro-

[20] *United States Magazine,* p. 343; and *Gazette Publications,* p. 162. The Eulogium was published as a book in 1779, and a German translation was issued the same year. It has been reprinted in H. H. Brackenridge's *Speeches on the Jew Bill,* pp. 183-91; and F. Moore's *American Eloquence* (1857), Vol. I, pp. 358-60.

[21] "The Saxon letter." (Brackenridge's note.)

[22] *United States Magazine,* p. 313.

fessional studies we only know that he "repaired to Annapolis and placed himself under the celebrated Samuel Chase."[23]

In December 1780 he was admitted to practise in the court of common pleas in Philadelphia.[24] He did not remain in that city, however, but, fulfilling the prophecy which he had uttered at Princeton in 1774, migrated to the frontier village of Pittsburgh. There, years later, he said:

When I left Philadelphia, almost twenty years ago, I saw no chance of being anything in that city, there were such great men before me, Chew, Dickinson, Wilson &c. I pushed my way to these woods where I thought I might emerge one day, and get forward myself in a congress or some other public body.[25]

[23] *Biographical Notice*, p. 156.
[24] J. H. Martin, *Bench and Bar of Philadelphia*, p. 281; and H. H. Brackenridge, *Law Miscellanies*, p. 511.
[25] *The Echo*.

CHAPTER VIII

THE SECOND FRONTIER

SO BRACKENRIDGE, in the spring of 1781, at the age of thirty-three, turned his back on the stimulating life of America's political and intellectual metropolis. We may in imagination see him, with Blackstone, Coke, and the Laws of Pennsylvania in his saddle-bags, and hopes of a brilliant future in his heart, set out to follow the old York road which narrowed to a mere horse trail as it crossed the Allegheny Mountains toward Pittsburgh.

The journey was tedious and difficult, punctuated by nights spent in primitive taverns or outdoor camps. One night which Brackenridge always remembered was spent at the home of Herman Husbands "in the glades of the Allegheny mountain." This eccentric had just completed a commentary on a part of the prophet Ezekiel.

It was the vision of the temple; the walls, the gates, the sea of glass, &c. Logger-head divines, heretofore, had interpreted it of the New Jerusalem; but he conceived it to apply to the western country; and the walls were the mountains, the gates, the gaps in them, by which the roads came, and the sea of glass, the lake on the west of us. I had no hesitation in saying, that the commentary was analagous to the vision. He was pleased; and said, I was the only person, except his wife, that he ever got to believe it. Thought I, your church is composed, like many others, of the ignorant and the dissembling.[1]

Once across the mountains, Brackenridge followed the partially settled Monongahela Valley to the forks of the Ohio, where there had been a settlement since the days of Fort Duquesne. He later said:

[1] *Incidents of the Western Insurrection,* Vol. I, p. 95.

I took up my residence in the town of Pittsburgh:

> "If town it might be called, that town was none
> Distinguishable by house or street"

But in fact a few old buildings, under the walls of a Garrison, which stood at the junction of two rivers. Nevertheless it appeared to me as what would one day be a town of note, and in the mean time might be pushed forward by the usual means which raise such places.[2]

The community to which he had come was in many respects like the York County of his boyhood.[3] Many of the settlers, in fact, had migrated from the Barrens district and other inland sections of Pennsylvania.[4] The population was composed largely of Scotch-Irish, Scotch, and Germans. They had created an environment which Brackenridge could readily understand but not one which he could find really congenial after his years in the more sophisticated society of Princeton and Philadelphia. Admittedly, he had come to the West in the hope of advancing his professional career, so that he might eventually "emerge."[5] His first concern, therefore, was to secure admission to practise at the bar.

Pittsburgh, although the most important settlement in Western Pennsylvania, was not the county seat, and Brackenridge had to travel to Hanna's Town, some thirty miles away, to attend court. Here, in April 1781, he was admitted in the quarter sessions court of Westmoreland County[6] and he appeared as attorney in four cases tried at the April session. In October he was admitted to practise in the first term of the court of Washington County, which had just been organized.[7]

Almost at once his legal work and his interest in public affairs brought him into intimate relation with the many-sided life of the Western frontier. The Indian wars, the separatist movement,

[2] *Gazette Publications*, p. 7.

[3] Joseph Doddrige's *Notes of the Settlements and Indian Wars of Virginia and Pennsylvania from 1763 to 1783* gives the fullest contemporary account of the pioneer life of Western Pennsylvania.

[4] *Biographical Notice*, p. 151.   [5] See above, p. 57.

[6] *Appearance Docket of Westmoreland County*, Vol. I.

[7] Boyd Crumrine, *Courts of Justice, Bench, and Bar of Washington County, Pennsylvania*, p. 262.

land-title disputes, road-making, the scarcity of money, and other frontier problems were to occupy his attention as lawyer and writer for the next few years.

It will be remembered that when Brackenridge started west in search of a career, the Revolutionary War was still in progress. In the East, Yorktown was yet to be fought; and in the West there were to be further forays against the Indians, such as had been frequently undertaken by the frontiersmen during the war. The last of these exploits provided the occasion for Brackenridge's first literary contribution from the frontier.

In the summer of 1782 Colonel Crawford led a punitive expedition from Western Pennsylvania against the Indians on the Sandusky River. The campaign ended in a rout of the Americans, several of whom were captured and tortured. John Slover, a typical illiterate frontiersman, and Dr. Knight, a physician, escaped from their captors, and succeeded in making their way back to Pittsburgh. Brackenridge secured accounts of their experiences, which he edited and sent to the *Freeman's Journal or North American Intelligencer,* of which Freneau was editor.[8] In introducing the documents Brackenridge said:

With the narratives enclosed, I subjoin some observations with regard to the animals vulgarly called Indians. It is not my intention to write any laboured essay; for at so great a distance from the city, and so long unaccustomed to write, I scarcely have resolution to put pen to paper. Having an opportunity to know something of the character of this race of men, from the deeds they perpetrate daily round me, I think proper to say something on the subject.

He then stated his belief that the Indians, as savages, had no natural right to the soil, and that it was quite useless to form treaties or make peace with them.

In the meantime more important political issues were attracting Brackenridge's attention. At the time when he took up his residence in Pittsburgh there was considerable disaffection toward the

---

[8] *The Narrative of the Perils and Sufferings of Dr. Knight and John Slover* was published in the *Freeman's Journal* serially in the issues of April 30, May 7, May 14, and May 28, 1783. It was also issued as a pamphlet in 1783 and was frequently reprinted.

State government among the frontiersmen. They felt that they had not been given sufficient support by the State in their defense of the border against the Indians.[9] Then, too, many inhabitants of the district were originally Virginians and they were dissatisfied with the boundary settlement of 1779 which had given the Pittsburgh region to Pennsylvania. These two causes of disaffection resulted in the inauguration of a movement to declare their independence of both Pennsylvania and Virginia and set up a western State bounded by Lake Erie, the Allegheny Mountains, the Kanawha River, and the Muskingum River. Brackenridge vigorously opposed these secessionist activities by appealing to members of the State assembly of Pennsylvania. He demonstrated to the legislators that secession would unjustly deprive the commonwealth of public lands in the west which were needed for raising the large sum pledged in compensation to the charter proprietaries.[10] On this basis a law was passed declaring treasonable any agitation for setting up a new State.[11]

Such was Brackenridge's first attempt to oppose the will of the frontiersmen. The result was disillusionizing. He later wrote:

If I had known the little account to which this turned afterwards by the mismanagement of the legislature and the land office, and speculators . . . and all these things obstructing the improvement and population of the country, I might have thought less of the value of my efforts on this occasion. Whatever they were, certain it is, that I encountered some danger in opposition to the popular current, on the Virginia side of the state.[12]

This first act of participation in the political life of Western Pennsylvania prefigured many aspects of Brackenridge's political activities during his twenty years' residence in the community. Although he was to be attentive to local Western interests, he was, by education and experience, also able to view issues from the State and the national points of view. His frequent disagree-

[9] *Law Miscellanies*, p. 512.   [10] *ibid.*, pp. 511-12.
[11] Smith's *Laws of Pennsylvania*, Vol. II, pp. 60-2.
[12] *Law Miscellanies*, p. 512.

ment, now with the Eastern, now with the Western political phi-
losophies, was to make him often unpopular.

In his legal practice, too, Brackenridge was often called upon
to handle cases which involved a clash between the Eastern and
the Western points of view. Much of the litigation in the Western
courts arose from the confused state of land titles in the pioneer
community. The settlers often squatted on the land and improved
it; and when, later, legal title to the same soil was acquired by
Eastern speculators, the numerous ejectment cases which followed made the courts the scene of conflict between the financial
seaboard and the agrarian frontier. Brackenridge, as a lawyer,
took cases on both sides. It is probable that his sympathies were
on the whole with the dispossessed settlers, but his interests as a
lawyer prompted him at times even to solicit cases in support of
the Eastern financiers, as the following letter to Bernard Gratz, a
Philadelphia capitalist, shows:

I have given up the people in this country against whom you have
brought your ejectments, all of whom have applyed to me. True I
expect that sooner or later you will make me an ample compensation.
I have also declined many suits against the estate of Col. Groghan. I
shall soon begin to think it time the executors give me a handsome
retaining fee to indemnify me; and also for the trouble I have taken
with regard to the lands and those upon them in the neighborhood of
Pittsburgh.[13]

Whether or not the handsome retaining fee was forthcoming
has not been recorded. There is, however, record of a case in which
Brackenridge defended thirteen settlers who had squatted on property which General Washington had bought from Colonel Groghan,
and whom the general sought to eject after they had refused his
offer to allow them to purchase or lease the tracts on which they
were living.[14] Brackenridge based his case for the settlers on the argument that Colonel Groghan had acquired his rights by purchase

[13] Manuscript in Autograph Collection of Simon Gratz, in Ms. Department of
the Historical Society of Pennsylvania.
[14] *The Diaries of George Washington,* ed. by John C. Fitzpatrick, Vol. II,
pp. 297-8.

from the Indians,[15] at a time when neither Virginia nor Pennsylvania had recognized "rights by Indian purchase."[16] Whatever the merits of this point may have been, Brackenridge lost the case, and "the general did not offer to make compensation" for the "cultivated fields, meadows, orchards, and buildings" with which his property had been improved.[17]

Another source of popular discontent and litigation in the West was the taxation system of Pennsylvania. In 1756 and again in 1772 the province of Pennsylvania had laid an excise duty on alcoholic liquors manufactured in the colony.[18] After the Declaration of Independence this tax was continued by an act of February 18, 1777.[19] From the beginning the excise was resisted in the West. Brackenridge explained this position as follows:

Collectors were appointed in the western country from time to time, but no attempt made by any of them, that I can trace, to collect the duties. It was thought to be an ignominious service; the name of an excise was odious. Whence the origin of this prejudice? Doubtless from the dominions of Great Britain. This country [Western Pennsylvania] is peopled by emigrants from North Britain and Ireland. The excise duties of those countries are extensive, they embrace almost every object of consumption; the people are in the habit of eluding them by every means possible. They hate excise officers and consider them as men having a distinct interest from that of the community. . . . Amongst the common people there is a horror of them, not only on account of the drawback which they make, but on account of the power which they have to enter houses, to search, and make seizures. . . . The people from these countries brought these impressions with them, when they came to America; and attach the same odium to excise laws and excise officers here, which they were accustomed to entertain before their emigration. Independent of these abstract prejudices, the people of the western country not having a market for their grain, had recourse to the distillation of it; and under the acts, all beyond what

[15] Boyd Crumrine, *History of Washington County, Pennsylvania*, p. 859; and B. A. Konkle, *Life and Times of Thomas Smith*, pp. 173-83.
[16] Boyd Crumrine, *History of Washington County, Pennsylvania*, p. 859.
[17] *Law Miscellanies*, pp. 257-8.
[18] *Incidents of the Western Insurrection*, Vol. III, p. 5.
[19] *ibid.*, Vol. III, pp. 5-6.

was for private use, was liable to the duties. Thus it became still more an object to evade the law, or oppose it.[20]

On account of these prejudices, the council of the State found it impossible to employ Westerners to collect the excise duties in the back country. In 1783, they appointed William Graham, a bankrupt tavern keeper of Philadelphia, as collector general for the district beyond the Alleghenies. Graham was unable to collect any taxes, although some of the farmer distillers gave him a few shillings to get rid of him. Still worse, he was subjected to persecution. The people "amused themselves at his expense, singeing his wig, cutting the tail of his horse, putting coals in his boots, and every other imaginable prank they could devise." In Westmoreland County in 1784, he was besieged in a public house a whole night, by persons who affected to be about to kill him. Fleeing to Washington County, "he was openly attacked by a mob of upwards of an hundred persons, and was shaved, and had his hair cut off, and was conducted and put over the Monongahela into Westmoreland, with threats of death if he returned to the Washington side of the river any more.[21]

Twelve of these rioters were brought to trial in 1785. Brackenridge was employed as their attorney, but his clients were convicted and fined. Later he said of this case:

It is to be presumed that I had been of the same opinion with my clients, that excise laws were odious, and that an honest fellow ought not to be severely treated, who had done nothing more than to shave the underhairs from the head of an excise man, who wore a wig at any rate.[22]

With respect to the excise, then, it appears that Brackenridge's views were in harmony with those of the back-country people. He pushed their interests, too, in the matter of road building. One of the most serious handicaps to the economic development of the West was the lack of means of transportation to the seaboard markets. Brackenridge saw that no attention could be given to the improvement of the roads between Philadelphia and Pittsburgh

20 *Incidents of the Western Insurrection,* Vol. III, p. 6.
21 *ibid.,* Vol. III, pp. 6-8.   22 *ibid.,* Vol. III, pp. 8, 13.

during the war, as the defense of the frontier against the Indians was the principal concern. But as soon as the war was over, he drew up a petition to the State assembly, and discussed the problem with Western members of the house. Also he appealed to the judges of the supreme court when they were on circuit in the Western counties in 1783.[23] Although this effort brought no immediate result, it shows that Brackenridge was early assuming leadership in the practical affairs of the Pittsburgh district.

However, it is not to be supposed that his life during these first years in the West was all spent in preoccupation with prosaic law suits and matters of public welfare. It is pleasant to turn from these to a poetic interlude which took place at Warm Springs, a popular watering-place in Virginia, where Brackenridge spent some days in the fall of 1784. We may readily imagine the excitement that seized the little community when word came that the Springs was to be honored for a day by the presence of George Washington, who was on a tour of inspection of his lands in Western Virginia and Pennsylvania. Brackenridge, no doubt the only poet and man of letters among the guests, at once took the lead in planning for the general's entertainment, and hurried to compose a masque in the style of the courtly productions of Ben Jonson and Milton,[24] such a performance as might have graced an Elizabethan progress. The Genius of the Springs, the Potomac, the Delaware, and the Ohio appropriately served as the dramatis personae. The style and content of the masque are well represented by the following speech by "Potomack" and the song of the Naiads:

> Go tell the naiads and the jocund deities,
> To cull their choicest flowers; a noble name,[25]
> Has come this day to do them honour.
> That chief whose fame has oft been heard by them,
> In contest with Britannia's arms; that chief

[23] *Pittsburgh Gazette,* May 17, 1788.
[24] *A Masque, Written at the Warm-Springs in Virginia, in the Year 1784.* Published in the *Pittsburgh Gazette,* June 16, 1787, and in *Gazette Publications,* pp. 35-40.
[25] "Washington." Brackenridge's note.

Whom I myself have seen quitting the farm,
By no ambition, but by virtue led,
Arising at his country's call, and swift
The challenge of the vet'ran foe receiving.
My brother streams have told me his atchievements.
The oak-crown'd Hudson told me that he saw him,
Walk like a God upon his well fought banks.
The Raritan in Jersey told me of him;
But most the Delaware, whose noble tide
Roll'd his indignant waves upon the bank
And triumphed on the heroic days
Of Brandywine, of Germantown and Monmouth;
The Rappahannock told me of the chief
When great Cornwallis yielded. With him I shed
A tear of lucent joy. The Chesapeake,
O! bay divine, thou heardst the victory,
And through thy hundred islands far and wide,
Rejoicing, there was gladness.

But when the rage of horrid war had ceas'd
My son return'd; I mark'd his character. . . .
No scorn appear'd upon his furrow'd brow,
His air was dignity and graceful ease
The same as when he left us, save that now
His visage worn with care shews more of age
I hail'd my son and bade him come with me
To taste the water of the healthful springs.

The Naiads in a Dance.
Purest streams that gently flow
    From the rock that covers you,
No decrease of tide you know,
    Summer suns do not subdue.

Nor do storms, fierce winter's brood,
    Rain or snow that comes with them,
Swell your current to a flood;
    You are still, pure streams, the same.

Emblem this of that great chief,
WASHINGTON who made us free,
Shewing 'midst our joy and grief
Equal equanimity.[26]

Unfortunately for the poet, General Washington was hardly in the mood for poetry on that September day in Warm Springs. He had had an unsatisfactory journey; his tenants, all along the line, had found a thousand excuses for non-payment, or very partial payment, of their rents and dues; excessive heat had galled the horses during the first days of travel, and on the day of his arrival at Warm Springs he had ridden from early morning till three o'clock through a drizzling rain.[27] Whatever impressions he may have formed of the masque and of the poet, he did not choose to confide to posterity. His diary for the day records that the hours were spent in the examination of a model mechanical boat, in making arrangements for the construction of buildings on the lots which he owned in the town, and in discussions relating to the project of the Potomac Navigation Company.[28] Of Brackenridge, he makes no mention, and it seems probable that his reception of the masque must have been a keen disappointment to its author.

Paulding relates how Brackenridge fell victim a second time, probably on this same day, to the "equal equanimity" which he had noted as a major characteristic of General Washington. He says:

The judge [Brackenridge] was an inimitable humorist, and, on a particular occasion, fell in with Washington at a public house, where a large company had gathered together for the purpose of discussing the subject of improving the navigation of the Potomac. They supped at the same table, and Mr. Brackenridge essayed all his powers of humour to divert the general; but in vain. He seemed aware of his purpose, and listened without a smile. However, it so happened that the chambers of Washington and Brackenridge adjoined, and were only separated from each other by a thin partition of pine boards. The general had retired first, and when the judge entered his own room, he was

[26] *Gazette Publications*, pp. 37-9.
[27] *The Diaries of George Washington*, ed. by John C. Fitzpatrick, Vol. II, p. 279.
[28] *ibid.*, Vol. II, pp. 282-5.

delighted to hear Washington, who was already in bed, laughing to himself with infinite glee, no doubt at the recollection of his stories.[29]

The reader cannot help wondering whether these successive disappointments may not have barbed Brackenridge's tongue with a sharper irony than usual when he appeared to defend the general's ejected tenants at the next quarter sessions. If so, it was in vain; the verdict was a third disappointment.

Another incident of this period is worth telling, both for the vivid picture it gives of certain aspects of frontier life, and for the light that it throws upon the character of Brackenridge himself. Across the river from Pittsburgh where the city of Allegheny now lies, there was situated at this time an Indian camp, where the Indians and the rougher element among the whites met for trading, drinking, gaming, and general brawling. Here, in 1785, an Indian called Mamachtaga murdered two white men in a drunken quarrel. He was at once arrested and flung into the black hole, an underground dungeon, to await the inevitable meting out of frontier justice. Some macabre whim led Brackenridge to interest himself in the case, to which his attention had probably been drawn by the fact that one of the murdered men had been recently in his employ. Ascertaining that Mamachtaga had a store of beaver skins which would suffice for a lawyer's fee, he visited the Indian's cell in company with an interpreter and offered to defend him. The poor savage, however, was so ignorant of the enlightened laws of the white man, that he could not be made to understand the offer. He knew that he was guilty, the world knew it too, and the idea embodied in a plea of not guilty was quite beyond his power to grasp. He was quite willing to surrender his beaver pelts to the lawyer, but supposed in doing this that he was paying for a commutation of sentence. Despairing at last of making himself understood, Brackenridge abandoned the idea of taking a fee, but arranged through the sale of the pelts to provide the prisoner with food and blankets until the time of his trial.

As payment for his pains, evidently, Brackenridge decided to secure some ethnological information from his client. "I had a curiosity," he said, "to know the force of abstract sentiment, in preferring greater evils to what with us will be less; or rather the force of opinion over pain." On a visit to the prisoner, he found an Indian woman who spoke English sitting by the trapdoor of Mamachtaga's cell, out of sympathy. Knowing the idea of the Indians with regard to the disgrace of hanging, he requested the squaw to ask Mamachtaga whether he preferred to be hanged or burned. But she seemed to be "struck by the inhumanity of introducing the idea of death," and "she not only declined to put the question, but her countenance expressed resentment." Brackenridge then recollected that it was a custom of the Indians never to tell a condemned person that he was to be put to death. He was not to be foiled by a tribal taboo, however, and he then put the question to the victim through an interpreter. The Indian replied that he would rather be shot or tomahawked than either hanged or burned.

The lawyer's desire to find diversion in this case was further hindered by the prejudices of the frontiersmen.

In a few days it made a great noise through the country that I was to appear for the Indian, and having acquired some reputation in the defence of criminals, it was thought possible by some that he might be acquitted by *the crooks of the law,* as the people expressed it; and it was talked of publickly to raise a party and come to town and take the interpreter and me both, and hang the interpreter, and exact an oath from me not to appear in behalf of the Indian. It was however, finally concluded to come into the garrison and demand the Indian, and hang him themselves. Accordingly, a party came, in a few days, and about break of day summoned the garrison, and demanded the surrender of the Indian; the commanding officer remonstrated, and prevailed with them to leave the Indian to civil authority. Upon which they retired, firing their guns as they came through the town. . . .

It did not appear to me advisable to relinquish the defence of the Indian, fee or no fee, lest it should be supposed I yielded to the popular impression, the fury of which, when it had a little spent itself, began to subside, and there were some who thought the Indian might be cleared, if it could be proved that the white men killed had made the Indian drunk, which was alleged to be the case.

This was, indeed, the line of argument that Brackenridge followed at the trial, but in spite of the lawyer's eloquence, Mamachtaga was convicted and hanged.[30]

From Brackenridge's narrative of the case of Mamachtaga it appears that he had acquired considerable local note as a lawyer. He had been in Pittsburgh over four years and was making preparations to become a householder in the village. He had purchased a number of building lots in 1785[31] and it was probably on one of these that he was building the house which he mentions as having been shingled by one of the men murdered by Mamachtaga. Brackenridge's first marriage probably took place about this time, although there are no extant records of it.[32] On May 11, 1786, his son Henry Marie Brackenridge was born.[33] Although both father and son embodied many autobiographical facts in their writings, they neglected to describe, or even to name, Brackenridge's first wife, who died before Henry Marie was eighteen months old.[34]

With the summer of 1786 a period of broader activity begins in the Western career of Brackenridge. During the first five years of his residence on the frontier he had achieved a good legal practice, had lent a hand now and then in the public affairs of the Western country, had become a householder, had married, and had become the father of a son who was to be a man of note.

[30] Loudon's *Indian Narratives*, Vol. I, pp. 38-50.

[31] Deed Book B, p. 92 (Westmoreland County, Pennsylvania). Brackenridge sold several of these lots the next year; *ibid.*, pp. 93-4.

[32] No church had yet been established in which records could be kept, and records of marriages were not kept by the county clerks of this period.

[33] H. M. Brackenridge, *Recollections of Persons and Places in the West* (1868), p. 10.

[34] *ibid.*, p. 10.

CHAPTER IX

POLITICS AND JOURNALISM

ON JULY 29, 1786, the first number of the *Pittsburgh Gazette* was published. Brackenridge said of his part in this journalistic venture:

One of the earliest things which I thought of on going to reside in the western country, was the encouragement of a public paper. An establishment of this nature was accomplished after some time, and a good deal by my exertions. With a view to assist it I wrote some things serious and some ludicrous. . . . I had an ambition; or rather I obeyed the impulse of my mind in being among the first to bring the press to the west of the mountains; so that in a small instance I might say with the poet,

> Primus ego in patriam mecum. . . .
> Aonio rediens deducans vertice musas.[1]

He of course made full use of the newspaper, and it played no small part in his activities during the next fifteen years. It was an essential medium for publishing his literary bagatelles, for promoting the interests of the Pennsylvania frontier, and for advancing his own political ambitions.

For the first issue of the *Gazette* he wrote an idealized description of the Pittsburgh of his day, "intended to give some reputation to the town with a view to induce emigration to this particular spot."[2] It is interesting to compare the publicity writing of the 1780's with that of present-day promoters.

You will see in a spring evening the banks of the rivers lined with men fishing at intervals, from one another. This, with the streams gently gliding, the woods, at a distance green, and the shadows lengthening towards the town, forms a delightful scene. . . .

This bank [of the Monongahela] is closely set with buildings for the distance of near half a mile, and behind this range the town

---

[1] *Gazette Publications,* pp. 23-4.   [2] *ibid.,* p. 7.

chiefly lies, falling back on the plains between the two rivers. . . .
The town consists at present of about an hundred dwelling houses,
with buildings appurtenant. More are daily added, and for some time
past it has improved with an equal but continual pace. The inhabitants,
children, men and women are about fifteen hundred;[3] doubling almost
every year from the accession of people from abroad, and from those
born in the town. . . .

There is not a more delightful spot under heaven to spend any of
the summer months than at this place. . . . Here we have the breezes
of the river, coming from the Mississippi and the ocean; the gales that
fan the woods, and are sent from the refreshing lakes to the north-
ward; in the mean time the prospect of extensive hills and dales,
whence the fragrant air brings odours of a thousand flowers and
plants, or of the corn and grain of husbandmen, upon its balmy wings.
Here we have the town and the country together. How pleasant is it
in a summer evening, to walk out upon these grounds; the smooth
green surface of the earth, and the woodland shade softening the late
fervid beams of the sun; how pleasant by a chrystal fountain in a
tea party under one of those hills, with the rivers and the plains
beneath. . . .

In the fall of the year and during the winter season, there is usually
a great concourse of strangers at this place, from the different states,
about to descend the river to the westward, or to make excursions into
the uninhabited and adjoining country. These, with the inhabitants
of the town spend the evening in parties at the different houses, or at
public balls, where they are surprised to find an elegant assembly of
ladies, not to be surpassed in beauty and accomplishments perhaps by
any on the continent.

It must appear like enchantment to a stranger, who after travelling
an hundred miles from the settlements, across a dreary mountain, and
through the adjoining country where in many places the spurs of the
mountains still continue, and cultivation does not always shew itself,
to see, all at once, and almost on the verge of the inhabited globe, a
town with smoking chimnies, halls lighted up with splendor, ladies
and gentlemen assembled, various music, and the mazes of the dance.
He may suppose it to be the effect of magic, or that he is come into a

---

[3] More sober statistics give the figure as between four hundred and five hundred
in 1788. N. B. Craig, *History of Pittsburgh*, p. 192. The population at the census
of 1800 was only 1,565.

new world where there is all the refinement of the former, and more benevolence of heart.[4]

In another series of articles entitled "Observations on the Country at the Head of the Ohio" Brackenridge sought to attract public attention to the needs of the West, laying particular emphasis on the commercial importance of Pittsburgh's location as a reason for encouraging the development of the city.[5] While in these articles Brackenridge was ostensibly appealing to the State legislators, he was really preparing the way for a political campaign of his own. A week after he had completed his series of observations on the Pittsburgh region, he proposed himself as a candidate for the State assembly, and published a detailed statement of his policies. To the electors of Westmoreland County he said:

The time of electing persons to represent you in the assembly of the state being near, I have been led to reflect a little on the subject. You would wish them no doubt to attend to the general interests of the commonwealth; but there are local interests of this Western Country to which it is necessary that a particular attention be paid. Next April is the time limited within which we are to take out patents for our lands. That time must be extended. Such is the scarcity of money in the country, that few will be able to take out patents before that period.

We entertain the hope that even this session a law will be enacted enabling us to patent on the applications of 1769, and on the old warrants, by certificates, as is now done on the new warrants. But if that point should not be gained this session it ought to be strongly urged at every session until it is gained. . . .

It is the interest of the public that titles to real property should be settled, and I believe in general that office rights should prevail. Nevertheless there are special cases where great iniquity is done, unless settlement can be given in evidence before the courts of justice. It is therefore in my opinion expedient that a law be enacted enabling the judges to receive such testimony.

I conceive it to be a public good to this country that the town of Pittsburgh be encouraged, that it be made a borough, that it have a seat of justice, that it have a school endowed in it.

[4] *Gazette Publications*, pp. 7-19.   [5] *Pittsburgh Gazette*, August 25, 1786.

But there is a point of still greater moment which interests us at present. It is said the court of Spain has lately made a proposition to the states of America, to give them a free trade to all the Spanish ports in our own bottoms, on this condition, that we relinquish all idea of a trade by the Mississippi for the space of 25 years. It becomes the representatives of this Western Country to remonstrate in the strongest terms in the assembly of the state against such agreement, that Pennsylvania may instruct her representatives in the Congress to oppose it.

It is natural for those who have an object at heart to be disposed to put a hand to accomplish it. From this cause it has happened that the writer of these thoughts has reflected with himself what it would be in his power to do in this special crisis.

He thinks it may be convenient for him to serve during the ensuing year as a representative in the assembly, and as he resides in Westmoreland would offer himself for that county. . . .[6]

In thus stating his program Brackenridge clearly formulated the problems that were causing unrest in the Western counties: scarcity of money, conflicting claims on land tracts, and the aggravation of the transportation problem caused by the closing of the Mississippi to Americans. In touching upon this last topic he brought forth from a correspondent to the *Gazette* a strong expression of the local feeling:

I observe in the last Pittsburgh Gazette in Mr. Brackenridge's address to the electors of Westmoreland county, that there has been a proposal made by the court of Spain to the United States of America, offering them a free trade to all Spanish ports, in American bottoms, provided they relinquish any *idea* of a trade down the Mississippi for the space of 25 years . . . it is feared that Congress will adopt the measure, for several reasons. Should that be the case, you are in a ruined and undone situation. After all the dangers, difficulties and fatigues you have undergone in removing to, and settling this wild and uncultivated desart, through difficulties and dangers innumerable . . . the only channel is to be shut up thro' which you can ever expect to have any regular trade to bring your produce to market.[7]

[6] *Pittsburgh Gazette*, September 9, 1786.   [7] *ibid.*, September 16, 1786.

The only record of pre-election discussion is in a few such letters to the *Gazette*. Brackenridge himself contributed one under the pseudonym of "Angus MacMore" in which he criticised the Western members of the assembly.

We have read over the extract of the debates in the house of assembly. I would wish to see a great deal less said, and more done. The vanity of talking appears to be visible in many of them. There are two or three of them that are up and down every minute like the elbow of a man playing on the fiddle. It makes my heart sore to hear the members from our own county jankling about small points, until land jobbers are running away with our property, by laying warrants on improvements. Honest Thomas Macmurrowky has lost his plantation, unless a law is made to exclude these rights. All last year was taken up about the bank. The devil take them and the bank both. The concerns of the western country are being neglected on account of this bank, when it might have stood another year, till we had time to consider the consequences of the institution.[8]

After a successful campaign, Brackenridge went to Philadelphia in the autumn of 1786 to represent his county in the State assembly. At that time the State legislatures were relatively much more important than they are now. The moribund Congress under the Articles of Confederation had little authority and less force; hence many functions now performed by the national government and many problems now considered as national ones were left to the States, which still retained much of their colonial individuality. Then, too, the persistent conflict between the financial East and the agrarian West was waged between the two halves of States rather than between the sections of a continent. It was natural, therefore, that many of the most important statesmen should be found serving in the local governments. In Pennsylvania, Benjamin Franklin was President of the Executive Council, and Robert Morris a State legislator. At this particular time the great issue in Pennsylvania was the conflict over the radical constitution which had already puzzled Brackenridge in 1779. The parties, formed on this issue, were the constitutionalists, or "radicals," and the

8 *ibid.*, September 30, 1786; and *Gazette Publications*, pp. 34-5.

anti-constitutionalists, or "aristocrats." In general the West favored the old radical constitution and the East opposed it, but party divisions were frequently disturbed by other sectional interests.[9] Brackenridge, by nature a free lance, refused, from the very first, to be bound to any single group. In consequence, he was destined, almost at once, to incur the wrath of his Western constituents.

The first session of the Eleventh General Assembly opened October 25, 1786, but Brackenridge did not present himself until November 13.[10] He did not have to wait long for an opportunity to work on the problems in which he was interested. On the day he took his seat, petitions from Washington County were read demanding that actual settlement be given preference over office rights in determining the ownership of Western land. On the next day he was named a member of the committee appointed to consider this question.[11] On November 17 he was put on the committee appointed to draw up a plan for the sale of the reserved lands opposite Pittsburgh,[12] some of which he hoped to have set aside as an endowment for the Pittsburgh Academy. A few days later, on November 30, he was nominated to the committee appointed to bring in a bill for the erection of a new county with Pittsburgh as its seat.[13] Thus during the first few weeks of his membership in the assembly he had kept literally his campaign promise to work for the Western country.

Meanwhile he had been considering the bill which was designed to permit settlers to pay for their lands partly in cash and partly in State certificates of indebtedness. He had promised to support this measure at the time of his election, but he had since been convinced, probably through the influence of Robert Morris, that it was unwise.[14] So, in spite of his campaign promises, he spoke

[9] The constitutional history of Pennsylvania for the period is most fully treated in B. A. Konkle, *George Bryan and the Constitution of Pennsylvania*, and S. B. Harding, "Party Struggles over the First Pennsylvania Constitution," *American Historical Association, Annual Report*, 1894, pp. 371-404.
[10] *Minutes of the First Session of the Eleventh General Assembly*, p. 32.
[11] *ibid.*, p. 33.   [12] *ibid.*, p. 42.   [13] *ibid.*, p. 57.
[14] *Pittsburgh Gazette*, April 28, 1787.

against the bill when the debate opened on December 1. His argument, as reported in the *Pittsburgh Gazette,* was as follows:

He thought, if adopted, it would be injurious to the interest of the people in the western country—and for this reason—the value of the certificates would rise in proportion to the demand for them, and the demand in proportion to the number of persons who came to the market. . . .

It was extremely difficult for people in his part of the country to obtain enough money to pay for certificates, to warrant the land they had a right to by occupancy, and as this measure would tend to raise them still higher, and so make it more difficult, he was opposed to it. Again, it would not only give to the speculation hinted at by a worthy member from the city (Mr. Morris) but would greatly encrease for a time the value of certificates, which he was directly opposed to. . . . He remarked upon the fortunes acquired by speculators, men devoid of honesty and principles, by getting measures of this kind adopted. For tho' it was held out to relieve those who owed arrearages to the state, it would not do it so greatly as expected. These certificates would rise in their value, and the poor farmer, instead of getting them for two and six-pence, or five shillings the pound, would be obliged to give ten or fifteen shillings.[15]

These arguments, felt by his constituents to be specious and insincere, were destined to convince no one. It is probable that Brackenridge's own conversion was an honest one, although it may have been the more easily effected because of the fact that he could not but feel himself more closely allied in spirit to men of cultivation and intelligence such as Robert Morris and others of the Eastern delegation, than to the crude and uneducated, if not simple, representatives of the frontier. However this may be, in that day as now a politician could not change his views after election without raising the cry of "traitor." In spite of the fact that Brackenridge continued to labor faithfully for the advancement of other measures dear to the West, the wrath of his constituents was not to be averted. But of this he was as yet unaware.

On December 6 he introduced the academy bill.[16] On December

15 *ibid.,* February 3, 1787.
16 *Minutes of the First Session of the Eleventh General Assembly,* p. 66.

7 he was appointed to a committee which was to prepare a bill providing that titles to improved land should be issued only to actual settlers.[17] On December 12 he was made a member of the committee to report on petitions for improving roads to the West,[18] and on the same day his bill for incorporating a "religious Christian Society" in Pittsburgh was introduced.[19]

On the next day, however, Brackenridge again allied himself with the "aristocratic" Eastern group by supporting the motion to restore the charter of the Bank of North America,[20] a measure unpopular with the West, and one which in his campaign writings he had seemed to disapprove.

A few days later the open conflict began among a small group of Western assemblymen[21] who had met at the house of Thomas McKean, the Chief Justice. David Redick and Brackenridge were arguing about the bank. Redick said that it was the opinion of some of the people "that Mr. Morris had it in view to make an advantage of the bank to himself and a few friends, rather than to serve the public." Brackenridge answered loudly, "The people are fools; if they would let Mr. Morris alone, he would make Pennsylvania a great people, but they will not suffer him to do it." Mr. Smiley overheard this injudicious remark and objected, saying that he did not think any man had a right to make such a declaration. Brackenridge angrily "dropped his brows" and refused to pursue the subject.

Later in the evening Redick asked Brackenridge whether he did not think the people of the Western country would be dissatisfied because he had not voted in favor of receiving certificates. Brackenridge answered that he would satisfy the people by making a statement of the case in the *Pittsburgh Gazette*.[22] Thus he committed the final folly of that unfortunate evening. However innocent in intention his words may have been, he had, in the presence of political rivals, expressed his opinion that the people were fools, and easily to be hoodwinked by anything he cared to tell them

---

[17] *Minutes*, p. 68.   [18] *ibid.*, p. 72.   [19] *ibid.*, p. 75.   [20] *ibid.*, p. 76.
[21] William Findley, David Redick, John Smiley and Brackenridge.
[22] *Pittsburgh Gazette*, April 21, 1787.

through the medium of the press. For this was the way in which his hearers were to interpret his words to the public. Taken in connection with his about-face on the certificate bill and his support of the bank, these remarks were sufficient to complete the wreck of his political hopes.

On December 16 his promised statement appeared in the *Gazette* in the form of a letter in which he gave a full report of his work on legislation which concerned the West, and explained why he had changed his opinion regarding the measure for paying land arrearages with certificates.[23]

In the interval between the first and second periods of the legislative term, the storm broke over his head. The people were furious at his opposition to the land payment bill. "A Farmer," writing to the *Gazette,* suggested that he had treacherously "sold the good will of his country for a dinner of some stockholder's fat beef." He added:

Must I quit my title to a most excellent tract of land after my pains of having it surveyed, riding to Philadelphia, entering my survey, with the addition of considerable expence, and no small fatigue of body? What must my feelings be at such a prospect? Nay, the very horse I rode, poor Jack . . . were he alive, would groan to hear I had lost both my labour and purse, and all to satisfy the voracious maw of some greedy broker.[24]

And now William Findley, the other representative from Westmoreland County, a vociferous champion of the people, came forward with a letter to the *Gazette* in which, after referring to Brackenridge's statement as a "pompous account" of recent legislative transactions, he put before the public his own version of Brackenridge's recent activities and of the conversation on that unfortunate night at Justice McKean's. He said:

When a member is chosen who doth not solicit the trust, nor perhaps expects it, which is the case generally with modest, disinterested men, his not having determined his own mind, or having changed sentiments even respecting known cases, is not very strange; but when

23 *ibid.,* January 6, 1787.
24 *ibid.,* January 20, 1787.

a gentleman who professes the greatest acquired abilities, and most shining imagination, makes a prey of the people's confidence, betrays their interests, and trifles with his own solemn professions, he may expect the people to look upon him with indignation and treat him with contempt. After the aforesaid vote, upon the gentleman being asked how he would reconcile his conduct with his professions to his constituents? he replied, that the people were all fools, and by putting a few lines in the newspapers he would easily reconcile them to his views; this, however, I would have passed over as an explosion of unguarded vanity, had I not seen his delusory attempt to impose upon the people by his insidious observations on this business in your newspaper.[25]

Thus began a controversy between Brackenridge and William Findley which was to have important consequences in Brackenridge's political and literary career.

The second session of the assembly, which sat from February 20 to March 29, 1787, was not so provocative of popular resentment, since most of the business was a continuation of work on bills introduced in the first session. Brackenridge's chief contribution to the proceedings was a powerful presentation of the Western view of the projected Spanish treaty, which involved the closing of the Mississippi to American commerce. During the first session he had not been able to get the house to debate this question. When vigorous petitions from the West were introduced they were merely "ordered to lie on the table" and a committee was appointed.[26] When it became evident, during the second session, that the report of the committee would be unfavorable to the Western demands, Brackenridge feared that he had lost his chance of getting a hearing on the subject. So, in order to secure a debate, he tried to introduce certain resolutions in place of the report. He described this attempt as follows:

It was difficult to obtain leave because . . . a number of the eastern members, especially of the mercantile interest, were in favor of admitting the Spanish proposition, and they are much disgusted with the greater part of our western members in what has respected trade. This

[25] *Pittsburgh Gazette,* February 10, 1787.
[26] *Minutes of the First Session of the Eleventh General Assembly,* p. 105.

gives them a prejudice against the country in general. They say that we come down like Huns, Goths and Vandals upon them, and join with those who tear up charters, and the most sacred engagements of government. I reasoned a great deal with them on this subject, and they have paid me the compliment to say that I had discovered a liberality, and they would yield that to me which they would not to any other, viz. they would not oppose my obtaining leave to offer my resolutions, and to support them with my arguments on the floor, but I could not expect they would vote for them.[27]

Having thus obtained an opportunity to speak on the question, Brackenridge made a forceful plea for justice to the West. After dealing with the legal aspects of the subject he said:

It is laid down by some merchants with whom I have conversed, that a trade with the western country would be more profitable than a trade with Spain. This country will be the Germany of America; officium gentium, the great birthplace of nations, where millions yet unborn shall exist: it will be the Russia of America in point of trade which will be carried on. Iron, lumber, hemp, hides, fur and other things will be carried hence by the merchants of these very towns on the sea coast, and like the towns in Holland and England by the Russian trade, they will be enriched and aggrandized. Not until the population of the western country is extended will even Philadelphia become a great city. I have seen this during the war; the traders coming from this city, planting themselves on our rivers with merchandise and stores, and collecting the produce of the country, descending by the Ohio River, and vending their cargoes at New Orleans, or in foreign markets—returned again to this city, and laid out the money which they had acquired. . . . Since the decline of trade, even at this time, the whole country languishes: the wheat of last year lies in the barn: there is no object to prompt industry—we are sinking to the pastoral and bordering on the barbaric state.

Later in his speech Brackenridge maintained that failure to listen to the West would rouse the separatist spirit of the frontier:

Will it not alienate the affections of this infant country? Will they not bind themselves with Canada, or endeavour to detach some of the southern states? Is it of no service to preserve the affections of this

[27] *Pittsburgh Gazette*, April 28, 1787.

infant country? . . . Make peace with the young lion; an injury in distress is not easily forgotten—favours to the unprotected are more gratefully remembered. The western country may long be preserved by the maternal embrace of the eastern part of the continent. . . .

It is my voice that we instruct our delegates, that with firmness they expostulate with Spain on this point, and obtain an instant relinquishment of the unjust claim, an instant opening of this river to our trade. It is my voice, and there are two hundred thousand people on the west of the mountains . . . who, were they present, would shout the same language.[28]

Brackenridge's eloquence was not powerful enough to break the resistance of the East. His colleague Findley was indifferent to this measure, and the resolutions were saved from downright defeat only by the device of securing postponement of action on them.[29]

During the interval between the second and third sessions of the assembly the discussion of Brackenridge's political conduct was resumed in Pittsburgh. "A Farmer" defended Brackenridge against Findley's attack:

I have been at Philadelphia, in different sessions, and resided there some time as a spectator, and have had an opportunity of observing the conduct of both of these gentlemen and the assembly in general. I can with the greatest boldness assert, that I never knew a member from any county possessed with greater zeal to serve his constituents. . . .

Mr. Brackenridge did not join Mr. Findley's party. I am well convinced that Mr. Brackenridge went to Philadelphia divested of any party views, and meant to take that advantage of the parties as might best enable him to serve the county he represented.[30]

Brackenridge's services were also noted in the capital. A gentleman in Philadelphia wrote to a friend in Pittsburgh:

I cannot omit this opportunity of testifying how much Mr. Brackenridge has done for the advancement of your part of the state. By accommodating in one or two particulars to the members of the eastern district of the state in matters of no concern to the back counties, he has acquired an influence which has enabled him to render you

[28] *Pittsburgh Gazette*, May 5, 1787; and *Gazette Publications*, pp. 41-52.
[29] *ibid*.   [30] *ibid.*, April 14, 1787.

great and essential services. His colleagues perhaps complain of his separating himself from them in sundry votes, but you may rest satisfied that by doing so he has secured friends to his constituents in matters of more consequence. In the opinion of all candid people he has acted the part of an honest, independent man. His speeches on the bank and the Mississippi business, shew him to be an enlightened and sensible legislator. They were admired by good judges, and thought to be equal to any of the speeches of Pitt and Fox in the house of commons in England.[31]

Brackenridge did not, however, leave his defense to his admirers. He himself answered the charges of Findley. On April 21, 1787, the *Pittsburgh Gazette* published the first instalment of an address "To the Inhabitants of the Western Country." Succeeding instalments appeared in the next seven issues of the paper. In this address Brackenridge gave an elaborate exposition of the legislative proceedings on bills which interested the West, and attempted to show that he had been faithful to the Western interests, while Findley, who posed as the man of the people, had, on account of ignorance, incapacity, and spite, refused to work for them.

To Findley's accusation that he had betrayed the people by not keeping his campaign promise on the certificate question, Brackenridge replied:

If my proposing, implied a promise to endeavour to accomplish, that promise implied a condition that it should be found consistent with the general good. On taking a seat in the house, I conceived myself to possess the power of deliberation, to act as I thought proper. . . .

If the representative had not a latitude of reflection notwithstanding every former sentiment, how could he act consistent with his oath when he takes his seat in the house. . . . From this oath it must appear that a representative is not supposed to be a mere machine, like a clock wound up, to run for many hours in the same way; he is sent to hear from others, & to think for himself, as well as to vote. . . .

I proposed a number of points to the people, and this case of certificates is the only one with respect to which I changed my mind: I have labored diligently to accomplish all the rest: nevertheless this was a point with respect to which I thought myself clear. . . . I knew that I

[31] *ibid.*

should bring upon myself the railing of the interested and the uninformed, and both might do me damage. But what I did I still approve, and were it a new case, I would do it again.

It is certain the people do not always know their own interest, nor do individuals know. It is the prayer of philosophy, give us those things which suit us, though we ask them not, and deny us what is hurtful to us even though we ask it.

To know what is a proper public measure in any state requires a perfect knowledge of the whole system of finance. The people at home know each man his own wishes and wants. Had they the same opportunity which we enjoy, in our present situation, doubtless they would be equally informed.

It is the height of ability to be able to distinguish clearly the interests of a state; the system is oftentimes complex, intricate and involved. . . .

The maxim is, every man is greatly to be trusted in his own province or course of knowledge. I pay great regard to any man in a particular case of whose knowledge of the subject in general I have a high opinion.[32]

In thus defending his exercise of independent judgment and in stating the limitations of the average citizen, Brackenridge made his first definite formulation of the political philosophy which was to dominate his writings for the next score of years, and was to be largely responsible for his political failure. A few weeks of experience in the assembly had taught him that the people were jealous, suspicious, and intolerant. Pursuing his attempt to placate them, however, he showed how he had worked for the welfare of the Western counties. In answer to Findley's accusation that he had sought election to the assembly for selfish purposes he said:

I had strong *interest* to prompt me to *offer* myself to that place. The same interest which prompts me to wish the wealth and happiness of the western country, in every point of view. My residence, and all the property I have is here, and in proportion as it is rendered flourishing, I profit by it; wealth cannot be drawn from a poor country. My object was to advance the country, and thereby advance myself.[33]

[32] *Pittsburgh Gazette,* April 21, 1787.
[33] *ibid.,* April 28, 1787.

In later instalments of his defense, he related with great fulness his labors for the land-title bill, the road bill, and other measures related to the welfare of the West. He also showed that Findley had refused to support these measures. His apology did not satisfy the people, however. In fact, Findley's attack had placed him in a dilemma from which there seemed to be no escape. The more he protested, the more it must have appeared to his constituents that he was attempting to hoodwink them with fair words and sophistical arguments. Several years later, referring to this dispute with Findley, he said:

I had thought to have defended myself by writing, but only made the matter worse, for the people thought it impossible that a plain simple man could be wrong, and a profane lawyer right.[34]

When the assembly met for the beginning of the third session on September 5, 1787, "the Honorable Mr. Speaker represented to the House, that the room they usually sat in was, at present, occupied by the Federal Convention,"[35] and requested them to continue their regular order of business upstairs. The new Federal Constitution was to be the most important subject for discussion during this session, but the Assembly continued to occupy itself with local affairs until the last week in September, and Brackenridge was busy pushing the bills in which he was interested.

On September 7 he succeeded in getting five thousand acres of land set aside as an endowment for the Pittsburgh Academy.[36] On September 14 the bill for erecting a new county with Pittsburgh as its seat was passed.[37] On September 21 the bill for the incorporation of a non-sectarian church in Pittsburgh, which he had introduced in the first session, came up for consideration. Meanwhile, however, a Presbyterian minister in Pittsburgh had, without consulting Brackenridge, manoeuvered to "alter the firm to Presbyterian Congregation."[38] When the amendment was moved, Brackenridge said to the assembly:

[34] *Incidents of the Western Insurrection*, Vol. III, p. 13.
[35] *Proceedings and Debates of the General Assembly of Pennsylvania*, Vol. I, p. 3.
[36] *ibid.*, Vol. I, p. 7.   [37] *ibid.*, Vol. I, pp. 30-48.   [38] *ibid.*, Vol. I, p. 74.

The people of Pittsburgh now wish many of them to have the term Presbyterian in the bill. I have no objections; there will another bill be brought forward at a future time, to incorporate an Episcopal church; it is the wish of some that I should have brought it forward in this session, but I did not chuse to give myself further trouble in ecclesiastical affairs. It is a delicate thing to touch the ark. I might make a blunder, and the less consequence anything is of, there is the more noise made about it. The people of that town were all well disposed to remain under one roof; but wherever priests come they make trouble.[39]

So Brackenridge's first year as a legislator drew toward its close. Only one great question now remained for consideration during the final days of the session, that of the Federal Constitution. To the casual eye the year may at first seem to have been a failure for Brackenridge. He had become further alienated from the church, had reached a profound disillusionment as regards the political wisdom of the people, and had sown the seeds of his own eventual political failure. But from this bitter brew of disappointment and frustration he was in time to distil the pungent wit of *Modern Chivalry*, and thereby to achieve a recognition denied to the more successful politicians who flouted him. Moreover, in the field of local politics, his services to his constituents had not been negligible, and, before the final adjournment of the house, he was to contribute materially to the stability of the national government through his support of the Federal Constitution.

[39] *Proceedings and Debates of the General Assembly of Pennsylvania,* Vol. I, p. 76.

CHAPTER X

THE FEDERAL CONSTITUTION

THE Federal Constitution was submitted unofficially to the assembly by Pennsylvania members of the convention on September 17. It was to meet stubborn opposition from the State "constitutionalist" party, which included most of the Western members, and was to be defended by the Eastern "aristocratic" group.[1] In this party and sectional struggle, Brackenridge was to show his characteristic independence.

On September 24, 1787, the discussion of the Constitution was begun in the assembly. The first day's activities rather strangely found Brackenridge and William Findley in agreement. Findley moved that "the House would direct one thousand copies in English, and five hundred copies in German, of the Constitution. . . . to be printed and distributed among the citizens of Pennsylvania." Brackenridge added an amendment to provide for "a proper person to translate the Plan into the German language."[2]

The only function of the State assembly in determining the reception of the Constitution was to provide for a State ratifying convention. It was not until September 28, the day before the close of the session, that the debate on this question began. During the two days of discussion, Brackenridge was one of the most effective supporters of the new plan of government, and he had the best of opportunities to turn his wit and eloquence against Findley and his party.

The first step toward acceptance of the Constitution was the introduction of resolutions calling for elections in October to choose delegates to the State ratifying convention.[3] The opposition, led by Findley and Whitehill, immediately protested against

[1] S. B. Harding, "Party Struggles over the First Pennsylvania Constitution," *American Historical Association, Annual Report (1894)*, p. 393.

[2] *Proceedings and Debates of the General Assembly of Pennsylvania*, p. 85.

[3] *ibid.*, pp. 115-16.

taking action at once, saying that the house ought to have more time to consider the subject. The "Federalists" were anxious to secure action before the end of the session, and Brackenridge was one of their chief spokesmen. Answering Findley and Whitehill he said:

With respect to this point, every member must have made up his mind fully, because it is a measure, that from the first was apparent, and must have occupied the attention of every individual who had but seen the plan. This has been on your table many days, and from its magnitude and importance must have been a subject of reflection to the members, who wished to perform the duty they owed to their God, their conscience, and their fellow-citizens—so that voting now on a subject already well understood, cannot be difficult. . . .[4]

Whitehill replied to Brackenridge, maintaining that it was improper to take action until the Constitution was officially referred to the assembly by Congress, and that the matter should be left for the next assembly to determine.[5] After further arguments from Brackenridge and other Federalists, the vote was taken, and the movement to postpone was defeated. Then Brackenridge answered the point regarding the propriety of acting before the house had received the Constitution from Congress. He argued that the movement for a new constitution did not originate with Congress, and that, therefore, it was perfectly proper to proceed without reference to congressional action:

I don't see, for my part, what Congress have to do with it—though doubtless I should not object to waiting a few days to hear of their opinion. This has been done even until now, which is so near the close of our session, as to make a longer delay improper:—therefore, waiting their recommendation is no argument for prolonging the consideration of the subject before us. But there is certainly strong reasons, why we should call up and determine the question, whether a convention should be called or not? The advantages to the state are, that it will be to her honour to take the lead in adopting so wise a plan, and it will be an inducement for other states to follow. . . . Every person who should hear we had the subject ten days before us, and notwithstanding avoided entering upon it, must conclude we are unfriendly to it; and it

[4] *Proceedings and Debates,* p. 120.　　　[5] *ibid.,* p. 121.

will be cause of triumph to our enemies, who wait only to see us refuse that government, which alone can save us from their machinations.[6]

In replying to the protests of Findley and his party against hasty action,[7] he said:

All efforts to restore energy to the federal government have proved ineffectual, when exerted in the mode directed by the 13th article of the confederation, and it is in consequence of this, that recourse is once more had to the *authority of the people*. The first step toward obtaining this was anti-federal, so far as it was not conducted in the manner prescribed by articles of union. But the first and every step was *federal* inasmuch as it was sanctioned by the *people of the United States*. The member from Westmoreland[8] pleases his fancy with being on federal ground, pursuing federal measures, and being a very federal sort of person, he concludes we are not in a state of nature, because we are on federal ground. But, Sir, we are not on federal ground, but on the wild and extended field of nature, unrestrained by any former compact, bound by no peculiar tye, at least so far are we disengaged, as to be capable of forming a constitution, which shall be the wonder of the universe. It is on the principle of self-conservation that we act. The former articles of confederation have received sentence of death, and though they may be on earth, yet are inactive, and have no efficacy: but the gentleman would still have us to be bound by them, and tells you your acts must correspond with their doctrine. . . . He will not suffer the old to be dissolved, until the new is adopted; he will not quit his old cabbin 'till the new house is furnished, not if it crumbles about his ears.[9]

After further discussion by Findley and Whitehill, a vote was called on the question: "Will the House take the proper means to have a convention of the people called, to deliberate on the propriety of receiving or refusing the new plan of government?" It was passed by a vote of 43 to 19.[10]

When the house met in the afternoon the nineteen members who had voted in the negative absented themselves in order that there

[6] *ibid.*, pp. 123-5.   [7] *ibid.*, pp. 125-6, 132-3.   [8] William Findley.
[9] *Proceedings and Debates of the General Assembly of Pennsylvania*, pp. 134-5.
[10] *ibid.*, p. 135.

might not be a quorum present to transact business, and no legal method could be discovered to compel attendance. On the next day the assembly received the Constitution from Congress with an official letter of transmission and recommendation; so there could no longer be offered any formal objection to completing the arrangements for electing delegates to the State ratifying convention. The sergeant at arms and the assistant clerk were dispatched to carry the news to the absconding nineteen members and to request their attendance again.

With praiseworthy zeal the clerks pursued the absentees through the highways and by-ways of Philadelphia, while the latter, setting a brisk pace, dodged around corners and into hallways, attics, and cellars to escape. Such as were overtaken or were bearded in their own homes, fell back upon their native strength of Scotch-Irish character and roundly said, with the unanimity of a Greek chorus, that they would not attend.[11] However, a group of citizens at length succeeded in forcing two of the truants, M'Calmont and Miley, into the chamber, and when the roll was called a bare quorum was found to be present. It was the last day of the existence of the eleventh assembly and arrangements for the State constitutional convention must hastily be completed. In this crisis "Mr. *M'Calmont* informed the House, that he had been forcibly brought into the assembly room, contrary to his wishes, this morning by a number of citizens, whom he did not know, and that therefore, he begged he might be dismissed the House."[12]

In the discussion concerning the legality of detaining Mr. M'Calmont which followed, the letter of the law received scant attention. The attitude of the Federalist majority, in the face of necessity for quick action, was ironically stated by Brackenridge:

It may be a proper question for the House to discuss, whether their officers by force have brought this Member here, or whether other Members have by violence compelled him. I suppose in either of these cases, the House might have cognizance. But if the Member has been conducted by the citizens of Philadelphia to his seat in the legislature and they have not treated him with the respect and veneration he de-

---

[11] *Proceedings and Debates*, p. 140.   [12] *ibid.*, p. 138.

serves, it must lie with him to obtain satisfaction, but not with us. The gentleman by answering to his name, when the roll was called, acknowledged himself present, and forms a part of the House. Well, Sir, I conceive the question is, what is to be done now he is here—for how he came here, can form no part of our enquiry, whether his friends brought him (and I should think they could not be his enemies, who would compel him to do his duty, and avoid wrong) I say, Sir, whether his friends brought him, or by the influence of good advice persuaded him to come, and he did come; or whether to ease his difficulty in walking to this room, they brought him in a sedan chair, or by whatever ways or means he introduced himself among us.—All we are to know, is, that he is here, and it only remains for us to decide, whether he shall have leave of absence—now if the gentleman can shew, that his life will be endangered by staying with us (for I should think the loss of health on the present occasion, an insufficient reason) we may grant him the indulgence he asks for—waving the whole story of his coming, I presume the House can immediately decide, whether he may retire or not.[18]

M'Calmont had, however, made up his mind not to await the house's decision. He "rose, and made towards the door. Mr. *Fitzsimmons* addressed him, but so as not to be heard—and the gallery called out *stop him*; there being a number of citizens at the door he went toward. The commotion subsided in a few seconds, and Mr. *M'Calmont* returned to his seat, to wait the decision of the house. Mr. *Fitzsimmons* informed the Speaker, that Mr. *M'Calmont* had told him, he had occasion to go out, and was willing to go in company with the sergeant at arms: He thereupon hoped the gentleman's wish might be complied with.

"The *Speaker* put the question, shall Mr. *M'Calmont* have leave of absence? which was determined almost, if not quite, unanimously, in the negative."[14]

The way was now clear to pass the resolution regarding the time of electing delegates to the State ratifying convention. "Mr. *Brackenridge* moved to insert the first Tuesday in November, to be the day throughout the State."[15] This was the date settled upon.

[18] *ibid.*, p. 139.   [14] *ibid.*, p. 142.   [15] *ibid.*

Then the assembly adjourned, and Brackenridge returned to Pittsburgh.

In the assembly, Brackenridge had been the only member from the three southwestern counties to vote for the convention resolutions. He had been the only representative from the frontier among the leading Federalist spokesmen. After he returned to Pittsburgh he continued to labor for the Constitution by using all his talents for satire and eloquence in an effort to overcome the popular prejudice against the new instrument of government. For that purpose he wrote a large number of contributions to the *Pittsburgh Gazette* in both prose and verse.

The first of these journalistic productions was devoted to the activities of the intransigeant nineteen. Soon after the close of the assembly, sixteen members of the group issued an address to the people of Pennsylvania criticizing the new Constitution and the methods used in drawing it up and securing its adoption.[16] Brackenridge immediately published some "Observations on the Address of the Sixteen Members." Replying to the accusation that the Pennsylvania delegates to the Constitutional Convention were all aristocratic and had financial rather than agrarian interests, he remarked:

It is said that our delegates in the late convention were "all of one *political party* and opposed to that *constitution* for which you have on every occasion manifested your attachment."[17] How long will the cry of *constitution* be made use of by designing men to sanction bad measures, or prevent good? . . . It is true that the delegates were "all citizens of Philadelphia," and all men of understanding, and against whose characters in private life nothing can be shewn. Why not consider the work and let the man alone? "None of them calculated to represent the landed interest of Pennsylvania." I believe all these delegates have land in the state, and understand the landed interest, if that can be supposed distinct from any other interest, as well as any men in the state; some of them have more land than all the sixteen remon-

16 The *Address* is reprinted in McMaster and Stone, *Pennsylvania and the Federal Constitution*, pp. 73-9. It was printed in the *Pittsburgh Gazette* on October 21, 1787.
17 The reference is to the State constitution of Pennsylvania.

strants put together; one of them has more land even in Washington county, than the representatives of that county have there or anywhere else. The truth is, Whitehill and Findley were offended that they or those who direct them, were not appointed in the convention; and this is the ground of the whole disturbance.

In closing his "Observations," Brackenridge expressed again the distrust of the populace and popular leaders which he had acquired during the past year:

It is possible that the arts used may prejudice the people, and prevent the adopting this system. In this case it will be owing to their inacquaintance with it. If that should be the melancholy result of all the pains that has been taken for their good in bringing it about; all I can say is in the language of the prophet, "O Israel thou art destroyed for lack of knowledge."[18]

To supply the desired knowledge he published a "Narrative of the Transactions of the Late Session of Assembly, so far as they respect the System of Confederate Government, proposed by the General Convention of the States at Philadelphia."[19] Then, in his next contribution, he covered this same subject again, this time in Hudibrastic verse. Writing ironically he thus attempted to make the absconding assemblymen, Findley in particular, appear ridiculous:

> Away from me all jests and slurrs,
> On Pennsylvania senators,
> Save those alone the worthless few,
> Who from the senate house withdrew
> When was proposed new government,
> For as if demon had been sent,
> To strike them with phrenetic fury,
> They ran off headlong hurry scurry;
> Some ran to cellars, or absconded
> In kitchens, and were there impounded.
> 'Mongst these there ran a western wight,[20]
> Who took the fore way in the flight;
> He got a garret by his clambering,

[18] *Pittsburgh Gazette*, October 27, 1787.
[19] *ibid.*, October 27, 1787. Reprinted in *Gazette Publications*, pp. 53-7.
[20] Findley.

And lay all day in his mind hammering
Escape from danger and alarms
Of furious, fiery sergeant at arms,
Aided by tumultuous rabble,
Who from the gallery slipt cable
To take and bring him to the house,
While here he lay entrenched like mouse.

Then a group of the truant members is presented in consultation about plans for further resistance. When it appears that there are no sound objections to the Constitution, Findley proposes a plan of attack:

Now at this critical non plus,
Our wight arose and argued thus:
Though constitution's almost done,
There's still some picking in the bone,
A new occasion gives new use,
And lets the prejudices loose,
No writing can be understood,
Or read at once by the multitude,
And in obscurity there's fear;
So, we can get a foot-hold here,
Say that this novel government,
Is form'd by them with an intent
To eat up the offices of the state,
And make each one of themselves great;
That under this outrageous system
No man alive will dare say peas t' them,
That soldiers arm'd with battle axes,
Henceforward will collect the taxes;
That the convention in great fury,
Have taken away the trial by jury;
That liberty of press is gone,
We shall be hang'd each mother's son;
Say Lord knows what, as comes in head,
Pretences for a scare crow made.

One of the conspirators, Grogram, warns the group that opposition will be difficult and tells them that the convention which framed the Constitution contained better men than can be found among the nineteen—Washington and Franklin, for instance—, and reminds his colleagues that they are not experts in statecraft. Of Findley he says:

> There's Wight himself just come from mooring,
> His anchor on the upper flooring
> Is in reality but a weaver,
> Though at his trade he may be clever.

Findley is, of course, resentful of this reference to his lowly origin. Brackenridge took this opportunity to rename him "Traddle," thus performing the first operation in the transformation of Findley into the "Traddle" of *Modern Chivalry*.

> This gave offence to signior WIGHT,
> Was almost angry enough to bite,
> For true he was of the occupation,
> Nor did he think it a degradation,
> Unless when waggs, just fiddle faddle,
> In way of talk, would call him, TRADDLE.
> But being now assemblyman,
> He wish'd to put it off his hand,
> And keep the mystery from view;
> But we shall call him Traddle too.
> Just for the whim of the odd name,
> For what we call him 'tis the same—
> Provided we but know what's meant,
> Which of all language is the intent;
> Then as he means to speak BE IT KNOWN,
> TRADDLE is the name he must own.[21]

Brackenridge was not content to support the Constitution merely by writing. He also offered himself as a candidate for the State ratifying convention. As might have been expected, he was defeated. He himself was now unpopular at home, and, in spite of his arguments in its behalf, the Constitution was still considered in the West to be a scheme drawn up for the advantage of the "aristocratic" and financial groups of the East. The only local

[21] *Pittsburgh Gazette,* November 3 and November 10, 1787; and *Gazette Publications,* pp. 58-69. Findley had been a weaver.

record of the election, which occurred on Tuesday, November 6, is the following scant note in the *Pittsburgh Gazette*: "At an election held on Tuesday last for persons to serve in convention to consider the new plan of government proposed by a convention of the states lately held in the city of Philadelphia, the following gentlemen were elected for Westmoreland county: William Findley, William Todd, John Beard."[22]

Brackenridge was infuriated by the people's choice of "Traddle" in preference to himself. Six weeks after the election he published another Hudibrastic satire on Findley entitled "On the Popularity of ———."

> Whence comes it that a thing like this,
> Of mind no bigger than a fly's
> Should yet attract the popular favor
> Be of his country thought the saviour,
> Sent to *assembly* and *convention*
> With votes almost without dissention, . . .
>   Whence comes it say you? Is it odd,
> That men should make a beast a God?
> Did not Egyptians worship bulls?
> And were the Jews a whit less fools,
> In setting up the god Ball Peor
> To be an object of their prayer?
> For even legislator Moses,
> And Aaron, spite of both their noses,
> Could not restrain the multitude
> Say they were stocks, do what they would.
> For after such, while sage was snoring
> The people still would run a whoring.
>   What wonder then that this Teague Regan,[23]
> Like Asteroth, or idol Dagon,
> Should here receive our reverence,
> In spite of truth and common sense;
> Men in all ages are the same,
> And nature is herself to blame,

[22] *Pittsburgh Gazette*, November 10, 1787.

[23] Teague Regan was the early American generic name for Irish laborers—the precursor of the modern Pat and Mike. William Findley was an Irishman by birth.

Who has not given to all an eye,
Of sapience and philosophy.
What though he wished to damn the motion,
Of opening passage to the ocean
By Mississippi; and what's more
Of making roads, to our own door;[24]
And voted with a stubborn will,
Against the *Pittsburgh County* bill.
What though constituents be disgrac'd
By *flying from his post in haste,*
And taking shelter in a garret,
Like vile rat catcher, or grey ferret;
This circumstance has done him good,
With th' injudicious multitude;
They wish to justify their choice
In sending such a thing to the house,
And so the more he runs a stern,
They hold him up with new concern,
A kind of partnership in shame,
That binds the faster him and them. . . .
 The circumstance of running off
Has had a good effect enough,
It gave the populace a hint,
The devil was in new government;
For sure the system must be bad,
Could make a senator run mad;
Assume the postures of a cat,
And on his marrow bones ly squat—
What eloquence could not produce,
Is done by turning tail to the house;
'Tis thus that rowers make`boat swim,
By turning backside to the stream.
But why aloft did Traddle rise,
As if he wanted wasps or flies?
A cellar was the proper place,
To hide himself in his disgrace;
There he could weave; and while at work,

[24] Findley had not supported Brackenridge in his efforts in the Mississippi affair, and had voted against the Philadelphia-Pittsburgh road bill, giving specious objections to the method of taxation which it involved.

Be thought a Paddy just from Cork;
For who would ask, let who would come,
What Senator is that at the loom?[25]

. . .   .

But men relinquish proper station,
As oft they do their occupation,
Though punish'd in the self same case,
With a connatural disgrace;
They rise, but shew defects the more,
The things that covered were before,[26]
And hence the subject of lampoon,
As Sawney said of the racoon,
Ah man! "ya climb; and aw the farce
Is but the mare ta shaw yar. . . ."
Had Traddle staid at home and woven,
Who would have known he had foot cloven?
Who would have laugh'd at the incident,
That such should judge of government,
As if it were a web which woman,
Complaining (not a thing uncommon)
That it was badly put together,
Not close enough to keep out weather,
Should have agreed; the customer,
With tradesmen, not to make a stir,
But settle difference and account,
By putting neighboring weavers on't.[27]

In the State convention, Findley and his party opposed the adoption of the Constitution, although they had maintained in the assembly that they objected only to hasty action on it. Brackenridge, of course, observed their activities closely, and although the Pennsylvania convention ratified the Constitution promptly,[28] he continued to satirize the opposition.

[25] This is the beginning of the evolution of the "Traddle" material in *Modern Chivalry* (edition of 1792), Vol. I, Book II. Henry Marie Brackenridge refers to Findley as "'Traddle the Weaver,' the name under which Findley is alluded to in 'Modern Chivalry.'" *The Western Insurrection in Western Pennsylvania*, p. 189.

[26] The preceding six lines state the theme developed in *Modern Chivalry*: let the cobbler stick to his last.

[27] *Pittsburgh Gazette*, December 1, 1787.   [28] On December 12, 1787.

In the ironical "Apology for the dissentients in the State Convention" he again expressed his low opinion of Findley and his backwood constituents.

> As natural bodies are made up,
> Of Higher, lower, bottom, top,
> In other words, of head and tail,
> So bodies politic as well,
> Of upper, nether, end should be,
> Why then indignant do we see,
> Such things as Traddle and humbugum,
> And Tadry hash and hogum mogum,
> 'Mongst managers of state affairs,
> Of which they know no more than bears?
> Will not a sample such as these,
> With sense not half so much as geese,
> Serve properly to represent,
> The ignorance by which they're sent,
> And show that in the common weal,
> There is a head as well as tail?

After satirizing the demand for a bill of rights and other points in the argument of the "dissentients" he continued his anatomical analogy with special reference to the position of the frontier in the body politic:

> But whence is it that most of these,
> Were of the Western Country geese,
> Because 'tis reasonable that we
> The legislative tail tree be.
> Let Philadelphia be the head,
> And Lancaster the shoulder blade;
> And thence collecting in a clump,
> A place called Stoney ridge the rump,
> The tail will naturally stretch,
> Across the Allegheny ridge,
> While we submit to stubborn fate,
> And be the backside of the state.

Arguing from this analogy, he closed with an ironical plea for charity in judging the Western politicians:

Why then complain that ignorance,
Of state affairs should come from hence,
That F[indle]y should hate making roads,
And leave us to trot down like goats—
That S[mile]y should advise t'oppose,
The general government with blows,
Who never handled sword or bodkin,
Or else thing but a spoon or noggin.[29]

After these Hudibrastics, Brackenridge turned to prose satire. In some short ironical papers of the Swiftean type he continued to ridicule the opposition to the Constitution. The first and most important of these pieces was the "Cursory Remarks on the Constitution," in which he caricatured the popular criticisms of the plan. Inventing absurd objections, he wrote:

The first thing that strikes a diligent observer, is the want of precaution with respect to the sex of the president. Is it provided that he shall be of the male gender? The Salii, a tribe of Burgundians, in the 11th century, excluded females from the sovereignty. Without a similar exclusion, what shall we think, if in progress of time we should come to have an *old woman* at the head of our affairs? But what security do we have that he shall be a *white* man? . . .

A senate is the next great constituent part of the government; and yet there is not a word said with regard to the ancestry of any of them; whether they should be altogether Irish or only Scotch Irish. If any of them have been in the war of the White Boys, Hearts of Oak or the like, they may overturn all authority, and make the shilelah the supreme law of the land. . . .

I would submit it to any candid man, if in this constitution there is the least provision for the privilege of shaving the beard? or is there any mode laid down to take the measure of a pair of breeches? Whence then is it that men of learning seem so much to approve, while the ignorant are against it? the cause is perfectly apparent, viz. that reason is an erring guide, while instinct, which is the guiding principle of the untaught is certain.[30]

[29] *Pittsburgh Gazette*, March 8, 1788. Reprinted in *Gazette Publications*, pp. 72-6, with the omission of the passage beginning "Why then complain that ignorance."

[30] *Pittsburgh Gazette*, March 1, 1788. Reprinted in Carey's *American Museum*, April 1788; *Gazette Miscellanies*, pp. 77-9; and A. B. Hart, *American History Told by Contemporaries*, Vol. III, pp. 237-9.

Another instalment of the "Cursory Remarks" followed two weeks later. It gives an ironical account of the suggestions of forcible resistance which had been made by some of the back-country leaders.

Having seen the mischief of this government, it remains to be considered how it shall be opposed. Doubtless by the force of arms. Reasoning having failed, the bayonette is now the alternative.

This being settled, it remains to be enquired under what leader the war shall commence. F[indle]y and S[mile]y are the only two on this side of the mountain between whom the choice must rest. With respect to the first of them, his abilities are undoubtedly great, but I should suppose he would be deficient in personal activity. I do not know to what it may be owing, but I observe that his legs are stiff; and if in a battle he should happen to have his horse shot under him, he might be unable to make his escape, and so fall into the hands of the enemy. . . .

A third thing comes into view, viz. how we shall commence our operations; whether wait on these low grounds until this government is organized, and begins to exercise some acts of jurisdiction over us, or to meet it in Cumberland Valley, and there give it battle. I would be for adopting a middle resolution, that is to seize the passes of the Alleghany mountain, and wait there for its arrival. By rolling rocks upon it, we might be successful in greatly annoying it on its approach.

It will be asked how shall we be able to subsist our troops in that quarter, carriage on the mountains being difficult and expensive. Indeed if we go all to war, as in so glorious a cause, who would wish to stay at home, I don't know how the ground will be cultivated and provisions raised. In this case, should it happen, a very great support may be derived from the racoons and opossums, which the soldiers may knock down with their spontoons at pleasure. . . .

The writer of these remarks is not a man of great estate. It might be said of me at any time, as to the sick of the palsy, "take up thy bed and walk," and I could in three hours settle my affairs, and be ready for Kentucky. This shews that I am not one of your overgrown men, but have a fellow feeling for the common people, who will have no more chance under the government, than toads under a harrow. Who is it that drives a shuttle or keeps a school, can expect to be elected president of the United States? This government is made for men of property, and those who have nothing to lose have no business with

it. Nay, it will prevent those revolutions where men have an opportunity of scrambling for a living. It is a hard thing to be obliged to
drudge on from day to day, and make a fortune by the common
means of industry. I should like to live in the same state with the
children of Israel, before the time of the judges, "where every man
did what was right in his own eyes." If this should come to be the
case amongst us, I know what I shall do. I will make a grab on the
stores at Greensburgh.

It is in order to prevent a thing of this kind that your monied men
are chiefly in favor of this constitution. They know that without it
we shall soon be at the ears with one another, and they will have no
security for what they have acquired.[31]

Having used the ironical manner in his Hudibrastics and in the
"Cursory Remarks," Brackenridge next adopted more direct
methods of attack on the enemies of the Constitution. In a series
of lay sermons published in the *Pittsburgh Gazette* he castigated
Findley and the other popular leaders of the West.

For the first sermon he took as his text, "Oh, my people, they
which lead thee cause thee to err, and destroy the way of thy
paths."[32] Discussing the cause of the local opposition he said:

No people were ever more mistaken than we are, at the present
time, with respect to the new constitution of federal government. I
have been led to consider whence it is that we so disgrace ourselves
with sentiments unfavorable to a system, which a convention of the
greatest and best men in any age or nation, have devised, and which
the good sense of America seems disposed to approve.

The answer is easy: a few men who have obtained a fortuitous and
temporary influence amongst us, are the cause of this. The people have
naturally as much good sense as those of any other country, but honest
and unsuspecting, they are imposed on by individuals, who by attention and flattery have gained their favor. It is well known who it is
about the center of Westmoreland that carries up from below pal-
pable falsehoods, and disseminates ideas unfavorable to this government.[33] It is well known who it is in Fayette county, that in an open
harrangue, has inveighed against a Washington, and proposed the
bayonette in opposition to those councils in which he has had a great

---

[31] *Pittsburgh Gazette*, March 15, 1788.   [32] Isaiah iii. 12.   [33] Findley.

share.[34] These and some others of the same spirit, are those who "lead the people" of this country and cause them to err. . . .[35]

In his second sermon Brackenridge further developed the same theme. Taking as his text, "My people are destroyed for lack of knowledge,"[36] he said:

I ask them why it is that so many of the inhabitants of this country are opposed to the new federal constitution. It is from the want of knowledge. I do not mean to say that they are less capable of judging than their neighbors, on the contrary, from the experience which I have had of their understanding in the capacity of magistrates, jurymen, or in the common concerns of life, I have conceived as highly of them in this respect as of any other people. But they are distant from the means of information, and are at the mercy of vague reports and the judgment of others. How else could they be led to oppose a government which must so greatly advance their own interest. For without the energy of such a constitution, how can we expect the opening of the Mississippi river, the surrender of the posts on the lakes, the support of troops on the frontiers, and the protection of settlements about to be made on Muskingum. . . .

The simplicity of those whom we send to represent us in the public bodies, is at the bottom of this misfortune. There is a knot in Philadelphia consisting of a few persons whom I could name, who, under pretence of great affection for the western country members, associate with them at the sign of the black bear, and play them off, sometimes to revenge themselves on the richer merchants, or for purposes of private advantage, by obtaining local laws, &c. This is the origin of the funding system, the attacks upon the bank, the breaking up the assembly, &c.

Our representatives coming home communicate the same impressions to their countrymen, and we become the laughing stock of the commonwealth.[37]

Brackenridge wrote two more such sermons,[38] and also resumed his satirical campaign against Findley and his group.[39] The later contributions were merely restatements of ideas which he had already used.

[34] Smiley.   [35] *Pittsburgh Gazette*, March 22, 1788.   [36] Hosea iv. 12.
[37] *Pittsburgh Gazette*, March 29, 1788.   [38] *ibid.*, April 5 and April 12, 1788.
[39] *ibid.*, May 10 and May 17, 1788.

In writing for the Federalist cause, he had been sharply satirical and had freely expressed his opinion that the backwoods people were ignorant and their representatives incapable. His literary manner and his ideas were of course resented. An ardent Anti-Federalist, "Sommers," contributing a criticism of the Constitution, said with reference to Brackenridge's articles:

What have you heard in support of this system, but buffoonery and scurrillity, passionate harangues founded on shallow & selfish principles, & honest men brow beat and insulted by the advocates for power and prerogative.[40]

Brackenridge replied in a few lines of tart verse. Then "Sommers" or one of his friends answered:

The writer of SOMMERS . . . as a citizen and freeman of Pennsylvania, has an equal right with the governor of the state, or the President of Congress, to speak and write his sentiments on the general government, or any other subject, *scurrillity and defamation excepted,* these subjects being monopolized by the *Western Oracle* or *Modern Hudibras.* . . . The writer Sommers being perfectly independent in principle, and easy in circumstances, is far above the calumny of a doggrell rhymist, who would *bark at the sun and bay at the moon* could he thereby secure a smile from his federal-leagued patrons.[41]

The controversy over the Constitution was naturally brought to a close in June 1788 when the ninth State ratified and adoption was assured. During the spring friends of the new plan had been anxiously awaiting the action of New Hampshire and Virginia, as acceptance by one more State was necessary. On June 20, news was received in Pittsburgh that Virginia had ratified. Not knowing that New Hampshire had adopted the Constitution a few days before, the Pittsburgh Federalists took this occasion to celebrate the victory of their cause. The next evening about fifteen hundred inhabitants of Pittsburgh and the surrounding country assembled on Grant's Hill, "a beautiful rising mount to the east of the town." "Occupying the verge of the hill they were addressed by Mr. Brackenridge as follows:"

[40] *Pittsburgh Gazette,* March 15, 1788.   [41] *ibid.,* April 19, 1788.

CHAPTER XII

"MODERN CHIVALRY"

AFTER his unfortunate venture into politics and journalistic satire, Brackenridge had seen the necessity of holding himself aloof from public affairs in order to regain his legal practice. But while he was occupied with private business and with the education of his infant son and the second Mrs. Brackenridge, he did not forget the bitter experiences of 1786-88. Instead, he elaborated the satire on demagogues and voters which he had begun in his newspaper Hudibrastics. The results were *The Modern Chevalier*, a narrative in verse, and *Modern Chivalry*, the novel on which his fame chiefly rests.

His literary preparation for these compositions had begun during his student years when his reading of Lucian had contributed to the formation of a satirical habit. "Afterwards," he said, "when I came to have some acquaintance with the modern wits, such as Cervantes, Le Sage, and especially Swift, I found myself still more inclined to an ironical, ludicrous way of thinking and writing."[1] Rabelais, Sterne,[2] and Samuel Butler were also formative influences in this development.

In the Hudibrastics contributed to the *Gazette*, Brackenridge had taken the first steps toward generalizing his satire when he transmogrified William Findley into "Traddle" and "Teague Regan," and when he saw a typical democratic populace in the electorate of Westmoreland County. Then, having ceased to participate in topical controversy as soon as the Constitution was adopted, he further developed this theme in a long Hudibrastic narrative entitled *The Modern Chevalier*, which was composed in 1788-89.[3] In this poem, which is important only as a preliminary version of the *Modern Chivalry* material, the "chevalier" appears

---

[1] *Modern Chivalry* (edition of 1792), Vol. I, pp. 82-3.
[2] *ibid.*, Vol. I, p. 84.   [3] *Gazette Publications*, p. 311.

brimstone, tar and feathers thrown into it; yet still some boughs of wood that were at the bottom, catched the flame, purged off the noxious vapour and materials. That of New-York and North Carolina at length took fire, and exceeded even the other piles. The youths of the village danced round them on the green; and the Indians who were present, the chiefs of several nations, on their way to the treaty at Muskingum, stood in amazement at the scene; concluded this to be a great council, seeing the thirteen states kindled on the hill.[43]

The Constitution had won, but its Pittsburgh champion suffered for his support of it. A few years later, reviewing the results of his venture into politics, he said:

Another circumstance had taken place during the session,[44] which accumulated odium upon me; that was the calling a convention to new model the federal government. I supported that measure; and when the convention had sat and published a constitution, I supported the adoption of it. All my colleagues from the westward came home antifederalists, and held me up in worse point of view than before. My character was totally gone with the populace. My practice was lost; and James Ross and David Bradford and others, whom I left at the bar just beginning, got it all. Pride and good policy would not permit me to leave the country, until I had conquered the prejudice; I knew that to be practicable, by lying by until the popular fury should waste itself; it required time but I had patience. But it was necessary for me to be silent, and add nothing more to the popular odium. It was the first experience, I had ever had in my life, of unpopularity, and I found it a thing more painful to sustain, and more difficult to remove than I had thought it to be. Had I possessed an independent fortune I would have cared less about it; but I had just laid the foundation of making something, by the practice I had established, and this was now taken from me.[45]

[43] Pittsburgh Gazette, June 28, 1788.   [44] Of the assembly.
[45] Incidents of the Western Insurrection, Vol. III, pp. 13-14.

CHAPTER XI

PRIVATE LIFE

IT WAS not only in his political and professional career that Brackenridge met with misfortune at this time. Soon after he returned from the assembly in the autumn of 1787 his wife died, leaving him with a son not yet eighteen months old.[1] After her death he took up his residence at the home of a certain Madame Marie,[2] where Albert Gallatin spent Christmas Day with him in 1787.[3]

His young son was placed in charge of a cobbler, who lived in a cabin belonging to Brackenridge. Although this man was, according to Henry Marie's later testimony, a respectable citizen, the child did not receive good care in his home. He was half starved, half clad, and "well scorched and meazled in the hot embers." Luckily the kindly Madame Marie one day called to see him, and was "touched with compassion" for him. Securing his father's consent, she took the child into her own house, but he presented so unpromising an appearance on account of neglect, that "she almost repented of the step she had taken." Under a course of gentle treatment, however, "a favorable change was soon effected."

Brackenridge himself at first gave little attention to the boy. He spent most of his time in his office, being "entirely devoted to books and business." One day, however, an incident occurred which aroused his interest in his son. Henry Marie, who was barely past two years of age, was taken to church and was much struck by what he saw. When he came home he attempted to imitate the clergyman, putting his hands together, closing his eyes, and repeating some words of the service. His father, "who was too much of a philosopher to be moved by the mere yearnings of nature," was now interested. He had discovered that the boy had "an

[1] H. M. Brackenridge, *Recollections of Persons and Places in the West,* p. 10.
[2] *ibid.*   [3] Henry Adams, *Life of Albert Gallatin,* p. 68.

improvable intellect" and was worth attention. Soon after, when Henry Marie came near his father's chair in his play, he took his eyes from his book and said:

"Well, boy, can you do anything for your living?"

"I can make shoes," Henry Marie replied, and then proceeded to go through the motions which he had observed when he was living with the cobbler.

"You must learn to read," concluded Brackenridge.

Accordingly he procured a hornbook for the two-year-old boy and forced him to apply himself to it. Henry Marie's screams under this exacting discipline often brought Madame Marie in to protest. She always interposed and saved him from the rod—but not from the terror that his ambitious father's methods produced.[4]

This life in the home of Madame Marie continued for about three years. Then Brackenridge remarried. The circumstances of the event are amusingly related in the journal of John Pope, a Virginian, who visited Pittsburgh in October 1790.

Apprehending a Return of the Rheumatism, I resolved to await the Event in Pittsburgh. . . . Here I saw the celebrated *Hugh Henry Breckenridge*. . . . He had been lately married to a Miss *Sabina Wolfe*, Daughter of an old *Dutch* Farmer in *Washington* County. The circumstances of his Courtship, Marriage, and subsequent Conduct I shall relate, with some slight Reference to the Person, Temper and Disposition of the Man.

Mr. Breckenridge on his Way from Washington Court, called in to have his horse fed and escape a Rain which was then descending. The Horse was fed, the rain had subsided, and Mr. *Breckenridge* to avoid wet feet, ordered his Horse brought to the Door; Miss *Wolfe* was directed to perform that office.

> Nut brown were her Locks, her shape was full strait,
> Her Eyes were as black as a Sloe;
> Milk white were her Teeth, full smart was her Gait,
> And Sleek was her Skin as a Doe.

These allurements made a deep Impression upon the susceptible Heart of *Breckenridge*—He prevented her in the servile Office,

---

[4] H. M. Brackenridge, *Recollections of Persons and Places in the West,* pp. 10-11.

mounted his Nag and off he went. He had not gone more than a Sabbath Day's Journey, (for such his really was) before his Horse, at the Instigation of the Rider, turned short about and revisited Mr. Wolfe's. A familiar Application was made to the old Gentleman for his Daughter, which he considered nothing more than Pleasantry in Mr. *Breckenridge,* for which he is so remarkable. Mr. *Breckenridge* declared that he was serious, that his Intentions were honorable, and that his future Happiness rested on the Event of his then Application. Miss *Sabina* had been employed in shrubbing the old Man's Meadow, which saved him the annual Expence of about ten Dollars. This with him was an insuperable Objection to parting with his Girl—Mr. *Breckenridge* obviated the Difficulty by paying down a Sum of Money, obtained the Young Lady's Consent, married her, and sent her to *Philadelphia,* where she now is under the Governance of a reputable female Character, whose business will be to polish the Manners, and wipe off the Rusticities which Mrs. *Breckenridge* had acquired whilst a Wolfe. . . .

After recapitulating in verse the wooing of Miss Wolfe by Brackenridge, Mr. Pope proceeded to give some interesting comments on Pittsburgh.

In company with this Gentleman [Brackenridge] I viewed the Fort and neighboring Eminencies of *Pittsburgh,* which will one Day or other employ the historic Pen, as being replete with strange and melancholy Events. The Town at present, is inhabited with only some few Exceptions, by Mortals who act as if possessed of a Charter of Exclusive Privilege to filch from, annoy and harass her Fellow Creatures, particularly the incautious and necessitous; many who have emigrated from various Parts to Kentuckey can verify this Charge—Goods of every Description are dearer in Pittsburgh than in Kentuckey, which I attribute to a Combination of pensioned Scoundrels who infest the Place.[5]

John Pope was not the only visitor to Western Pennsylvania in 1790 who found Brackenridge a curious character. Jean Badollet, an emigrant from Geneva, met him in the village of Cat Fish, and reported to Albert Gallatin:

"I can declare in all conscience that in all my days I have never seen such an impertinent cox comb." He then gave an account of a

[5] John Pope, *Travels through the Southern and Western Territories of the United States,* pp. 14-18.

dialogue between Brackenridge and some unknown person, indicated as Mr. N., who, he supposed, was merely trying to draw Brackenridge out.

"I think, Mr. Brackenridge," remarked Mr. N., "you are one of the happiest men in the world."

"Yes, sir," replied Brackenridge, "nothing disturbs me. I can declare that I never feel a single moment of discontent, but laugh at everything."

"I believe so, sir," continued Mr. N., "but your humor—"

"Oh, sir, truly inexhaustible," Brackenridge answered in a tone of immense self satisfaction, as he pulled at his cuffs and frill, rubbed his face, and smiled like a Narcissus, "yes, truly inexhaustible, truly inexhaustible. Sir, I could set down and write a piece of humor for fifty-seven years without being the least exhausted. I have just now two compositions agoing—"

"Happy turn of mind," commented Mr. N.

"You may say that, sir," agreed Brackenridge. "I enjoy a truly inexhaustible richness of mind."[6]

Evidently grotesque exaggeration had already become a characteristic of Western humor, so much so that the Genevan Badollet was completely mystified by Brackenridge's talk and set him down as an absurd boaster.

Brackenridge's second marriage brought a change of environment to his five-year-old son. Henry Marie was removed from the home of Madame Marie and sent to live for a year on the farm of his step-grandfather. In his new home he learned to speak a German patois which was the family tongue. When he returned to Pittsburgh his father, not knowing that he had acquired only a low dialect, was much pleased that he had learned German, as he placed a very high estimate on linguistic accomplishments. He often said that a man doubled himself by learning another language. For this reason he conceived the idea of sending the boy to a village in Louisiana to acquire a familiar knowledge of French. A Frenchman, John S. B. Lucas, was about to make a visit to St.

[6] Henry Adams, *Life of Albert Gallatin*, p. 134. I have translated freely the French portions of the account.

Genevieve, near St. Louis, and Brackenridge arranged to have him take the boy on the journey and place him in a French family. So Henry Marie, less than seven years old, was forced to make a long and dangerous journey to satisfy a rather whimsical educational scheme of his father's. Later he passed judgment on the incident as follows:

Although nothing could have been better intended than this measure, it is one which few persons will approve. It is true I learned the French language, from which I afterward derived both pleasure and advantage, and it was my fortune to fall into good hands; but it might have been otherwise. The risk I ran was certainly great, both to my future character and personal safety; and it is very questionable whether the advantages to be expected were equivalent to that risk. Although I escaped many dangers, both physical and moral, yet I think it probable that a direction was given to my feelings rather unfavorable to my success in life.[7]

It would seem, from this account, that in spite of his good intentions, Brackenridge's philosophic temperament was less fitted to develop in his child a healthy disposition toward happiness and success than would have been the "yearnings of nature" which he despised. That he was feared and respected, we may well believe, but the reader can scarcely forbear a pang of pity for the little Henry Marie, weeping over his hornbook, or travelling with strangers through the terror-haunted wilderness to find shelter among aliens speaking an alien tongue.

[7] H. M. Brackenridge, *Recollections of Persons and Places in the West*, pp. 13-14.

Oh my Compatriots, I have great news to give you. A union of nine states has taken place, and you are now citizens of a new empire: an empire, not the effect of chance, nor hewn out by the sword; but formed by the skill of sages, and the design of wise men. Who is there who does not spring in height, and find himself taller by the circumstance? For you have acquired superior strength; you are become a great people. . . .

Yet this noble fabric rises as it were from the marshy ground? Instabilis terra, inabilis unda . . . amidst popular opinions and the discord of states, it ascends and acquires a solid foundation by its own weight. O noble pile! On the four sides of thy pedestal are the names of the patriots who framed thee. At a distance are the shades of Plato, Montesquieu, and Hume. They rise from Elysium, and contemplate a structure which they may have imagined, but could never have expected to see upon the earth. Thy base overspreading our extensive tract of country, is broader than the pyramids of Egypt. Thy age bids fair to outlast their date. In vain shall the rains beat upon thee, and the elemental fury of the winds.

But who are those fell monsters who growl at the shadow of thy structure. They are the opponents of the new system. O, Ignorance, where is thy cave? Whence do thy vapours and thy fogs arise? . . .

What inferior race is that which croak along the bog? animals which live by the credulity, the want of discernment, and the changing temper of the populace. Ranae palustres, O, frogs of the marsh, local demagogues, insidious declaimers, your pond is about to be dried up, no more amongst the weeds, and in the muddy fluid, shall you lift your hoarse voice. The marsh is drained; the dome aspires, and the bright tinges of the rising day, gild its summits.[42]

A spectacular display followed Brackenridge's oration.

Three cheers were now given, and hats thrown into the air. Nine piles of wood were then alighted, representing the nine states which had adopted the constitution. At intermediate distances, four piles were left uninflamed, representing those which had not adopted it. Fire was kindled in them, but oppressed by green leaves and heavy boughs; in spite of all that could be done the pile of New Hampshire burst out, and gave a luminous splendor; that of Rhode Island, not having sent delegates to the convention, or called a convention of their own, had

[42] *ibid.*, June 28, 1788; and *Gazette Publications*, pp. 271-3. The reprint in *Gazette Publications* does not include the whole oration.

as a spokesman for Brackenridge, and "Traddle" is of course a political weaver.

The Modern Chevalier was not published at the time when it was written, but was later included in *Gazette Publications* (1806). The published poem is probably only a fragment of the whole work, however, as it is only thirty pages long, and Brackenridge said in 1792 that this piece was about "two parts in three as large as Butler's Hudibras."[4]

The extant portion of *The Modern Chevalier* presents a shadowy modern "knight errant" travelling about the country, evidently for the purpose of critically observing American politics and society. It begins with an account of a visit to Traddle the Weaver.

> Not far from hence there was a cabbin
> Inhabited by a great Rabbin,
> A weaver who had serv'd the state,
> Which Chevalier did not know yet,
> And therefore having heard the loom,
> Just as he had that way come
> More out of humour than of ire
> Began to feel a great desire
> T' accost the manufacturer,
> And ask him what was doing there;
> A breed that earth themselves in cellars,
> Like conjurors or fortune tellers;
> Devoid of virtue and of mettle;
> A sort of subterranean cattle,
> Of no account in church or state,
> Or ever think of being great,
> As warriors or as politicians,
> But lurk in dungeons as magicians.[5]

The chevalier ironically chides the weaver for being without ambition and urges him to become a statesman.

> Are you enchanted by some gipsey,
> Who on your heart has cast a sheep's eye,
> And fain would hug you to her amours

[4] *Modern Chivalry* (edition of 1792), Vol. I, p. 150.
[5] *Gazette Publications,* pp. 311-12.

In low and subterranean chambers,
That thus you linger in sick mansion
Where never has the light of sun shone?

. . .   .

Is that a loom that stands before ye
That keeps you from the walks of glory?
It ill befits that men whom nature,
Hath favour'd with such parts and feature,
Should waste the taper of existence,
In meaner arts, when their assistance
Is wanted both in field and council,
To help our politics at groundsell,
And make some new and wholesome laws.[6]

The chevalier finds, however, that Traddle has already had a career in politics, much to the annoyance of his wife. Then another character, a writer, requests the chevalier to instruct the people regarding the folly of electing mechanics to public office.

It would do service to the state,
If such a noble Knight as you
Would teach them what they ought to do,
And give them seasonable lessons
Respecting such their crude creations,
That on the one hand while they pass
The ignorant though monied ass,
So on the other should avoid
The chusing such amongst the crowd
As are unqualified, though less,
They may in property possess.[7]

Brackenridge rightly had some doubt about the quality of his Hudibrastics. Perhaps he saw, as we do, that he was unable to combine successfully Hudibrastic verse and English syntax, and that a lack of clearness resulted. So he rewrote the book as *Modern Chivalry*, "thinking that it might be more acceptable in prose."[8] In writing this work he gave close attention to composition. Of the prose style he said: "This I have formed on the model of

[6] *Gazette Publications*, p. 312.   [7] *ibid.*, p. 328.
[8] *Modern Chivalry* (edition of 1792), Vol. I, p. 150.

Xenophon, and Swift's *Tale of a Tub,* and *Gulliver's Travels.* It is simple, natural, various, and forcible."[9] He also maintained that he had written in the pure, simple, Attic taste of Addison, Arbuthnot, Tillotson, and Bolingbroke.[10]

Brackenridge's remark to Badollet indicates that he was working on *Modern Chivalry* in 1790. The first two volumes were published in Philadelphia in 1792. In this quiet period of his life Brackenridge had abundant leisure for writing. Thus *Modern Chivalry* was composed not only for the education of the voters of Pennsylvania but as a literary pastime. He said: "It is a good deal owing to my solitary residence in the Western country, at a distance from books and literary conversation, that I have been led to write at all. It was necessary to fill up the interstices of business."[11]

Composing deliberately, Brackenridge was able to make his prose narrative much stronger than *The Modern Chevalier.* The shadowy "Chevalier" was transformed into Captain Farrago, a well read farmer and militia officer of Western Pennsylvania. This change put the book into close relation with its basis in Brackenridge's experience and provided a character well adapted to express the author's opinions. Traddle remained unaltered in his transfer to *Modern Chivalry,* but Teague O'Regan, an illiterate Irish servant, became the chief butt of the satire. The setting was likewise improved. The events in *The Modern Chevalier* seem to occur in an abstract world of political thought. In *Modern Chivalry,* Captain Farrago and his servant, Teague O'Regan, make a journey from Western Pennsylvania to Philadelphia just as Brackenridge himself had often done.

The narrative plan of *Modern Chivalry,* like that of *The Modern Chevalier,* is borrowed from *Don Quixote* and *Hudibras.* Also it follows the scheme of Swift's *Tale of a Tub* in interlarding chapters of philosophical comment between the incidents of the narrative. These structural formulas Brackenridge adapts to a satirical and realistic representation of American, particularly

9 *ibid.,* Vol. I. p. 152.   10 *ibid.* (edition of 1926), p. 202.
11 *ibid.* (edition of 1792), Vol. I, p. 152.

Western, society and politics. So *Modern Chivalry,* which is our first back-country book, is the result of using classic European literary traditions in an attempt to impart "seasonable lessons" to the tousle-headed frontier democracy.

As Brackenridge leads Captain Farrago and Teague O'Regan along the road from the frontier to Philadelphia, he makes one episode after another illustrate his thesis that "the people" are fools.

The first incident shows the Captain and Teague at a horse race. Some of the sporting men assume that the Captain is going to enter his nag in the races, but he denies having any such intention. From this episode the author extracts a moral:

> The first reflection that arises, is, the good sense of the Captain; who was unwilling to impose his horse for a racer; not being qualified for the course. Because, as an old lean beast, attempting a trot, he was respectable enough; but going out of his nature, and affecting speed, he would have been contemptible. The great secret of preserving respect, is the cultivating and showing to advantage the powers that we possess, and the not going beyond them. Every thing in its element is good, and in their proper sphere all natures and capacities are excellent. This thought might be turned into a thousand different shapes, and cloathed with various expressions; but after all, it comes to the old proverb at last, *Ne sutor ultra crepidam,* Let the cobbler stick to his last; a sentiment we are about to illustrate in the sequel of this work.[12]

The next chapter applies the same thesis to American politics, and is Brackenridge's final version of William Findley's victory of 1786-88. Captain Farrago and Teague, arriving at a village on election day, found a weaver and "a man of education" to be the candidates for the State legislature. As the weaver seemed to be the popular favorite, his opponent addressed the villagers as follows:

> Fellow citizens, I pretend not to any great abilities; but am conscious to myself that I have the best good will to serve you. But it is very astonishing to me, that this weaver should conceive himself

[12] *Modern Chivalry,* Vol. I, p. 22.

qualified for the trust. . . . The mechanical business which he pursues, must necessarily take up so much of his time, that he cannot apply himself to political studies. I should therefore think it would be more answerable to your dignity, and conducive to your interest, to be represented by a man of at least some letters, than by an illiterate handicraftsman like this. It will be more honourable for himself, to remain at his loom and knot threads, than to come forward in a legislative capacity: because, in the one case, he is in the sphere where God and nature has placed him; in the other, he is like a fish out of water, and must struggle for breath in a new element.[13]

Captain Farrago, always Brackenridge's *alter ego,* overheard this speech, and of course, seized the opportunity to expose the weaver's incompetency. Addressing the villagers, he said:

I have no prejudice against a weaver more than another man. . . . But to rise from the cellar to the senate house, would be an unnatural hoist. To come from counting threads, and adjusting them to the splits of a reed, to regulate the finances of a government would be preposterous; there being no congruity in the case. There is no analogy between knotting threads and framing laws. . . . Not that a manufacturer of linen or woolen, or other stuff, is an inferiour character, but a different one, from that which ought to be employed in affairs of state.[14]

While the opponents of the weaver were thus discoursing, Teague O'Regan "took it into his head that he could be a legislator himself." "The thing was not displeasing to the people, who seemed to favour his pretensions; owing, in some degree, to there being several of his countrymen among the crowd; but more especially to the fluctuation of the popular mind, and a disposition to what is new and ignoble."[15]

Captain Farrago, annoyed by this turn of the affair, resumed his harangue to the villagers:

This is making the matter still worse, gentlemen: this servant of mine is but a bog-trotter; who can scarcely speak the dialect in which your laws ought to be written; but certainly he has never read a single treatise on any political subject; for the truth is, he cannot read at all. . . . A free government is a noble possession to a people: and this

[13] *ibid.,* Vol. I, p. 25.   [14] *ibid.,* Vol. I, pp. 27-8.   [15] *ibid.,* Vol. I, p. 30.

freedom consists in an equal right to make laws, and to have the benefit of laws when made. Though doubtless, in such a government, the lowest citizen may become the chief magistrate; yet it is sufficient to possess the right; not absolutely necessary to exercise it. Or even if you should think proper, now and then, to shew your privilege, and exert, in a signal manner, the democratic prerogative, yet is it not descending too low to filch away from me a hireling, which I cannot well spare, to suit your purposes? You are surely carrying the matter too far, in thinking to make a senator of this hostler; to take him away from an employment to which he has been bred, and put him to another to which he has served no apprenticeship: to set those hands which have been lately employed in currying my horse, to the draughting bills, and preparing business for the house.[16]

The people, resentful of this interference, insisted on their right to elect Teague. One of the crowd angrily replied to the Captain:

It is a very strange thing, that after having conquered Burgoyne and Cornwallis, and got a government of our own, we cannot put in whom we please. This young man may be your servant, or another man's servant; but if we chuse to make him a delegate, what is that to you? He may not be skilled in the matter, but there is a good day a-coming. We will impower him; and it is better to trust a plain man like him, than one of your high flyers, that will make laws to suit their own purposes.[17]

So Teague O'Regan would have been sent to the legislature, had not the Captain induced him to withdraw his candidacy.

In his chapter of comment on this episode Brackenridge gave the following succinct statement of the central doctrine in his political philosophy:

A Democracy is beyond all question the freest government: because under this, every man is equally protected by the laws, and has equally a voice in making them. But I do not say an equal voice; because some men have stronger lungs than others, and can express more forcibly their opinions of public affairs. Others, though they may not speak very loud, yet have a faculty of saying more in a short time; and even in the case of others, who speak little or none at all, yet what they do say containing good sense, comes with greater weight; so that,

[16] *Modern Chivalry*, Vol. I, pp. 30-1.   [17] *ibid.*, Vol. I, p. 32.

all things considered, every citizen, has not, in this sense of the word, an equal voice. But the right being equal, what great harm if it is unequally exercised? Is it necessary that every man should become a statesman? No more than that every man should become a poet or a painter. The sciences, are open to all; but let him only who has taste and genius pursue them. . . . A ditcher is a respectable character, with his over-alls on, and a spade in his hand; but put the same man to those offices which require the head, whereas he has been accustomed to impress with his foot, and there appears a contrast between the individual and the occupation.[18]

Although Brackenridge did not share his frontier neighbors' fondness for Traddles and Teague O'Regans, he was equally unsympathetic with the Federalists' predilection for men of wealth. Continuing his comments on the village election he said:

I would not mean to insinuate that legislators are to be selected from the more wealthy of the citizens; yet a man's circumstances ought to be such as afford him leisure for study and reflection. There is often wealth without taste or talent. I have no idea, that because a man lives in a great house, and has a cluster of bricks or stones about his backside, that he is therefore fit for a legislator. There is so much pride and arrogance with those who consider themselves the first in a government, that it deserves to be checked by the populace; and the evil most usually commences on this side. Men associate with their own persons, the adventitious circumstances of birth and fortune: so that a fellow blowing with fat and repletion, conceives himself superior to the poor lean man, that lodges in an inferior mansion. But as in all cases, so in this, there is a medium. Genius and virtue are independent of rank and fortune; and it is neither the opulent, nor the indigent, but the man of ability and integrity that ought to be called forth to serve his country: and while, on the one hand, the aristocratic part of the government, arrogates a right to represent; on the other hand, the democratic contends the point; and from this conjunction and opposition of forces, there is produced a compound resolution, which carries the object to an intermediate direction. When we see, therefore, a Teague O'Regan lifted up, the philosopher will reflect, that it is to balance some purse-proud fellow, equally as ignorant, that comes down from the sphere of aristocratic interest.[19]

18 *ibid.*, Vol. I, pp. 41-2.   19 *ibid.*, Vol. I, pp. 42-3.

As Captain Farrago and Teague proceeded toward Philadelphia, the bog-trotter continued to be a favored candidate for honors. He was almost elected to membership in the American Philosophical Society, an organization for which Brackenridge had scant respect.[20] Then, in spite of his ignorance and lewdness, Teague barely escaped being made a preacher. In his comment on this ecclesiastical episode, Brackenridge, the skeptic, gives his ironical view of the state of the church:

The overtures made by Teague, to be admitted to the ministry, and the simplicity of the ecclesiastics in listening to his pretensions, made a great noise through the neighborhood; in as much as the young man laboured under a want of education, and was not qualified by theological reading. But I do not see, why it should be thought blamable; provided the matter was not too much hurried and hastily brought forward. For give him a little time, and he might have been instructed to preach as well as some that I myself have heard. . . .

I acknowledge, that in the regular churches, such as that of the Presbyterians, there is still kept up some opinion of the necessity of literature. But do we not see that with other denominations, such as the Quakers, the Methodists, and Anabaptists, it is totally disregarded and thrown out? Because, when human gifts or acquirements are absent, that which is supernatural more evidently appears. . . .

This being the case, I feel myself disposed to agree with those who reject human learning in religious matters altogether. More especially as science is really not the fashion at the present time. For as has been before seen, even in the very province of science itself, it is dispensed with; that of natural philosophy, for instance. In state affairs, ignorance does very well, and why not in church? I am for having all things of a piece; ignorant statesmen, ignorant philosophers, and ignorant ecclesiastics.[21]

As the journey draws near its conclusion matters other than democratic foibles call for comment. Brackenridge shows his contempt for the duel,[22] satirizes the Indian treaties of the Federal government,[23] and criticizes the aristocratic tendency of the Order

[20] *Modern Chivalry,* Vol. I, p. 46. See also his ironical "Memoir to the American Philosophical Society," *Gazette Publications,* pp. 256-64.

[21] *Modern Chivalry* (edition of 1792), Vol. I, pp. 79-81.

[22] *ibid.,* Vol. I, pp. 88 *ff.*   [23] *ibid.,* Vol. I, pp. 106 *ff.*

of the Cincinnati. Captain Farrago's address to a "Cincinnati gentleman" is clear evidence that Brackenridge's criticism of the frontier democracy did not spring from any sympathy with aristocracy.

But for my part, the principal objection that lies with me against your institution, is that which lies against all partial institutions whatsoever; they cut men from the common mass, and alienate their affections from the whole, concentring their attachments to a particular point and interest. A circumstance of this kind is unfavourable to general philanthropy, giving a temporary and artificial credit to those who are of the body, amongst themselves; so that while some lend character, others borrow; and the individuals do not stand on the natural basis of their own merit.[24]

The chapters on Captain Farrago's adventures and observations in Philadelphia again show that Brackenridge was not in sympathy with Hamiltonian Federalism. Teague disappeared, and the Captain, fearing that he was once more running for office, looked for him among the politicians. The office seekers in the metropolis were in striking contrast to the backwoods candidates, but were just as far from the philosophical ideal.

The candidates were all remarkably pot-bellied; and waddled in their gate. The captain inquiring what were the pretensions of these men to be elected; he was told, that they had all stock in the funds, and lived in brick buildings; and some of them entertained fifty people at a time, and ate and drank abundantly; and living an easy life, and pampering their appetites, they had swollen to this size.

It is a strange thing, said the captain, that in the country, in my route, they would elect no one but a weaver or a whiskey-distiller; and here none but fat swabs, that guzzle wine and smoke segars. It was not so in Greece, where Phocion came with his plain coat, from his humble dwelling, and directed the counsels of the people; or in Rome, where Cincinnatus was made dictator from the plough. Something must be wrong, where the inflate, and pompous are the objects of choice; though there is one good arising from it, that there is no danger of my Teague here. He could not afford to give a dinner; and as to funds, he has not a single shilling in them. They will make him neither mayor nor legislator in this city.[25]

[24] *ibid.*, Vol. I, pp. 140-1.   [25] *ibid.* (edition of 1792), Vol. II, pp. 51-2.

The Captain's search for Teague continued several days and took him to the University,[26] to Congress,[27] and to the American Philosophical Society.[28] The absconding Irishman was finally discovered as an actor in the theater. The outcome of Teague's theatrical episode was a severe beating administered by the manager, which Captain Farrago thought would cure his ambition to make unseemly advances in his station in life.[29] His aspirations were, however, only transferred to a new profession: he determined to become a lawyer. After the Captain had foiled this aim, he was persuaded by a tavern acquaintance to allow Teague to enter the public service in the executive branch of the Federal government. The second volume ends with a statement of the plans to prepare Teague for a presidential levee as a first step in obtaining a government post for him. "The state of politics at this time, and the prospect of Teague's advancement, we shall leave to the Third Volume of this work," said Brackenridge.[30]

The third volume was published at Pittsburgh in 1793. The small pamphlet of ninety-nine pages was the first literary work both written and published west of the Allegheny Mountains.[31] It opens with a long Hudibrastic poem on the Order of the Cincinnati. The chapters of the prose narrative which follow are mostly devoted to Teague's amazing success at the Republican Court and in the fashionable society of the capital, in which he for some time passes as the popular "Major" O'Regan. Obviously this section is inspired by a contempt of both parvenu favorites and legitimate "society."

[26] *Modern Chivalry*, Vol. II, pp. 92 *ff.*   [27] *ibid.*, Vol. II, pp. 88 *ff.*
[28] *ibid.*, Vol. II, pp. 71 *ff.*   [29] *ibid.*, Vol. II, pp. 123 *ff.*, 139.
[30] *ibid.*, Vol. II, p. 154.
[31] The following advertisement, probably the first of its kind in the West, appeared in the *Pittsburgh Gazette* of February 9, 1793:

> Modern Chivalry
> Volume III
> By H. H. Brackenridge
> Just published and to be sold by the Printer
> Price—Three Shillings & Nine Pence
> Pittsburgh, February 23, 1793.
> N.B. A few copies of the first and second
> Volume may be had in this town.

With this third volume of *Modern Chivalry* Brackenridge rested his case against the ignorant interlopers in American social institutions. New manifestations of popular folly were later to call forth additions to his work.

CHAPTER XIII

TOWARD DEMOCRACY

I N THE five years during which Brackenridge had been satirizing extreme democracy in *The Modern Chevalier* and *Modern Chivalry* he had gradually become alienated from the Federalist party, and by the time *Modern Chivalry* was published he had become a spokesman for the opposition.

His rupture with the Federalist party of the State of Pennsylvania occurred immediately after the ratification of the Constitution. When he learned that William Findley was to be selected as a candidate for the first Congress by the Anti-Federalist party, he determined to seek nomination as a Federalist candidate in order to oppose his old rival. The Federalist convention, however, refused to put his name on the ticket. He was indignant, and, as he later said, considered himself "absolved from all engagement to the party" as far as State politics were concerned.[1]

This new attitude found practical expression immediately. In 1790 the Federalists of Pennsylvania attempted to revise the old radical State constitution of 1776. Brackenridge, who had been an "anti-constitutionalist," opposed this movement. In a newspaper article he said:

We have carried the new federal government, and driven, as it were our chariot wheel over the belly of much opposition. Let us wait some time before we attack the State government, to new model or amend it. . . .

Is there no danger that a convention now called would in the enthusiasm of a reform go too far, and instead of lopping and pruning the tree of liberty to make it grow and flourish and bear fruit more abundantly, they might grub it up wholly by the roots?[2]

In two important legal cases also Brackenridge revealed his sympathy with a certain aspect of democratic as opposed to Fed-

[1] *Incidents of the Western Insurrection*, Vol. III, pp. 29-30.
[2] *Gazette Publications*, p. 84.

eralist feeling. In 1790 a collector of the State excise tax seized a quantity of liquor belonging to distillers in the Pittsburgh region. Brackenridge, as attorney for the distillers, had the seizures declared illegal. In the same year he appeared as attorney for seventy distillers who had refused to pay the excise tax and succeeded in quashing the writs which had been served against them. In handling these cases Brackenridge freely made use "of arguments drawn from the odious nature of the excise laws."[3] In so doing he was not merely availing himself of the lawyer's privilege of playing on prejudices; he was expressing his own feelings.

Although he had not repudiated the national party when he quarrelled with the State Federalists in 1789, he early objected to the policies of Alexander Hamilton. Later he summarized his relation to the Federalists at this period as follows:

I was with you, on the adoption of the *Federal Constitution.* I was against you, in some of the leading acts of the *administration*; the providing for the payment of the *aliened certificates,* at something not far short of par; the establishment of the United States banks, increasing the inequality of the gain; the *assumption* of the state debts, and the internal taxes the consequence of it.[4]

Although Brackenridge was soon to enter frankly into the Western opposition to the excise law, which was a phase of Hamilton's financial system, he at first refused to be involved with the issue. He did not wish to break off all connections with his former friends in the assembly, all of whom were Federalists. Also he desired to retain the friendship of several influential Federalists in the Pittsburgh district: Thomas Scott, Congressman; Judge Alexander Addison; and the wealthy Neville family. Furthermore he was embarrassed by the fact that his political enemies, Findley and Smiley, "had come forward to reprobate the law." He said:

I did not like to be ostensibly in the same party with them, besides in my gazette writings against Findley and others, I had treated with such ridicule the arts of seeking popular favor, that I was afraid of

[3] *Incidents of the Western Insurrection,* Vol. III, p. 8.
[4] *The Freeman's Journal,* August 3, 1805; and *The Standard of Liberty,* p. 51.

being suspected of that myself. . . . If I had not been shackled by the terms on which I stood with the Neville connection particularly, it is not improbable that I might have exercised at least attempts at wit, at the expense of the officer or the office; and excise duties might have been sung here, as Wood's half pence in Ireland.[5]

For these reasons he not only refrained from gazette satire, but also refused to enter openly into the more active forms of protest against the excise.

The first organized demonstration against the whiskey tax was a meeting of committees from the Western counties at Redstone Old Fort (Brownsville) in August 1791. At this meeting a general committee was appointed to meet at Pittsburgh on September 7 in order to draw up resolutions, circular letters, and an address to Congress which would express "with decency and firmness" the "sense of their constituents on the subject of the excise laws." Brackenridge was urged to get himself elected a member of this general committee, but declined the invitation. He did, however, consent to draw up for the committee "a sketch of resolutions and a draught of an address to Congress."[6] But when he later found that these documents had been radically altered by the committee he disclaimed all responsibility for them. Nevertheless his work is probably visible in the published resolutions, which condemn the funding system, the excise law, and the bank.[7]

Instead of joining openly with the local opposition to the Federalist policies in Pittsburgh, Brackenridge chose to carry his ideas to Philadelphia, where he went early in 1792 to see *Modern Chivalry* through the press and to secure admission to practise in the State Supreme Court. While he was in the capital, he expressed his opinions on current Western problems in a series of communications to the *National Gazette,* which Freneau had founded in 1791 as an organ of criticism of the Federalist régime.[8]

Brackenridge's first article, "Thoughts on the Present Indian War," charged the agents of the British with supplying the In-

[5] *Incidents of the Western Insurrection,* Vol. III, pp. 14-15.
[6] *ibid.,* Vol. III, p. 17.
[7] *Pennsylvania Archives,* Series II, Vol. IV, pp. 20-2.
[8] S. E. Forman, *The Political Activities of Philip Freneau,* p. 29.

dians with arms to attack the American frontier settlements. It also accused the Federal government of laxness in defending the frontier.[9]

In his next article, "Farther and Concluding Thoughts on the Indian War," he repeated his charge that British agents were responsible for the uprising of the savages, and caustically criticized the romantic view of the Indians.

I consider men who are unacquainted with the savages, like young women who have read romances, and have as improper an idea of the Indian character in the one case, as the female mind has of real life in the other. The philosopher, weary of the vices of refined life, thinks to find perfect virtue in the simplicity of the unimproved state. He sees green fields and meadows in the customs and virtues of the savages. It is experience only can relieve from this calenture of the intellect. All that is good and great in man results from education; and an uncivilized Indian is but a little way removed from a beast, who, when incensed, can only tear and devour, but the savage applies the ingenuity of man to torture and inflict anguish.[10]

In his next article Brackenridge dealt forcefully with the excise law. Here again he spoke as a representative of the West and revealed a philosophical understanding of the function of the frontier in American life. After informing his Eastern readers that

[9] *National Gazette,* February 2, 1792.
[10] *ibid.,* February 6, 1792. When this protest reached Hartford, the two Connecticut wits who were writing *The Echo* turned Brackenridge's observations into ironical verse, as follows:
> I view the men, who ne'er a savage saw,
> Like those young girls whose minds begin to thaw,
> In Fancy's spring, when wild romances start
> The mind to mischief, and to love the heart.
> The one is solely bent on plotting evil;
> The other thinks an Indian is the devil;
> The first employs her industry and art
> To raise a bobbery in the human heart;
> The last with pure devotion worships God
> By offering incense sweet of scalps and blood.
> The sage Philosopher, by ign'rance fir'd
> Of genteel vice, and common follies tir'd,
> Thinks Virtue's hallow'd form alone is found
> Where squaws cut capers o'er the desart ground.
> He sees green spring in their rude minds appear,

he had not "appeared in committees on this subject in the Western country," he proceeded to show that the excise tax was unjust to his part of the country. In support of this view he said that, on account of the closing of the Mississippi, the Western farmers could dispose of their grain only by converting it into whiskey; that, because of heavy carriage charges, prices on commodities were higher in the West than elsewhere; that agricultural implements and labor were abnormally dear on the frontier; that the border counties had suffered from prolonged trouble with the Indians; and that land titles were still unsettled. "This is therefore no country from which to raise a revenue," he maintained.

Then, in answer to those who would discourage the development of the frontier region, he said:

The idea of a new and unoccupied territory has drawn and will draw thousands not from the bosom of our settlements, but from the continent of Europe, the kingdom of France especially, who would never otherwise have thought of mixing and sitting down with our more populated settlements. We have now a small town Gallipolis, but may soon have a great city of this last polished people.

Those therefore who think and act on the contracted principles of checking emigration discover a contracted mind, and were I a great emperor, they should never be grand vizirs or ministers of state to me. I am for filling up the whole canvas of the United States territory, and for pushing out a column of inhabitants as speedily as possible to take the flank of Canada; and secure the western Indians in amity before they are made hostile by our rivals.

I consider the western country as the *tiers état,* or third estate of the union, and, as necessary to hold the balance in the interests of the east and south parts. There is nothing, in my contemplation, will contribute more to the duration of our empire than such a balance. It will also serve to counterbalance the weight of the monied interests and

---

And their brown skins disclose the falling year.
Experience only can the pill dispense,
Which purges off this calenture of sense.
All that is great in man, I do suppose,
From education and from College flows,
And these brown tribes, who snuff the desart air,
Are aunts and cousins to the skunk and bear.—*The Echo,* p. 36.

germ of aristocracy, in the richer capitals, by preserving a bed of simplicity and true republicanism.

Next, pleading for a suspension of the excise, he directly addressed Alexander Hamilton:

I profess, had I it in my power, and was answerable for the success of provision for the public debt, I would adopt this policy; because with respect to these people, the thing is palpably so unequal and oppressive that it cannot be borne. It amounts to a prohibition of distillation altogether; and opposition necessarily generated in one quarter may communicate to another, and take flame where there was not the same strokes of the steel originally to produce it. These thoughts I submit respectfully to the Secretary of the Treasury or the representatives of the people, if an eye should be cast on this paper.

Having hinted at the seriousness of the situation, he proceeded to advise Hamilton:

I have just to add farther; let peace be given to the western country; let the use of the waters to the ocean be established; let them have a little time to breathe and recover loss, and feel vigor, and if they do not submit to every demand of contribution to the revenue, I shall be the first to bear testimony against them in their country, as I have done heretofore when I thought them wrong. But I know the yeomanry are honest, though sometimes misled, and in due time that country will afford both by trade and tax a substantial revenue to these states, but oppression will make the wise mad, and induce them to resist with intemperance what they ought to resist with reason.[11]

In thus determining to act as champion of both the Federal government and the Western distillers, Brackenridge was characteristically preparing trouble for himself.

After returning to Pittsburgh early in 1792, he continued to hold himself aloof from the anti-excise activities. A second meeting of county delegates was held in Pittsburgh on August 21, 1792. Brackenridge was elected a delegate from Allegheny County, but declined to serve.[12] The committee, of which Albert Gallatin was chairman, passed resolutions recommending that the people take a firm stand against excise tax collectors. It was resolved "that in

[11] *National Gazette,* February 9, 1792.
[12] *Incidents of the Western Insurrection,* Vol. III, p. 20.

future we will consider such persons as unworthy of our friendship, have no intercourse or dealings with them, withdraw from them every assistance, and withhold all the comforts of life . . . and upon all occasions, treat them with that contempt they deserve." Brackenridge was asked by some of the members "whether the going so far could be construed treason." "I thought not," he said later. "It struck me, however, to be going to the utmost boundary of right preserved by the people. On the principle of political virtue, nothing but extreme necessity could justify it; it is the last step short of using actual force."[13]

So Western Pennsylvania was drifting rapidly toward the Whiskey Insurrection of 1794, and Brackenridge, embarrassed by divided sympathies, was being as discreet as possible in an attempt to avoid entanglements.

During the next year, 1793, he evidently had no connection with the campaign against the excise law. Perhaps it was policy that still held him aloof, but the records show him to have been occupied with a new interest—the French Revolution. During this period Federalists and Republicans were sharply divided in their attitude toward European affairs, and Brackenridge aligned himself frankly and openly with the Republican partisans of revolutionary France. Again he used Freneau's *National Gazette* as a means of publishing his ideas.

His first expression of sympathy with the revolutionists was issued when he learned that Louis XVI had been beheaded.[14] On April 1, 1793, he wrote in Pittsburgh, under the title "Louis Capet lost his Caput":

From my use of a pun, it may seem that I think lightly of his fate. I certainly do so. It affects me no more than the execution of another malefactor. Less indeed; because knowing the commiseration which will ensue on the false principle of estimating highly the misfortunes of great personages, I feel a contempt of this distinction of rank, and am disposed to commiserate less than in the case of some obscure and unpitied rogue that goes to the gallows without a thought to survive him. Because few pity him, I will be one of those few: but in the case

[13] *Incidents,* Vol. III, p. 20.   [14] Louis XVI was beheaded on January 21, 1792.

of Louis, because there are so many kings and queens, and aristocrats throughout the world to make a mountain of the matter, I disdain to join with them, or feel pity at all.

That he was guilty there can be no doubt. It was scarcely in human nature that he should not be guilty.—Who, ever parted with power when he could keep it? . . . A man that has been in the habit of dictating every thing but the power of thought to those of mankind around him, cannot have become such a philosopher, as to reduce his mind within his state, and be satisfied with a restricted controul. You may as well tame a grown up wolf, or a bear. To a certain extent Louis was willing; nay anxious, to procure for the people all the happiness he could give them under despotism: that is, a convention of the states, in order to choose their own ways and means of supplying them with money. But he had no idea of retrenching his prerogative. He was not sincere in the adopting the constitution. His oath was false; his councils insidious; his object subjugation by the assistance of his brother kings. It was at stake whether he should succeed and trucidate half a million of subjects; or whether his subjects should decapitate him. Had he succeeded, would his brother kings, and aristocrats, have felt commiseration at a recital of the trucidation of democrats? No: they would have sniffed the air that brought the account, as if fragrant with odoriferous odours. Why then such a noise even with republicans about the death of Louis?[15]

The next European event that aroused strong feeling in America was France's declaration of war on England on February 1, 1793. On this as on other aspects of the Revolution the Federalists and Republicans divided radically in their sympathies, and President Washington issued a proclamation of neutrality on April 22. Brackenridge at once wrote a sharp protest against the President's proclamation and urged American participation in the war.

To the President of the United States
Sir,

I have just seen your PROCLAMATION, written with your usual propriety and delicacy. But I do not accord with your idea, that "the duty and interest of the United States require, that they should

[15] *National Gazette*, April 20, 1793. The article is not signed. A Ms. note in the copy of the *National Gazette* in the library of the University of Pittsburgh assigns it to Brackenridge. Probably no one else in Pittsburgh could have written it.

with sincerity and good faith, adopt and pursue a conduct friendly and impartial towards the belligerent powers," leagued against France. It is not their duty, because, though bound by no express contract, yet there is an implied obligation to assist the *weak* against the *strong,* the *oppressed* against the *oppressor,* on the same principle as in the case of an individual in a state of nature, who sees another attempt an unjust force upon a third, and ought to interfere to preserve right. The cause of France is the cause of man, and neutrality is desertion.

It is "not our interest"; because despotism will give us thanks, and the republic of France which will assuredly triumph, will disdain her unfeeling *Sister,* who stood by with an unassisting hand, and saw her distress.

But how can we assist? We can make a push at one of her adversaries, England; and remove that power from Canada.—The losing of foot hold any where will contribute to reduce her force. It will be self defence for ourselves, as it will relieve from the hostilities of savages.

The independence of the islands in our neighborhood, will give an equal use of their productions, which at present, are engrossed by England.

Objection: Our commerce in the mean time will suffer, and the imposts be reduced. How so? instead of purchasing British cargoes, cannot we take them? If we have not duties, we can have the bulks.

If it is referred to the great mass of the people, I doubt much whether it is "the disposition" of the United States to preserve the conduct you enjoin.[16] It may be the disposition of those who draw from the funds; but of none else. The fact is, the American mind is indignant, and needs to be but roused a little to go to war with England, and assist France. Let all who think with me, SPEAK.[17]

[16] "If the British do not instigate the enemy, they furnish them with contraband articles of commerce—Is it constitutional in the President to declare the disposition of the people with regard to war; the declaring which is in the Congress? as the executive, it became him in the mean time to enjoin peace until the nation thro' its representatives, should have declared its sense." Brackenridge's note.

[17] *National Gazette,* May 15, 1793. This contribution is not signed, but there can be no doubt that Brackenridge wrote it. He probably had reference to this article when he wrote in 1805: "Nor were the measures of the government altogether to my liking in our relations with France. I was for striking Britain, and invading Canada, the moment that Britain declared war against France." *The Freeman's Journal,* August 3, 1805.

American enthusiasm for the French cause reached its climax during the spring and summer of 1793. At this time Brackenridge made his last gesture for the Revolution in an oration delivered on the Fourth of July in Pittsburgh. Citizen Brackenridge, as he was styled in the *National Gazette,* which published his oration, spoke as follows:

The celebration of the day introduces the idea of the effect of it beyond the sphere of these states. . . . The light kindled here has been reflected to France, and a new order of things has arisen. Shall we blame the intemperature of the exertions? And was there ever a great effect without enthusiasm? Thy principles, O! Liberty, are not violent or cruel; but in the desperation of thy efforts against tyranny, it is not possible to keep within the limit of the vengeance necessary to defence. . . .
Is it the duty of these states to assist France? That we are bound by treaty, and how far, I will not say; because it is not necessary. We are bound by a higher principle, if our assistance could avail; the great law of humanity. . . . Shall kings combine, and shall republics not unite? We have united. The heart of America feels the cause of France; she takes a part in all her councils; approves her wisdom; blames her excesses; she is moved, impelled, elevated, and depressed, with all the changes of her good and bad fortune; she feels the same fury in her veins. . . . Why not? Can we be indifferent? Is not our fate interlaced with hers? For, O! France, if thy republic perish, where is the honour due to ours? . . .
Can we assist France by arming in her favour? I will not say that we can. But could we, and should France say, United States, your neutrality is not sufficient; I expect the junction of your arms with mine . . . who is there would not say, it shall be so; you shall have them; our citizens shall arm; they shall attack; our oaks shall descend from the mountains; our vessels be launched upon the stream, and the voice of our war, however weak, shall be heard with yours.[18]

[18] *Gazette Publications,* pp. 121-4; *National Gazette,* July 27, 1793; and *A Political Miscellany,* pp. 27-31.

CHAPTER XIV

THE WHISKEY INSURRECTION

I N SPITE of the stimulation of the radical spirit through the enthusiasm of the friends of the French Revolution, the opposition to the excise appeared to be weakening during the year 1793. A few acts of violence, however, occurred in Western Pennsylvania. The collector for Fayette County was, for example, compelled by force to deliver up his commission and his books.[1] Nevertheless, Alexander Hamilton was able to report to President Washington, that "notwithstanding these excesses the law appeared during the latter periods of this year [1793] to be rather gaining ground."[2]

Soon, however, the conjunction of the French radical spirit with the other causes of discontent was to create an atmosphere of rebellion. In Western Pennsylvania, as elsewhere in the United States, democratic societies were being organized in imitation of the French revolutionary clubs. The first and most important of these organizations was formed at Mingo Creek, near Pittsburgh, on February 28, 1794.[3] The membership was composed of a battalion of militia,[4] and the society usually met in the Mingo meetinghouse.[5] Although the club stated that nothing in its constitution was "to be so construed as to prejudice any claims of the State, or United States," its principles were radical and it proposed to assume some of the regular functions of the government, particularly of the judiciary. It forbade any citizen of the district to sue any other citizen in court before applying to the society for redress.[6] Brackenridge later called this organization the "cradle of the insurrection."[7]

---

[1] November 22, 1793. See *Proceedings of the Executive of the United States respecting the Insurgents*, pp. 113-14.
[2] *ibid.*, p. 114.   [3] *Incidents of the Western Insurrection*, Vol. III, p. 148.
[4] *ibid.*   [5] *ibid.*, Vol. III, p. 25.   [6] *ibid.*, Vol. III, p. 149.
[7] *ibid.*, Vol. I, p. 86.

Meanwhile forcible resistance to the excise law was again breaking out, and it became unsafe for law-abiding citizens to pay the tax. The case of William Cochran reveals the prevailing temper. "His still was cut to pieces; and this was humorously called, mending his still; and the menders of course must be tinkers."[8] So these self-appointed regulators of justice assumed the name "Tom the Tinker, threatening individuals, or admonishing, or commanding them, in measures with regard to the excise law."[9] From such a state of affairs the so-called "insurrection" rapidly developed, and Brackenridge was unable to avoid being involved in it.

In July 1794 a United States marshal, David Lenox, came to Western Pennsylvania to serve writs on delinquent distillers and on the persons who had attacked the collector of Fayette County. On July 14 he visited Brackenridge in Pittsburgh and reported that he had "met with no insult, much less injury, in the execution of his duty." Brackenridge expressed surprise that he had expected any resistance, since the people were disposed to respect sheriffs and judicial officers, although they had no scruples about resisting excise officers.[10]

On July 15 Marshal Lenox rode out to serve the last of his writs in company with General John Neville. General Neville had previously been very popular with the farmers and had voted for the resolutions against the excise law in the State assembly.[11] Now, however, the people were bitterly resentful because he had accepted the office of inspector of the revenue for the Western Pennsylvania District. In spite of having an unpopular companion with him, however, Marshal Lenox was able to perform his duty without opposition until he came to serve the very last writ. It was evening when, leaving Neville on horseback in a lane, he rode into a harvest field to read a summons to a farmer named Miller. While the marshal was reading the writ, Neville shouted to him to make haste, as a party of men were running across the field as if to head

[8] ibid., Vol. I, p. 79.

[9] ibid., Vol. I, p. 79. See also Alexander Hamilton's report in Proceedings of the Executive of the United States respecting the Insurgents, pp. 113 ff.

[10] Incidents of the Western Insurrection, Vol. I, pp. 5-6.

[11] William Findley, History of the Insurrection, p. 79.

him off. He galloped off with Neville, and when they got to the end of the lane, the men fired on them.

The embattled farmers were, in fact, mad with rage. The summons meant that Miller had to leave his farm in the middle of the harvest and appear at the federal court in Philadelphia. The trip would cost him two hundred and fifty dollars at least. This was ruin. That night he and his friends hastily determined to go to Neville's farm and take Neville and the marshal.[12] Early on the next morning they appeared before the farmhouse—a group of about thirty-five men, including several members of the Mingo Creek democratic society. They were fired upon, and six of them were wounded, one mortally.[13]

The next day General Neville wrote to his son, Colonel Presley Neville, who lived in Pittsburgh, reporting that a large number of men were gathering at Couche's Fort, about four miles from his house. Presley Neville at once called on Brackenridge, read this letter to him, and expressed "his apprehensions for the situation of his father." Brackenridge asked Colonel Neville what he considered to be the intention of this mob. He answered that they were going to demand that his father "deliver up his commission."

"Deliver it," said Brackenridge.

"No," answered Neville.[14]

In giving such advice Brackenridge was attempting to calm the tempest by the exercise of "policy." He thought that the simplest way to insure peace was to "give the rioters a piece of paper which they had their minds set upon, and let the justices of the peace, the constables, the sheriffs, the grand juries of the courts, settle it with them afterwards."[15]

Refusing to accept Brackenridge's suggestion, Presley Neville went to John Gibson, major general of the militia, and John Wilkins, brigadier general, and demanded that they call out the militia to suppress the rioters. Wilkins came to Brackenridge and asked whether they had authority to call out the militia. After con-

[12] *Incidents of the Western Insurrection,* Vol. I, pp. 121-2.
[13] *ibid.,* Vol. I, pp. 6-7.
[14] *ibid.,* Vol. I, p. 6.   [15] *ibid.,* Vol. I, p. 7.

sidering the question a short time, Brackenridge expressed the opinion that they had not.

Disappointed in this attempt, Presley Neville next called upon Gibson and Wilkins, in their capacity as judges of the court, to raise "the posse of the county." Wilkins again consulted Brackenridge as to the legal aspects of the question. Brackenridge declared that the judges did not have authority to raise the posse.

"But," he said, "the sheriff can. He is in town; let him be called upon."[16]

Presley Neville then requested the sheriff to raise the posse. The officer, however, expressed doubt as to his power to do so, and, together with the justices, consulted Brackenridge about it. When Brackenridge had explained the law, the sheriff "was alarmed at the task . . . and thought it not practicable." Brackenridge agreed that it was not practicable, and the justices concurred in the opinion.

"This, however, can be done," said Brackenridge. "Ride out without arms, and address the people. Persuasion will avail more than force. If this is adopted, I will be one to go."

His suggestion was followed. In a few minutes he had returned to his house, mounted his horse, and joined the company which was assembling at the river crossing. In the company he found three men armed: Presley Neville, Marshal Lenox, and a certain Ormsby.

"What! Armed?" said Brackenridge to Ormsby.

"Yes," was the curt reply.

"You will not ride with us armed," Brackenridge said.

"You may ride as you please, I am armed," retorted Ormsby.

"We are not all born orators: we are going to fight; you to speak," added Presley Neville.

Then the crowd boarded a boat and started across the river. The boat being heavily loaded and the water low, they were soon stranded on a bar. In his anxiety to reach Neville's house before trouble began, Brackenridge leaped his horse overboard, rode

16 *ibid.*, Vol. I, p. 8.

over the bar, and swam the channel to the other side. Others followed his example.[17]

In spite of their haste, however, they were not able to take the main road, since they learned that guards were posted there, but they were forced to follow an old, unfrequented by-way. As they rode along many signs of the general excitement were in evidence. Brackenridge noticed that there were no men in the fields; only women were working. At a farmhouse at which they stopped, a woman was alarmed by their presence, considering them to be of the "Neville party," as she called it. It was clear that the presence of civil officers at Neville's would be resented. Therefore Brackenridge proposed to ride ahead alone so that it would be apparent that their intention was to dissuade, not to arrest.[18] Before he reached Neville's, however, he learned that it was too late to do anything. The mob had demanded General Neville's papers, and, when these were refused, they had ordered the women to leave the house, and then had attacked it. It was defended by ten or twelve regular soldiers from the Pittsburgh garrison under Major Kirkpatrick. In the battle the leader of the insurgents, a certain McFarlane, was killed; but the house was taken and burned, and the soldiers surrendered. When Brackenridge learned of this battle, he rejoined his party, and they returned to Pittsburgh.[19]

During the next few days various requests for advice continued to draw Brackenridge into the current of the insurrection. David Hamilton, leader of the Mingo Creek society, and John Black came to Pittsburgh to demand that Marshal Lenox give up his writs without returning them to court. They consulted Brackenridge, who gave the opinion that the marshal was required to return the writs, but that they were summonses only and that non-compliance would not bring judgment by default.[20]

On July 21 Brackenridge received a note from David Hamilton requesting him to appear at a meeting of a committee at Mingo meeting-house on July 24. Although he supposed that he was invited only for the purpose of explaining to the committee his

[17] *Incidents of the Western Insurrection*, Vol. I, p. 9.
[18] *ibid.*, Vol. I, pp. 9-10.   [19] *ibid.*, Vol. I, pp. 21-2.   [20] *ibid.*, Vol. I, pp. 23-4.

legal opinion regarding the writs, he was nevertheless unwilling to have any correspondence with the radical and treasonable Mingo Creek group. Therefore he tore up the note and threw the fragments into a closet with other scrap paper, "meaning never to make further mention of it."[21] But, for all his precautions, he was not able to avoid attending the meeting. The next day Presley Neville came to his office and asked him whether he had not received a note from David Hamilton.

"I have," answered Brackenridge, "but how have you come to the knowledge of it?"

"The young man that brought it mentioned it," replied Neville.

"I had never intended to have mentioned it," said Brackenridge, "but here it is."

Opening the closet, he took out the scraps, fitted them together, and gave the note to Neville to read. Now that his receipt of the note was no secret, he wished to have Neville as a witness of the contents.

"Do you mean to go?" asked Neville.

"No," replied Brackenridge, "this is high treason that has been committed; and in treason there are no accessories before or after the fact; all are principals; and I am aware of the delicacy of having anything to say to people in the predicament in which these are. I have reflected on the subject and think it not safe to go."

"I wish you would go," said Neville. "It might answer a good end."

Thinking that Neville wished him to attend the meeting in order to counsel moderation, Brackenridge, after being further solicited, said:

"I will go, provided you vouch with what sentiments I go."

"I will," Neville promised.

"And provided," Brackenridge added, "some person can be got to go with me to bear testimony of what I shall say or do on the occasion."

It was agreed that Brackenridge should be accompanied at the meeting by the chief burgess of Pittsburgh, the first assistant bur-

[21] *ibid.*, Vol. I, p. 29.

gess, one of the town regulators, and two of the leading merchants.

When Brackenridge and his companions arrived at the Mingo meeting-house on July 24, they found not only a committee representing those who had been concerned in the burning of Neville's house but also a large number of other people from all parts of the district. While they lay on the grass or strolled about before the meeting assembled, there was an atmosphere of tenseness and anxiety. Every countenance revealed "a strong sense of the solemnity of the occasion."[22] All were silent. Brackenridge did not exchange a word with anybody.

When the meeting opened, a letter was read from Presley Neville stating that his father and Marshal Lenox had left the district. This news gave great offense to the rebellious members, as the marshal had promised to surrender himself on demand, and Presley Neville had sponsored the agreement.

After this letter and others had been discussed, one of the radicals, Benjamin Parkinson, put the question:

"We wish to know whether what has been done is right or wrong; and whether we are to be supported in it, or left to ourselves."

When Brackenridge heard these words he was, he says, "impressed with an agony of mind."

A discussion of the question followed. First, David Bradford, a lawyer of Washington, spoke violently in support of the recent acts of rebellion. "After he had spoken there was a dead silence."[23] It was a difficult moment for Brackenridge. He saw that a vote would probably be called for on the question: "Support or not support." His own situation was delicate. To join with the insurgents would be treason; to vote against the proposition would incur popular odium which "might produce personal injury" before he left Mingo; and to withdraw from the meeting would be equally dangerous.

He had anticipated being called on to speak, and had outlined a speech in his mind. So, when he was solicited, he addressed the meeting. First, he gave a summary of recent events. In order to

[22] *Incidents,* Vol. I, pp. 29-30.   [23] *ibid.,* Vol. I, p. 32.

avoid giving a direct statement of his opinion of what had been done he attempted to distract the audience by giving a humorous account of the closing of the Pittsburgh inspection office. Then, trying to prevent a vote on Parkinson's question, he said for the Pittsburgh contingent:

"We were not delegated for the purpose of giving a vote, but simply to give a narrative of what had taken place there, with respect to the excise office, in order to calm the minds of the people, and render it unnecessary for any force to come and take it down."

Although, he said, the Pittsburgh delegation had no authority to vote, he himself was willing, as an individual, to give advice. Then he stated his opinion that "what had been done might be morally right, but it was legally wrong. . . . In construction of law it was high treason. It was a case within the power of the President to call out the militia." The guilty members of the audience were much impressed by this opinion, as they had considered that their actions were cognizable only in the county courts. Taking advantage of the embarrassment which he perceived in their countenances, Brackenridge continued:

"But the President will reflect upon the difficulty of getting the militia to march. They will be reluctant from the midlands of Pennsylvania, from the upper parts of Maryland and Virginia. It will probably be necessary to bring them from Jersey and the lower parts of the States. For this reason the President may be disposed to give an amnesty." In his opinion it would be necessary to make an application to the President in order to obtain amnesty, and he thought that such an application would come with better grace, and with better effect, from the innocent than from the guilty. Consequently, it was not prudent for those who were involved to involve others also; the innocent should be allowed to remain unentangled in order to act as mediators with the government.

At this point in his address Brackenridge saw rage in the countenance of Benjamin Parkinson and others, who perceived that he was attempting to avoid support of their scheme to make their own case a common cause. Therefore he proceeded to show that it was necessary to ask for amnesty because the Western Pennsylvania counties could not successfully make war against the whole country. Also he maintained that the President would in all probability grant an amnesty, since he had shown a disposition to avoid war. As evidence on this point he cited the recent Indian treaties. Not approving of the treaties himself, and eager to put his audience in good humor, he yielded to the temptation to become ironical at the expense of President Washington and the Federal government. Dramatizing the situation, he "introduced General Knox on one side, and Cornplanter on the other, and made them make speeches."

"Now," he said, "if Indians can have treaties, why cannot we have one or two?"

Then, gradually returning to seriousness, he concluded by proposing another meeting of representatives from all parts of the district. This body would, he suggested, send delegates to the President to effect "an arrangement with regard to what had been rashly, and, in legal construction, criminally acted." He also volunteered to serve as one of the emissaries himself if this measure should be adopted.[24]

Even while Brackenridge was speaking it had been apparent that he was not winning over all his audience. "Those not involved were greatly relieved and satisfied; and manifested this by the countenance, and by the nod of the head. Those involved . . . were dissatisfied; and manifested this by the countenance, and by the shaking of the head."

After he had finished speaking, there was a total silence, and most of the people left the house. Brackenridge went out and walked about, waiting to learn what the general impression was. His friends from Pittsburgh informed him that many of the people were dissatisfied, and that "there appeared to be a murmuring amongst them." One of the men who had been in the mob that burned Neville's house told him that Benjamin Parkinson and a brother of the man who had been killed in the attack

[24] *Incidents of the Western Insurrection*, Vol. I, pp. 32-4.

were stirring up the people against him. On hearing this Brackenridge went back into the meeting-house "to observe what was doing there." There he saw David Bradford and others "in a knot or globe, in the center of the house, conversing with their heads together, in a low voice." He walked slowly past them, but "was not asked to stop, or join in the deliberation." Walking back past them again he asked one of the group, James Marshall, "what they were concluding on." Marshall pointedly said that "he did not know." So Brackenridge, feeling himself distrusted, withdrew in alarm.

Finding his Pittsburgh company as soon as possible, he gave them warning, and they set off. He himself, lingering a few minutes and mingling with the people, gave out word that his company was going, and that, since he did not wish to miss them, he was going too. When they had proceeded a short distance, they were called back, but only hastened their pace forward. Coming to the house where they had left their horses, they stayed about an hour to dine and get the animals out of the pasture. They were now ready for the ride to Pittsburgh, but one of the company suggested that their abrupt departure might give the impression that they were spies, and that it might be well for Brackenridge to go back and show himself and make some apology. Brackenridge agreed, and rode back. Dismounting at some distance from the meeting-house and tying his horse in a creek bottom, where it would not be seen, he walked up to the meeting-house as if he had not been away at all. But most of the people had left or were just leaving, and so Brackenridge merely showed himself and then rejoined his company. Before they set out for Pittsburgh the owner of the farm at which they had been staying returned from the Mingo meeting and told them "that nothing had been done, but a large meeting agreed upon at another day."[25]

Three days later, on July 26, Brackenridge first learned of the arrangements for the meeting from an item in the *Pittsburgh Gazette*. The Mingo group recommended that township meetings of the Western Pennsylvania and Western Virginia counties

[25] *ibid.*, Vol. I, pp. 35-6.

should choose delegates to assemble at Parkinson's Ferry[26] on August 14 "to take into consideration the situation of the Western country." His first thought was that this call was the result of his own suggestion, and that the meeting was designed for "instituting a negotiation with the government, for the purpose of composing the disturbance." He was worried, however, when General Arthur St. Clair, who happened to be in Pittsburgh at the time, told him that "such a convention would be dangerous."[27]

At this same time the radical leaders, David Bradford and Marshall, took further steps toward open rebellion. They planned and caused to be executed a robbery of the Pittsburgh mail for the purpose of learning which of the Pittsburgh citizens were sending to Philadelphia unfavorable accounts of the insurgents. After reading the letters of their local critics, they planned to have the latter expelled from the community. On July 28 they sent circular letters to officers of the militia requesting them to bring volunteers fully armed to Braddock Field, about twenty miles from Pittsburgh, on August 1.[28]

The citizens of Pittsburgh were terrified by this maneuver, since they knew that the country people suspected them of favoring a policy of conciliation. The days preceding the gathering at Braddock Field gave abundant cause for alarm. Some of the country people who visited Pittsburgh talked of plundering it; others of burning it. "Sodom, they said, had been burnt by fire from heaven; but this second Sodom should be burned with fire from earth." "The shop-keepers were told at their counters, by persons cheapening their goods, that they would get them at a less price in a few days." Even women from the country, seeing Pittsburgh ladies, said, "That fine lady lives in a fine house, but her pride will be humbled by and by."[29]

During this period Brackenridge's personal situation was exceedingly trying. More and more clearly he perceived that his

---

[26] Now Monongahela City.
[27] *Incidents of the Western Insurrection,* Vol. I, p. 37.
[28] *ibid.,* Vol. I, pp. 39-44.   [29] *ibid.,* Vol. I, pp. 43-4.

address at Mingo had made him unpopular. To those who said that
the insurgents should have been supported he replied:
"What will be the consequence? A war will ensue."
"Well," they answered, "let those that do not choose to stand
with the country leave it; there will be enough behind without
them; what they leave will help to carry on the war."

Such being the temper of the people, Brackenridge could not
see any satisfactory escape for himself. His sentiments in this situation are best stated in his own words:

Knowing that the government could not possibly overlook the outrages committed, and finding these dispositions in the people to support them, I saw my situation perfectly, and canvassed in my mind, the
practicability of lying by, and remaining a spectator, or the necessity
of abandoning the country. I thought also of taking a part, but the
cause was not good; at the same time hazardous, and nothing to be
got by it. A revolution did not suit me, nor any man else that had anything to lose, or was in a way of making something. A secession of the
country from the government, presented nothing, that could be an
object with me. . . . For my part I had seen and heard enough of
revolutions, to have any wish to bear any part in one. But to lie by was
impossible; no man would be suffered to remain neutral. I thought,
therefore, of emigrating. . . . I thought of crossing the mountains
to Philadelphia: Nothing but the suddenness with which the march to
Braddock's fields came upon us, prevented my being out of the way, at
that time. It was impossible to make arrangements in so short a period.
When that came, I thought of nothing but weathering the blast, for
the moment, and then making my escape.[30]

Having decided to remain in Pittsburgh, Brackenridge was unable to avoid further entanglement in the insurrection. During the
next few weeks he followed the policy of appearing to take part
in the insurrectionist activities while actually attempting to render
them as harmless as possible.

On July 31, the day before the Braddock Field gathering, the
citizens of Pittsburgh held a town meeting "to take into consideration the present situation of affairs and to declare their sentiments
on this delicate crisis." Early in the proceedings it was announced

[30] ibid., Vol. I, pp. 41-2.

that "certain gentlemen from the town of Washington had arrived, and had signified, that they were entrusted with a message to the inhabitants of the town relative to present affairs." A committee of three, including Brackenridge, was appointed to receive their message. After conferring with the gentlemen from Washington this committee reported "that in consequence of certain letters sent by the last mail, certain persons were discovered as advocates of the excise law, and enemies to the interests of the country; and that a certain Edward Day, James Brison, and Abraham Kirkpatrick, were particularly obnoxious, and that it was expected by the country that they should be dismissed without delay." The meeting "resolved that it should be so done; and a committee of twenty-one were appointed to see this resolution carried into effect." Brackenridge was appointed a member of this committee also, along with such solid citizens as the chief burgess, an assistant burgess, the editor of the *Pittsburgh Gazette,* and some of the leading merchants. The town meeting, ostensibly capitulating to the demands of the rebels, further resolved: that the committee of twenty-one should go to Braddock Field the next day and assure the people that the proscribed persons had been expelled; that the inhabitants of the town should march out, and join the people on Braddock Field as brethren, to carry into effect with them any measure that might seem to them advisable for the common cause; that the committee should serve in the future as a committee of information and correspondence; and that, on August 9, delegates should be chosen at a town meeting to attend the meeting to be held at Parkinson's Ferry on August 14. Six hundred copies of these resolutions were printed for distribution in Pittsburgh and at the Braddock Field gathering.[81]

The next day, August 1, in accordance with the arrangements, the committee and a large number of citizens of Pittsburgh marched out to Braddock Field. Being in an apprehensive mood, they stopped about two miles short of the place of rendezvous and waited while some delegates from Washington carried copies of the handbills to the field and distributed them. In about an hour

[81] *Incidents of the Western Insurrection,* Vol. I, pp. 47-8.

these messengers returned and reported that the handbills had had a good effect on the crowd, who had been particularly gratified by news of the expulsion of their enemies.

Thus reassured the Pittsburghers proceeded, the committee marching in front unarmed. As they approached Braddock Field Brackenridge was very nervous; he really felt that he was in danger on account of what he had said at Mingo. Therefore he proposed that they advance with a flag, and, pulling out a white handkerchief, he attached it to his whip. But the other members of the committee thought that it would be imprudent to show distrust of the people, and so he put his handkerchief back in his pocket.[32]

When the Pittsburgh company marched on to the field, they were alarmed by the warlike appearance of the crowd. The Washington County militiamen were dressed as for a campaign against the Indians—in hunting shirts, and with handkerchiefs on their heads. "They were amusing themselves with shooting with balls at marks, and firing in the air at random, with powder only. There was a continual discharge of guns, and constant smoke, in the woods, and along the bank of the river. There appeared a great wantonness of mind, and disposition to do any thing extravagant."[33]

The Pittsburghers found themselves safe for the time, however, as their handbills had pacified Bradford, who assumed the rôle of chieftain, and his lieutenants. But during the whole day they were extremely anxious, fearing that their real sentiments might be discovered. On one occasion particularly Brackenridge was disconcerted. He was sitting under a tree with two or three of his friends when James Ross, a lawyer from Washington, passed by and said to him with a smile, "You have got a great deal of subtility, but you will have occasion for it all." Brackenridge was terrified, fearing that the remark might be overheard by some of the insurgents, but this, luckily, was not the case.[34]

[32] *ibid.*, Vol. I, pp. 49-51.   [33] *ibid.*, Vol. I, p. 52.
[34] *ibid.*, Vol. I, p. 54. (This page is incorrectly numbered 36 in the text.)

As the day wore on, it became evident that most of the people on the field were inclined to violence. Brackenridge noticed that the language and ideas of the French Revolution had been adopted by the crowd. "It was not tarring and feathering, as at the beginning of the revolution from Great Britain, but guillotining."[35]

Such being the temper of the crowd, the Pittsburghers were quite ready to find an excuse for going home. The insurgents were going to camp on Braddock Field all night, but the Pittsburgh delegation gave out word toward evening that, as they had brought no provisions, they were going to return to town and come back to the rendezvous the next morning. This news roused a great clamor. The country people said that the townsmen were deserting the cause. Brackenridge immediately rode after the Pittsburghers who had started home, turned them back to the field, and gave orders, on his authority as a committeeman, that they should stay on the ground all night, let their want of food be what it might, "rather than produce a dissatisfaction with the people . . . and bring them irregularly, and in bad humour, to the town."[36]

During the night he exerted himself particularly to prevent an attack on Pittsburgh. In so doing he pretended to fall in with the proposals of the insurgents, thinking that, if he got their confidence, he could direct the mob toward harmless manifestations of their wrath. Passing from group to group, he appeared to support the proposal to attack the garrison. The general type of conversation was as follows:

Insurgent. "Are we to take the garrison?"

Brackenridge. "We are."

Insurgent. "Can we take it?"

Brackenridge. "No doubt of it."

Insurgent. "At a great loss?"

Brackenridge. "Not at all; not above a thousand killed and five hundred mortally wounded."[37] This last remark, so lightly uttered, always appeared serious to the more thinking part of those to whom he spoke.

[35] *Incidents,* Vol. I, pp. 54-5.   [36] *ibid.,* Vol. I, pp. 55-6.   [37] *ibid.,* Vol. I, pp. 56-7.

Nevertheless, the militiamen and the people were determined to march to Pittsburgh. Since there was no stopping them, Brackenridge attempted to render the expedition as innocuous as possible. To the more radical of the militia battalions he said:

"The people of Pittsburgh wish to see the army; and you must go through it, and let the damn'd garrison see, that we could take it, if we would. It will convince the government that we are no mob, but a regular army, and can preserve discipline, and pass through a town, like the French and American armies, in the course of the last war, without doing the least injury to persons or property."

His proposal was accepted. "There was a general acclamation, and all professed a determination to molest no one."[38]

In the morning a general committee for the whole district was formed to carry out Bradford's demand for the expulsion of some other townsmen who were critics of the radical party. Brackenridge was made a member for Pittsburgh.[39] While the committee was deliberating, the crowd became very impatient, and it was apparent that they would have to be diverted into some activity at once. Bradford proposed that they should go to Pittsburgh.

Brackenridge replied, reiterating his former proposal, "Yes, by all means; and if with no other view, at least to give a proof that the strictest order can be kept and no damage done. We will just march through, and taking a turn, come out upon the plain of the Monongahela's banks; and taking a little whiskey with the inhabitants of the town, the troops will embark, and cross the river."[40]

So the "army" marched to Pittsburgh. Every effort was made to keep them in good temper, and when they reached the town, the members of the delegation plied them generously with whiskey and water. Brackenridge himself served out four barrels of his best old whiskey that day: he would rather spare that, he said, than a single quart of blood, and he thought it better to be employed in extinguishing thirst than fire.[41]

[38] *ibid.*, Vol. I, p. 58.   [39] *ibid.*, Vol. I, pp. 59-64.   [40] *ibid.*, Vol. I, p. 65.
[41] *ibid.*, Vol. I, p. 71.

Now it was necessary to maneuver the crowd out of town before it became unruly. Brackenridge tried the ford at the mouth of the Monongahela with his own horse, and then led the people who had come on horseback down to the crossing. Those who were on foot crossed in ferry boats. Thus the town was cleared except for about a hundred countrymen who remained all night. Their only serious misdemeanor was the burning of a barn belonging to Major Kirkpatrick, an officer of the Federal garrison.[42]

Pittsburgh was safe for the moment, but the townsmen had to continue their policy of conciliation. For this reason the "committee on expulsion" which had been appointed at Braddock Field met on August 4 and proscribed Presley Neville and General John Gibson, who had imprudently criticized the insurrectionists in letters sent to the East.[43]

Brackenridge still felt himself on the horns of a dilemma. He thus describes his state of mind at the time:

I canvassed my situation fully, and begun more seriously to think of emigration; but in that case, I would be considered in the light of a deserter, and my property become a sacrifice. I thought of disposing of my house, which was perishable, to some individual less conspicuous, and under his name save it. But that would be suspected or discovered. I thought of being absent on some pretence that might be plausible; and it struck me to prevail with the people of Pittsburgh to appoint me as an envoy to the executive, to state the motives of their conduct, and explain their situation.[44]

He decided, in the end, to await the result of the meeting at Parkinson's Ferry, which was to be held on August 14. Meanwhile he thought that it might be efficacious to lay before the government and the people of the East "a just idea of the situation of the country; the magnitude and extent of the opposition."[45] For that purpose he wrote to Tench Coxe, a politician of Philadelphia, reviewing in his letter the events of the "insurrection" down to the march on Pittsburgh. In conclusion, he said:

[42] *Incidents,* Vol. I, p. 67.
[44] *ibid.,* Vol. I, p. 78.
[43] *ibid.,* Vol. I, pp. 80-1.
[45] *ibid.,* Vol. I, p. 78.

The town of Pittsburgh will send delegates to the meeting of the 14th instant—what the result will be I know not. I flatter myself, nothing more than to send commissioners to the President with an address, proposing that he shall delay any attempt to suppress the insurrection, as it will be stiled, until the meeting of Congress. This will be the object, simply and alone, with all that labour to avert a civil war. On the part of the government, I would earnestly pray a delay until such address and commissioners may come forward. This is my object in writing you this letter, which I desire you to communicate either by the Gazette, or otherwise.

It will be said, this insurrection can be easily suppressed—it is but that of a part of four counties. Be assured, it is that of the greater part —and I am induced to believe, the three Virginia counties, on this side the mountain, will fall in. The first measure then will be, the organization of a new government, comprehending the three Virginia counties, and those of Pennsylvania, to the westward, to what extent I know not. This event, which I contemplate with great pain, will be the result of the necessity of self-defence. For this reason, I earnestly and anxiously wish that delay on the part of government may give time to bring about, if practicable, good order and subordination. By the time the Congress meets, there may be a favourable issue to the negociation, with regard to the navigation of the Mississippi, the western posts, &c. A suspension of the excise law, during the Indian war, a measure I proposed in a publication three years ago, in Philadelphia, may, perhaps, suffice. Being then on an equal footing with other parts of the union, if they submitted to the law, this country might also.

I anticipate all that can be said with regard to example, &c. I may be mistaken, but I am decisive in opinion that the United States cannot effect the operation of the law in this country. It is universally odious in the neighboring parts of all the neighboring states, and the militia under the law, in the hands of the President cannot be called out to reduce an opposition. The midland counties, I am persuaded, will not even suffer the militia of more distant parts of the union, to pass through them.

But the excise law is a branch of the funding system, detested and abhorred by all the philosophic men, and the yeomanry of America, those who hold certificates excepted. There is a growling, lurking discontent at this system, that is ready to burst out and discover itself everywhere. I candidly and decidedly tell you, the chariot of government has been driven Jehu-like as to the finances; like that of Phaeton, it has descended from the middle path, and is likely to burn up the earth.

Should an attempt be made to suppress these people, I am afraid the question will not be, whether you will march to Pittsburgh, but whether they will march to Philadelphia, accumulating in their course, and swelling over the banks of the Susquehanna like a torrent, irresistible, and devouring in its progress. There can be no equality between the rage of a forest, and the abundance, indolence, and opulence of a city. If the President has evinced a prudent and approved delay in the case of the British spoilations, in the case of the Indian tribes; much more humane and politic will it be to consult the internal peace of the government, by avoiding force until every means of accomodation are found unavailing. I deplore my personal situation; I deplore the situation of the country, should a civil war ensue.

An application to the British is spoken of, which, may God avert. But what will not despair produce?[46]

This exaggerated view of the martial potentialities of the Western counties was no doubt inspired partly by a desire to frighten the East into a conciliatory mood, and partly by the overwrought nerves of the writer. Later he described his feelings at this time: "I saw before me the anarchy of a period; a shock to the government; and possibly a revolution,—a revolution impregnated with the Jacobin principles of France, and which might become equally bloody to the principal actors. It would be bloody unavoidably to them; and to the people, destructive. Let no man suppose, that I coveted a revolution. I had seen the evils of one already, the American; and I had read the evils of another, the French. My imagination presented the evils of the last so strongly to my view, and brought them so close to a probable experience at home, that, during the whole period of the insurrection I could scarcely bear to cast my eye upon a paragraph of French news."[47]

In this apprehensive mood, Brackenridge feared that the only result of the approaching meeting at Parkinson's Ferry would be further violence. He therefore gave out word that he did not wish to be a delegate.[48] In spite of this, he was chosen at the town meeting as a representative from Pittsburgh.[49]

[46] Incidents, Vol. III, pp. 128-31.
[48] ibid., Vol. I, pp. 80-1.
[47] ibid., Vol. I, pp. 85-6.
[49] ibid., Vol. I, p. 82.

As the delegates rode toward Parkinson's Ferry on August 13, it was evident that the spirit of the country was far from pacific. "Liberty poles in abundance" had been set up.[50]

When the general committee assembled, the revolutionary party took the initiative. James Marshall introduced resolutions which savored of rebellion, and David Bradford proposed definite measures of preparation for war. Brackenridge and Albert Gallatin, who was named secretary, worked adroitly to eliminate the objectionable features of the proposals, and both of them were put on the committee of four which was appointed to frame new resolutions. At the end of the first day, Brackenridge perceived that he was again popular with the crowd. Much gratified by this appreciation, and yet unwilling to join the insurrection, he again faced a dilemma. That night, as he lay on the floor of a cabin with a saddle for a pillow, he was kept awake by the following uneasy thoughts about himself and the people, who were crying for war:

What suppose that, in the prosecution of the plan I have in view, arrangements cannot be made to satisfy them, and that a war must ensue; what shall I do? I am under no obligation of honour, to take a part in supporting them; for I have no way contributed to produce the disturbance. And though, on principles of conscience, it may be excusable in them to make war, for they think they are right; yet it would not be so in me, for I think them wrong. But, on the score of self-preservation, and personal interest, what am I to do? It is a miserable thing to be an emigrant; there is a secret contempt attached to it, even with those to whom you come. They respect more the valour, though they disapprove the principles, of those that stay at home. All I have in the world, is in this country. It is not in money; I cannot carry it with me; and if I go abroad, I go poor: and I am too far advanced in life, to begin the world altogether.

But as to these people; what chance have they? They may defend the passes of the mountains; they are warlike, accustomed to the use of arms; capable of hunger and fatigue; and can lie in the water like badgers. They are enthusiastic to madness; and the effect is beyond calculation.

The people on the east of the mountains are, many of them, dissatisfied, on the same principle; and will be little disposed to disturb

50 *ibid.,* Vol. I, p. 99.

the people here, if they should mean to defend themselves. It is true, the consequence of war, supposing the country independent of the United States, will be poverty, and a miserable state of things, for a long time; but still, those who stand by the country, where they are, have the best chance, and the most credit in the end. Should I emigrate, and the country be reduced, I cannot live in it again, for a thousand reasons. I am in a quandary; and in either case, the election is painful. The only thing that can suit me, is an accomodation, and having the matter settled without a civil war. But is there any prospect of this? Will the executive be disposed to act with mildness, or rigour, in this instance? The excise law is a branch of the funding system, which is a child of the secretary of the treasury; who is considered as the minister of the President. He will feel a personal antipathy against the opposers of it; and will be inclined to sanguinary counsels. The President himself, will consider it, as a more dangerous case than the Indian war, or the British spoilations; and will be disposed to apply more desperate remedies. He will see, that here the vitals are affected; whereas there, the attack was upon the extremities. Nevertheless, the extreme reluctance which he must have, to shed the blood of the people, with whom he is personally popular, will dispose him to overtures of amnesty.[51]

After a sleepless night Brackenridge went to the next day's meeting of the committee on resolutions with a renewed determination to work for an accommodation between the insurrectionists and the government. The resolutions which were adopted represented in general the views of Brackenridge and Gallatin, although Bradford forced some of his radical sentiment into the phrasing. They restated the objections to the excise law, called for a remonstrance to Congress, provided for "a meeting, either of a new representation of the people, or of the deputies here convened," and recommended supporting "the municipal laws of the various States."[52] The clause suggesting a new representation was introduced by Brackenridge, who was trying to make it possible to withdraw from all connection with the affair if he saw no prospect of accommodation with the government or submission on the part of the people. He was, however, chosen a member of the standing committee.

[51] *Incidents,* Vol. I, pp. 93-4   [52] *ibid.,* Vol. I, pp. 95-6.

At the last meeting of the delegates it was announced that commissioners from President Washington had arrived in the Western country. Brackenridge thereupon presented resolutions providing that a committee consisting of three members from each county be appointed to meet the Federal commissioners and to report the result of their conference to the standing committee. With much difficulty the adoption of his plan was secured.[53] Just before adjournment it was arranged that the local committee should meet the United States commissioners at Pittsburgh on August 20, and report to the standing committee at a meeting at Brownsville in September.

As soon as possible after the Parkinson's Ferry meeting Brackenridge made a personal call upon the Federal commissioners: James Ross, a lawyer of Washington, Pennsylvania; Jasper Yeates, a justice of the supreme court of Pennsylvania; and William Bradford, attorney-general of the United States, who had been Brackenridge's roommate at Princeton. They treated him very coolly, having heard from Major Craig the prejudiced accounts of Western affairs which Presley Neville had given in the East since his banishment from Pittsburgh. Brackenridge immediately began to imagine other consequences of the tale-bearing of the Nevilles and the other exiles. He saw that President Washington would be influenced by a version of the insurrection which would present his own actions as treasonable. Much disturbed by this new aspect of the situation, he went home in despair and spent another sleepless night. Reviewing the probable effects of setting up a separate government in the West he feverishly concluded:

But is it practicable to establish and support such a government? Perhaps it might claim these lands to the westward, and invite all the world to take possession of them. Collect all the banditti on the frontiers of the state, to help us fight for them; tell the Spaniards to come up to the mouth of the Ohio, and give us a free trade; let the British keep the posts, and furnish us with arms and ammunition; get the Indians of the woods to assist us; tell them, that the people on the east of the mountains want our whiskey, and their lands;—we might

[53] *ibid.*, Vol. I, p. 97.

urge war, and perhaps succeed. It is true, we should succeed to misery, for a while, and poverty at last. But even this would be more tolerable to me, than to live under any circumstances, suspected by the government, and treated with contumely by these people, when they had returned, loaded with the favours of the government, as having been the great defenders of it.[54]

But his desperate resolution to join the insurrectionists was short lived. The next day he met James Ross, who told him that Judge Yeates and Bradford had been satisfied with the explanation of his conduct which he had given them the day before. His failing courage was restored by this news. Since the commissioners showed an accommodating attitude, he saw the way clear "for the country to get out." There was then no further need for "concealment of intentions and half-way acquiescence," and he determined that the time had come for "an explicit avowal of opinions." Acting on this decision, he took the first opportunity of telling Marshall and David Bradford, in the presence of a member of the standing committee, his real opinion about the recent lawless acts, particularly the robbery of the mail and the gathering of forces at Braddock Field.[55]

The committee of conference met the United States commissioners in Pittsburgh on August 21, 22, and 23. The commissioners reported that they had authority "to suspend prosecutions for the late offences against the United States—and, even, to engage for a general pardon and oblivion of them."[56] The committee of conference presented to the commissioners a summary statement of the "causes of discontent and uneasiness which very generally prevailed in the minds of the people."[57] It is almost certain that Brackenridge was the chief spokesman for the Westerners, as the report of the committee's views which the commissioners sent to President Washington covers the same points as his letter to Tench Coxe.

In this conference it was arranged that a report should be made

[54] *Incidents*, Vol. I, pp. 101-2.   [55] *ibid.*, Vol. I, p. 103.
[56] *Proceedings of the Executive of the United States respecting the Insurgents,* p. 31.   [57] *ibid.*, pp. 18-19.

to the standing committee at Brownsville on August 28, and Brackenridge was appointed to draft this report. The means by which the violators of the laws could secure amnesty were formulated, and the committee promised to urge acceptance of the conditions.

In accordance with these plans the standing committee met at Brownsville on August 28. Brackenridge and his party, on their approach, were alarmed by signs of a riotous temper. A crowd of about seventy armed men had marched from Washington County to burn the house, barn, and mill of a Quaker farmer named Samuel Jackson, who had given offense by calling the standing committee a "scrub congress." The truculent frontiersmen were persuaded, however, to give up their design of burning Jackson's buildings and to permit him to be tried by the committee. This trial was the first business of the meeting. Brackenridge feared that it would strike a note of violence and lawlessness which would defeat the plans for accommodation with the government. Anxious to put the committee in a better temper, he spoke first when the trial was called, making use of his "usual expedient in such cases—pleasantry." He said:

I recollect to have read, that, in the time of Oliver Cromwell, lord protector of England, when he was in the height of his glory, a person came to him, and gave him information of words, used by another, greatly contemptuous of his dignity; viz. he has said, that your excellency may kiss his ——. You may tell him, said Oliver, that he may kiss mine. This Quaker has called us a Scrub Congress; let our sentence be, that he shall be called a Scrub himself.

This anecdote produced a loud laugh. The suggestion was adopted, and the crowd which had brought the Quaker to the meeting took him off to bestow the epithet upon him. The culprit got a bucket of whiskey and water for his accusers, and the incident was closed.[58]

Although Brackenridge was thus able to dissolve the bad temper of the crowd at the opening of the meeting, he soon perceived an intransigeant attitude toward the important issues. The people

[58] *Incidents of the Western Insurrection,* Vol. I, pp. 108-9.

expected an immediate repeal of the excise law and unconditional amnesty. They would evidently not be satisfied with the recommendations of the committee of conference. Brackenridge and Gallatin, therefore, in order to gain time to work for moderate counsels, secured an adjournment until the next day. So uncertain was the temper of the people that Brackenridge prudently crossed the river and spent the night at a farmhouse.[59]

The next morning it was evident that the spirit of the crowd had not improved. Brackenridge and Gallatin were both reluctant to venture the opening speech in the meeting, but Gallatin, who was secretary of the committee, eventually agreed to do so. In a masterly and complete exposition he covered all the reasons for submission, appealing particularly to the sentiment of patriotism. Brackenridge followed Gallatin. Having nothing material to add to the argument, he spoke partly to show that he had the courage to speak. Also, having little confidence in the ability of the crowd to understand Gallatin's logic, he attempted to play upon their feelings. After showing that it was impossible to "remain a part of the government, and yet wage war against it," he said:

But is it our interest to secede? having no sea coast, we are at the mercy of the imposts all around us, even for the necessaries of life. If the weight of the union, in the scale of nations, cannot procure us the surrender of the western posts, peace with the Indians, and the navigation of the Mississippi; how shall a half uninhabited, uncommerced extent of an hundred and fifty miles square, command it. There is no manner of question, but the time will come when the western country will fall off from the eastern, as north will from the south, and produce a confederacy of four; but surely it is our mutual interest to remain together as long as possible; to bear with inequalities, or local and partial grievances, while we enjoy general advantages, and avoid general evils. In due time the situation of affairs will provide for itself; and as in nature, so here dismemberment or subdivision, will maturely take place, with consent and mutual adjustment of interests. But these disjointings are yet premature, and will produce convulsions and death to the part that attempts it.

[59] *Incidents of the Western Insurrection*, Vol. I, pp. 109-11.

But are you able to secede? Can you fight the United States? Can you beat the 15,000 that are in requisition by the President? Grant it. Perhaps 30,000 in the passes of the mountains, for a heat. What of that? Are you able to beat a second 15,000 or a second 30,000? Are you able to beat a third army of that number, or of a superior force to these? Can you maintain a war of years against numbers, and the purse? you must do that, or be in the same situation with the Miami Indians, that beat Harmar, beat St. Clair, and are now lately driven into the lake by General Wayne. I know your spirit, but condemn your prudence.

But do you know, that you are mistaken in your support at home? Do you think that all are sincere, who have been clamouring for war? Some clamour, because they are cowards, and wish to be thought brave; because they are ignorant enough not to expect a war. Others, because they have not estimated the fatigues of campaigning, and do not consider how soon they will be tired. Others because they have contracted for the sale of their lands, and are about to remove to Kentucky or elsewhere. Others, and this class numerous, because they have nothing to lose, and can make their escape by the floods. If you depend upon these, you will by and by have to take the same course, *and descend the current with the frogs.*

But men affect to be for war, because they are afraid to speak their real sentiments. I have my eye upon those, here present, and could name them, who are thought to be strenuous for the most violent measures; and yet, in the course of our committeeing, have acknowledged to me, what they really think; and it is their earnest desire, to get out of the scrape, upon almost any terms. After what has happened, any terms, short of life, ought to be accepted.

The outrages have been grievous, wanton, and useless; in construction of law amounting to high treason. *Having had no privacy with these transactions, or concern in the perpetration,* but disapproving, when and where I could speak with safety; nevertheless, for the sake of those involved, I have laboured hard to bring them out; and have ever looked forward to that amnesty, which is now before you. If I, who have nothing to apprehend for myself, have been ready to embrace it; surely those, in a different predicament, well may.

I have heretofore felt myself embarrassed, in knowing what to do. I considered the feelings of the country with partiality of heart; knowing the ground of them to be, the unequal law in question. I made excuses for these breaking into acts; knowing it to be the error of judgment, not distinguishing between what feelings are, and what acts ought to be. I was impressed with the reflection, that the disapprobation of the law having been general, in the country, and expressed by almost every one, no man could tell how far, by words, he might have contributed to that current of resentment, which, at length, swelled beyond the constitutional banks of representation and remonstrance, and broke out into outrage. He must, therefore, have a disposition to repair the mischief; and save those, who have gone to an excess, not contemplated. Besides, living in the country for a number of years, and, in my professional capacity, having much acquaintance, and many attachments, it was natural for me, to wish to save, from error of conduct, and danger of life, those who had violated law, by accomplishing an accomodation, and settling terms of oblivion. If these are not accepted, I am done; and consider myself as discharged, in honour, and in conscience, from all further concern in the business. It is, therefore, the last and only advice I have to give, that you acquiesce with the propositions of the commissioners, and accept the amnesty offered you. It is the expedient left to save the country, which has been already impaired and reduced, by our late history. It was improving in agriculture, replenishing with buildings, becoming an object of emigration from abroad; and is now dejected from this height, to a considerable depth from what it was.[60] The value of property is

[60] Brackenridge's statement of the economic improvement in the West just before the insurrection is corroborated by a similar statement made by Judge Alexander Addison, of Washington, Pennsylvania, in September 1794: "The peculiar objection which lay in the mouths of the people on this side of the mountains to this law was this—that from our local circumstances it drew from us a sum of money which was disproportioned to our wealth and would soon exhaust our circulating medium. However necessary on these grounds an opposition to the excise law might be three years ago it is less necessary now. Since that period the progress of the country to wealth has been amazingly rapid. There has been more public and private building raised within this period than for nine years preceding, and fewer sheriff's sales for debt in the whole three than in any one of the nine. Three years ago I believe, there was not a burr millstone in the country; now there are many. The quantity of money circulating among us is since greatly increased,—and the value of property is thereby greatly increased—in other words, the value of money is greatly lessened and thereby the value of the excise to be paid is greatly lessened. *Then* there was hardly any trade to the Spanish settlements on the Mississippi; it was at any rate so small and confined to a few adventurers; the quantity of grain exported was but little of course, but little was withdrawn from our own consumption, and this little was generally bought with goods." Alexander Addison, *Charges to Grand Juries* ("Necessity of Submission to the Excise Law," September Sessions, 1794), p. 106.

reduced, from what it was. I do not consider what I possess, at this moment, as of more than one half of the value of what it was three months ago; but it will be still worse, unless the evils that are impending, are prevented by an immediate acquiescence.[61]

In the audience which listened to Brackenridge's speech was William Findley, who said later: "His argument was of the more importance that it was decisive; formerly he had temporized in such a manner as to induce the rioters to believe he was a friend to their cause."[62]

David Bradford answered Brackenridge and Gallatin. He violently opposed accepting the propositions of the commissioners. Then a motion was made that the conditions be accepted. It was defeated, only twelve of the conferees supporting it. A motion to take a secret vote was similarly defeated. Here Brackenridge feared that Bradford would come forward with his proposals for military preparations and for procedures modelled on the French Reign of Terror. But at this crucial moment Gallatin's presence of mind saved the day. He proposed that the committee take a vote by ballot merely to determine its own mind. Then another member wisely proposed that each member be given a slip of paper with Yea written on one side and Nay on the other so that he could cast his ballot without fear of having his handwriting recognized. The vote was thus taken without fear of public opinion. Thirty-four members declared in favor of accepting the terms of amnesty, and only twenty-three voted Nay.[63] After this fortunate turn of affairs, the standing committee adjourned *sine die.*

A mere vote of course did not settle the affairs of the country, nor did it clear Brackenridge in the eyes of the community. There had been a rumor that he had been bribed by the commissioners. After the adjournment of the committee he saw clear signs of enmity among groups of men on the ground, and a companion told him that mischief was afoot. He left Brownsville in haste.[64]

[61] *Incidents of the Western Insurrection,* Vol. I, pp. 112-16.
[62] William Findley, *History of the Insurrection,* p. 124.
[63] *Incidents of the Western Insurrection,* Vol. I, p. 117.
[64] *ibid.,* Vol. I, pp. 119-20.

Back in Pittsburgh he found the townsmen apprehensive of an attack by the country people. A town meeting was called on September 6 to discuss measures of defense. Brackenridge gave the opening speech, saying that the time had now come for the Pittsburghers to avow their real sentiments, and that it might be expedient to organize for defense against the insurgents. The idea "produced a revulsion in the minds of the people," and he suggested postponement. At an evening meeting, however, some of the citizens agreed to organize for protection against parties which might enter the town for plunder.[65]

About this time Brackenridge was alarmed by the activities of John Woods, an intriguing professional rival, who represented him to the commissioners as an instigator of the insurrection and an accomplice of David Bradford.[66]

On September 8 Brackenridge went to Greensburg to attend the county court. After three days, however, he asked for a few days' leave, and on September 11, the date set for signing the pledges of submission he went to Parkinson's Ferry in order to urge the people to sign. He found the inhabitants of the Parkinson's Ferry and Mingo Creek districts unresponsive, however, and, becoming discouraged, he rode to Pittsburgh in the evening. He arrived too late to sign the pledge himself, but, not considering himself an insurgent, he presumed that he had no need of amnesty. Nevertheless he signed on the next day, supposing that the government would not demand a strict enforcement of the date clause.[67]

The results of September 11 were disappointing to all who were working for conciliation. At Mingo Creek force was used to prevent the well-disposed from signing the promise of submission. In all districts there were some persons who openly favored war. In twenty-three townships the majority did not sign the pledge. "Here," said Brackenridge, "was what amounted to a declaration of war, by twenty-three townships; and put an end to all contem-

[65] Incidents of the Western Insurrection, Vol. II, pp. 11-13.
[66] ibid., Vol. II, pp. 24-5; and H. M. Brackenridge, History of the Western Insurrection in Western Pennsylvania, p. 302.
[67] Incidents of the Western Insurrection, Vol. II, pp. 14-20.

plation of a general and sincere acquiescence in the execution of the laws."[68]

It was now generally supposed that the President would send an army to Western Pennsylvania. Brackenridge, in a vain attempt to ward off this expedition and to clear his own reputation in the East, now wrote another letter to Tench Coxe:

In some expressions I had used in my letter, you have understood me as speaking of the excise law. Review it, and you will find that it was of the funding system in general. Of that system I have been an adversary from the commencement, in all its principles and effects. At the same time, I have never charged the Secretary, who was said to be the author of it, with anything more than an error in judgment. . . .

Were it possible that we could be freed from this system by a revolution without greater mischief, it is possible I might be brought to think of it. But that is impossible. The remedy would be worse than the malady; honest creditors would suffer, and we should lose the advantages of a general union of the States. These advantages are immense, and far outweigh all other considerations.

Though in a country of insurgency, you see I write freely; because I am not the most distantly involved in the insurrection; but deserve the credit of contributing to disorganize and reduce it.

From paragraphs in the papers I find that it is otherwise understood with you; but time will explain all things.

The arrival of commissioners from the government was announced to the delegates of the 14th at Parkinson's Ferry, when actually convened, and superseded what was contemplated, the sending commissioners from hence.

You will have heard the result.

By the measures taken, the spirit of the insurrection was broken. The government has now nothing to fear. The militia may advance, but will meet with nothing considerable to oppose them. But had it not been for the pacific measure on the part of the President, and the internal arrangements made by the friends of order here, which I cannot in a few words develope, affairs would have worn a different aspect, and the standard of the insurrection would have been by this time in the neighborhood of Carlisle. But I hope that this will always

[68] *ibid.,* Vol. II, p. 21.

remain matter of opinion, and [that we shall] have no experiment in the like case to ascertain the event.

My writing to you at first was owing to my having received a letter from you on an indifferent subject, and it struck me that through you government might receive information that might be useful, and if published, which was left to your discretion, it might operate as an apology for the government with the people, in adopting pacific measures, representing in strong terms the magnitude and extent of the danger; for it was not the force of this country I had in view, but the communicability to other parts of the Union, the like inflammable causes of discontent existing elsewhere. I am told my letter has been considered as intending to intimidate the government, and gain time until the insurrection should gain strength.

It might have been with that view; but that it was not so, will be proved by my conduct and sentiments here. No; from the tenor of my life, I expect to be considered as the advocate of liberty, a greater injury to which could not be, than by the most distant means endangering the existence or infringing the structure of the noblest monument it ever had, or ever will have in the world—the United States of America.

You will do me the justice to communicate this letter to the same extent with the first.

I have further to observe that I am in the meantime not without apprehension for the town of Pittsburgh. The moment of danger will be on the advance of the militia; if the insurgents should embody to meet them, they will, in the first instance, probably turn round and give a stroke here for the purpose of obtaining arms and ammunition; and, if resisted, and perhaps whether or not, will plunder the stores and set on fire all or some of the buildings.

Before sending this letter Brackenridge added the following postscript:

Since writing the within, which was two or three days ago, apprehension of danger, with ourselves, or opposition of force, considerably vanishes or diminishes.

. . .   .

As an instance of order gaining ground, I am just informed from the town of Washington that the liberty tree was cut down, and none came forward to erect another, or revenge the affront.[69]

[69] H. M. Brackenridge, *History of the Western Insurrection*, pp. 146-7.

By this time preparations had been made by the Federal government for a military expedition to the West. On September 20 the citizens of Western Pennsylvania read accounts of these arrangements in the *Pittsburgh Gazette*. The leading citizens of the section at once made further efforts to convince the President that the country was loyal and pacific in spite of the results of September 11. At this time Brackenridge had gone to Washington, Pennsylvania, to attend court. There he was invited to attend a meeting of citizens who passed resolutions declaring that order could be preserved without resorting to military force. Although he was not a resident of the county, he proposed that the original Parkinson's Ferry delegates be called together again in order to formulate assurances that the country was pacified and send them to the President. His suggestion was adopted.

On October 2 the proposed meeting was held at Parkinson's Ferry. Its proceedings included confident statements as to the ability of the insurgent region to manage its own affairs. William Findley and David Reddick were chosen as delegates to confer with President Washington. Brackenridge was disappointed in not being named as one of the emissaries, but he took pains to post copies of the resolutions to the President and to Governor Mifflin of Pennsylvania.[70]

The date of the elections for Congress, October 14, was now drawing near. Brackenridge was a candidate, but for several weeks he had been too much troubled to attend to the campaign; in fact, he had lost interest in it. John Woods, David Hamilton, and Thomas Scott now came forth as candidates, however, and Brackenridge was too proud to let the election go to one of them uncontested. Then, a few days before the day of voting, he heard a rumor that he had withdrawn his name. Immediately, on October 8, he published the following denial in the *Pittsburgh Gazette*:

Previous to the late convulsions, it was proposed to me to give my name, as a candidate for the Congress of the United States; I accepted

70 *Incidents of the Western Insurrection*, Vol. II, pp. 31-5. For Brackenridge's letter of transmission to Governor Mifflin see *Pennsylvania Archives*, Series II, Vol. IV, p. 393.

the compliment. It has now circulated that I have declined it; No. Considering the delicacy of the times, I might wish I had not thought of it, but as it is, it would imply a fear of submitting my conduct to investigation, to withdraw my name from the public; I have therefore not done it. I may, at present, have less popularity than I had, but the time will come, when I shall be considered as having deserved well of the country, in all the delicate conjunctures, in which we have been situated.[71]

This statement was either ineffective, or it reached the voters too late. Albert Gallatin, who entered the contest only three days before the election, was chosen, although he lived in another Congressional district. Brackenridge stood second, and Thomas Scott third. Rather surprisingly the leading advocates of submission proved most popular at the polls.[72]

Brackenridge was now free from fear of being troubled by the insurgents, but he was not yet to know peace of mind. Rather, he saw more and more reason to fear the army which was approaching from the East. The misapprehension of his first letter to Tench Coxe was causing mischief; he was considered to have defied the government. Also someone had published in the *Pittsburgh Gazette* a burlesque account of the conferences between the Western Pennsylvania committee and the United States Commissioners in which a "Captain Whiskey" had been made to say: "Brothers, you must not think to frighten us with fine arranged lists of infantry, cavalry, and artillery, composed of your water-melon armies from the Jersey shore; they could cut a much better figure, in warring with the crabs and oysters, about the capes of Delaware."[73] This squib was popularly attributed to Brackenridge, and the incensed Jersey militiamen, as they moved westward, slashed and bayoneted the bushes, calling them "Brackenridge."[74] These threatening gestures were reported to Brackenridge in Pittsburgh. At the same time, David Reddick, one of the commissioners sent by the Parkinson's Ferry meeting, returned and said that, although he had told Presi-

---

[71] *Incidents of the Western Insurrection,* Vol. II, p. 37.
[72] *ibid.,* Vol. II, pp. 44-5.   [73] *ibid.,* Vol. II, pp. 6-7.
[74] *ibid.,* Vol. II, pp. 45-56.

dent Washington that Brackenridge was innocent, many persons in the President's entourage appeared to have strong prejudices against him. Brackenridge assumed that these opinions were due to the misrepresentations of Presley Neville. At any rate it was evident that the spirit of the army was extremely hostile toward Brackenridge.[75]

His apprehensions, in this state of affairs, led him to write a number of letters to the principal officers, stating his fears and "representing the disgrace that it would bring upon their march, to injure a man who was, and in due time would appear to be innocent." Thinking, however, that the officers might not like to be addressed by one in his situation, he determined to appeal to the rank and file. Accordingly he wrote the following ill-advised plea, which he had printed on handbills:

Citizens of the Army advancing to the Western Country.

Serious intimations are given me, that I am considered by you as greatly criminal in the late insurrection in this country; and though I may have shielded myself from the law, by taking advantage of the terms of amnesty proposed by the commissioners, and sanctioned by the proclamation of the President, yet that I shall not escape the resentment of individuals. It would seem to me totally improbable, that republican soldiers would sully the glory of their voluntary rising, by a single intemperate act. Nevertheless, as it would wound me with exquisite sensibility, to be treated with indignity, by words or looks, short of violence, I beg leave to suggest to you, that it is a maxim of reason, that a man "shall be presumed innocent till the contrary is proved"; and I give you a strong presumption of my innocence, viz. that though having an opportunity of relinquishing the country, I stand firm, and will surrender myself to the closest examination of the judges, and put myself entirely on the merit or demerit of my conduct, through the whole of this unfortunate crisis.[76]

When Governor Howell, commander of the New Jersey troops, received a packet of these handbills he "threw them instantly into the fire." Only a few of them, through the agency of Reddick, were actually distributed among the soldiers. In this disregard of

[75] *ibid.,* Vol. II, pp. 46-7.   [76] *ibid.,* Vol. II, p. 52.

military etiquette Brackenridge laid himself open to the charge of stupidity as well as of villainy. He maintained, however, that he had not seen any impropriety in thus appealing to a republican army of citizens.

The right wing of the advancing forces had now crossed the Allegheny Mountains. As the militiamen drew near Pittsburgh, Brackenridge's courage began to fail, as he feared that the officers could not restrain the troops from violence against him. So he again meditated flight from Pittsburgh, feverishly thinking that he might take refuge with the Indians. He even made inquiries for the purpose of finding an Indian guide who could conduct him through the Western forest. But during a sleepless night he suddenly determined to stand his ground. Springing out of bed he declared that if he was to be assassinated, it would be in his own house. This decision was strengthened by his recollection of what he had said in his handbills to the army. He had not ceased to fear, however, and spent the next day or two in putting his papers in order and preparing a sketch of his conduct during the insurrection which might serve to clear his name if he should be murdered.[77]

About this time John Woods began to spread the word that Brackenridge had not signed the pledge of submission on the required day. Then, when the army went into camp near Pittsburgh, Woods at once put himself in touch with the judges who accompanied the troops, and officiously undertook to solicit testimony against Brackenridge.

Thus faced with the probability of an unfair trial, Brackenridge saw that Alexander Hamilton also would inevitably be prejudiced against him because of his published criticisms of the funding system. Furthermore he began to see how easy it would be to misunderstand his purposely equivocal conduct at Mingo and Parkinson's Ferry. So he did not hope to escape arrest.[78]

When detachments of the troops arrived in Pittsburgh, he saw that rumor had not exaggerated the feeling against him. General

[77] *Incidents,* Vol. II, pp. 52-5.   [78] *ibid.,* Vol. II, pp. 58-9.

Gibson, who had been exiled from Pittsburgh, told the troops not to speak to him. General Morgan, parading near Brackenridge's house with his suite, was heard to say, "Hang the rascal, hang him." The common soldiers were eager to do something. One evening some of the dragoons were seen watching the streets which led to his house, and some of them even came into his yard and peered through the windows. About eleven o'clock a body of them marched toward the house, evidently planning an attack. An officer met them and tried in vain to dissuade them. Then he ran to report the case to General Morgan, who was at Presley Neville's house. Morgan and Neville, in spite of their prejudices, ran out hatless, and faced the dragoons. Morgan told them that Brackenridge had stood his ground, and that they must let the law take its regular course. Thus mob violence was averted.

But Brackenridge suffered intensely from the thought of facing a trial. Under the excitement caused by thinking of the complications of his case, his nerves, never dependable since his illness of twenty years before, almost gave way. He really feared that he would die "under the sensibility of his affections," and that his death would be attributed to "consciousness of guilt" rather than to "the pain which the ingenuous mind feels when it is wronged by the world."[79]

During the night of November 13 the persons who were suspected of treasonable acts were arrested, and many of them were subjected to atrocious indignities.[80] That night and the next, Brackenridge, expecting arrest, lay on his couch dressed and ready to go when summoned. Reading Plutarch as he waited, he meditated on Solon's law requiring that a citizen who did not take some part in a "civil tumult" should be put to death, because moderate citizens, by mingling with the violent, could assist in bringing about an accommodation. He thought that he himself had acted on precisely that principle; but he also saw that conditions in America were not like those in Athens, because the center of government was so far from the extremes that the moderate men could not have an intimate understanding of each other.

[79] *ibid.*, Vol. II, p. 63.   [80] *ibid.*, Vol. II, pp. 68-72.

Now, while Brackenridge still awaited arrest, General Lee of Virginia, who had been in Princeton with him, moved into his house—not for the sake of old acquaintance, but because the house was a large one. Brackenridge had reserved one apartment for himself and his family, and he hoped that he would be able to avoid contact with Lee. The latter, however, called for him when he moved in with his suite. Brackenridge thought that the summons was for his arrest. When he faced the general he was almost overcome with humiliation. Twenty years before he had assisted Lee with his college compositions and orations; now he expected to be arrested by him on the charge of attempting to overthrow the government. Lee observed his panic, and inquired whether he was mistaken as to the house he was to occupy. Temporarily relieved, Brackenridge showed him his quarters, and immediately withdrew to his own apartment. The next day Lee invited him to dine. He was much pained by the prospect of sitting at table with the man who would probably be detailed to arrest him, but the situation was too delicate to be explained, and he was not able to decline the invitation. At dinner the officers behaved with perfect politeness, but he felt that they secretly viewed him as an insurgent who would soon be arrested as a criminal. He left the table as soon after dinner as etiquette permitted.

The next morning a subpoena from Judge Peters was read to Brackenridge commanding him to appear to give testimony. Considering that this hearing was to be an examination of his own conduct, and that the results would determine whether or not he was to be arrested, he presented himself to the judge, who referred him to Alexander Hamilton for examination.

Hamilton's first questions concerned the existence of a plot to overthrow the government. Brackenridge maintained that he knew of no such plan. Then, after some general questions to which the witness had no answer, Brackenridge himself proposed to give a general account of what he personally knew about the insurrection. Hamilton agreed, and began writing down the narrative from Brackenridge's dictation. In describing the events immediately following the burning of Neville's house, Brackenridge said that the people had demanded that Bradford and Marshall should support what had been done or be treated as Neville had been. At this point Hamilton laid down his pen and said:

Mr. Brackenridge, I observe one leading trait in your account, a disposition to excuse the principal actors; and before we go further, I must be candid, and inform you of the delicate situation in which you stand; *you are not within the amnesty; you have not signed upon the day*; a thing we did not know until we came upon this ground, I mean into the Western country; and though the government may not be disposed to proceed rigorously, yet it has you in its power; and it will depend upon the candour of your account, what your fate will be.

Brackenridge replied: *"I am not within the amnesty,* and am sensible of the extent of the power of the government; but were the narrative to begin again, I would not change a single word." Then he proceeded with his testimony. When he got to the point where Presley Neville had requested him to go to the Mingo meeting-house, Hamilton was called to dinner, and Brackenridge was told to return in the afternoon.

He went to his house, but declined General Lee's invitation to dinner, since he felt very doubtful about the outcome of the examination, and could not bear to show himself in official company in such a state of mind.

At three o'clock he returned to the examination. When Hamilton entered the room he appeared to have been reflecting, and said, "Mr. Brackenridge, your conduct has been horribly misrepresented." Brackenridge presumed that Hamilton had just been dining with Presley Neville, who had admitted that he himself had urged attendance at the Mingo meeting. Now he proceeded with his account of this meeting. Hamilton appeared not to be satisfied. "Mr. Brackenridge," said he, "you must know we have testimony extremely unfavourable to you, of speeches made at this meeting; in particular your ridiculing the executive."

Brackenridge saw then that his humorous dramatization of a scene between Cornplanter and President Washington had been misunderstood and misrepresented. So he replied to Hamilton: "Five persons were chosen to go with me to that meeting; for the express purpose of bearing testimony of what I should say; let these be called upon. Is it reasonable I should be at the mercy of the misconceptions, or a voluntary misrepresentation of weak or prejudiced individuals?"

Hamilton was silent. Brackenridge then went on to give an account of the town meeting at Pittsburgh, stating that he himself had proposed that the townspeople march out and join the people at Braddock Field. Hamilton appeared to be staggered by this, and sank into deep reflection. So Brackenridge added: "Was it any more than Richard the Second did, when a mob of 100,000 men assembled on Blackheath? The young prince addressed them, put himself at their head, and said, 'What do you want, gentlemen? I will lead you on.' "

He then continued with his narrative. After a short time Hamilton said, "My breast begins to ache, we will stop tonight; we will resume it tomorrow morning at 9 o'clock." Brackenridge withdrew, alarmed by Hamilton's expression. He was puzzled as to whether Hamilton's breast ached from sympathy or from writing. But, being in an apprehensive mood, he concluded that the secretary was suffering from compassion for his probable fate.

The next morning his fears were intensified. General Lee told Mrs. Brackenridge that for the sake of retirement he was going to move to a less central part of town. Brackenridge supposed that Lee was moved by the delicacy of his feelings—that he could not endure the spectacle of an old college friend "sinking into a melancholy situation just under his eye."

At nine o'clock Brackenridge's examination began again. In the course of the narrative Hamilton's countenance began to brighten, and when the recital was ended he said:

Mr. Brackenridge, in the course of yesterday I had uneasy feelings. I was concerned for you as a man of talents; my impressions were unfavourable; you may have noticed it. I now think it my duty to inform you that not a single one remains. Had we listened to some people, I do not know what we might have done. There is a side to your account; your conduct has been horribly misrepresented, owing to misconception. I will announce you in this point of view to Governor Lee, who represents the executive. You are in no personal danger. You will not be troubled even by a simple inquisition by the judge; what may be due to yourself with the public, is another question.

Hamilton then directed him to go and sign his narrative before Judge Peters. So great was Brackenridge's nervous excitement at this sudden change in his situation that he could scarcely hold a pen in his hand to write, and he cursed the circumstance of having to sign his name to each of the five sheets of his narrative, but he returned to his house in a better state of mind than he had known for a long time.[81]

Brackenridge's adversaries were enraged at his thus escaping so easily. When General Neville heard of it he exclaimed: "The most artful fellow that ever was on God Almighty's earth; he has put his finger in Bradford's eye, in Yates' eye, and now he has put his finger in Hamilton's eye too: I would not wonder if he is made attorney for the states, on the west of the Allegheny Mountain."

The feeling against him gradually cooled, however. Governor Howell called upon him, and General Lee invited him to dinner. But his popularity was not completely regained. His name was omitted from some lists of invitations to public entertainments given for the leaders of the expedition. One of these omissions caused an amusing little domestic flurry. A ball was given for General Lee by the citizens of Pittsburgh and the master of ceremonies did not send an invitation to Mrs. Brackenridge. Brackenridge, seeing "the flush of indignation in her cheek, and a sparkle of fire in her eye," reproved her thus:

What! Are you hurt at this? You insult me, because it is on my account you suffer the indignity. Did you not read to me the other evening the life of Phocion? After having rendered services to the state, and accused of treason by the arts of malignant individuals, and acquited by the people; suppose his adversaries to have taken their revenge, by getting a master of ceremonies to exclude his wife from a ball. Would you not think it more honourable to be the wife of Phocion, under these circumstances, than of a common Athenian, though you had received a card, and been called to lead down the first dance?

[81] *Incidents of the Western Insurrection,* Vol. II, pp. 75-8.

Would not Phocion have laughed at the indignity, as I do? And would not his wife have laughed too?[82]

After the departure of the main part of the army the Western Pennsylvanians settled down to their ordinary pursuits, disturbed only by the insolent behavior of some of the eight hundred militiamen who remained in the country.[83] Brackenridge spent the winter in professional pursuits and in collecting vouchers from prominent and respectable citizens relating to his conduct during the insurrection. These vouchers he later used as an appendix to his *Incidents of the Western Insurrection*. He was employed as attorney for the persons who had been arrested on a charge of treason.[84] For the defense he prepared a study of the treason laws of the United States in which he argued that the English treason laws were too severe to be applied in America, that there had already been a softening in the application of these laws in the United States, and that still further limitation of their application was desirable.[85] He was not able to make use of the argument he had prepared, however, as he was called as a witness for the government, and could not appear in the trial as an attorney.[86]

The trial was set for May 4, in the Federal Court at Philadelphia, and early in the spring of 1795 Brackenridge went to that city. There he suffered intensely from social ostracism. Colonel Neville and John Woods had spread prejudiced accounts of him with the result that everybody shunned him. Even on the streets men whom he knew changed their courses to avoid meeting him, or pretended not to see him. So Brackenridge was driven "to contemplate the buildings a good deal" as he walked, "casting his eyes to the upper stories of the houses." "A stranger," he said, "would have thought me a disciple of Palladio, examining the architecture."[87]

The rumors about Brackenridge were such that he was cut off

[82] *Incidents*, Vol. II, pp. 81-3.   [83] *ibid.*, Vol. III, pp. 30-2.
[84] *ibid.*, Vol. III, p. 33.
[85] This essay on the treason laws was published in *Incidents of the Western Insurrection*, Vol. III, Appendix, pp. 41-61; and in *Law Miscellanies*, pp. 475-502.
[86] *Law Miscellanies*, p. 475.
[87] *Incidents of the Western Insurrection*, Vol. III, pp. 34-5.

even from those who sympathized with the insurgents. They conceived that he had saved himself by turning state's evidence, that the commissioners had bought him off with a promise of immunity, had left him as a spy upon the people, and that he had now come to court "to fulfil that dark engagement of giving testimony to hang others." He attempted to amuse himself in the bookshops, but the booksellers were afraid to have him about their places, and so he had to spend his time walking about the shipyards and docks and looking over the improvements in the environs of the city.

When the trial began he found that the court and jury were suspicious of him. He was examined as a witness on only three occasions, being called on for relations of "the general history of particular scenes." But as the trial progressed, the spirit changed. As the evidence accumulated it appeared that he had contributed to "quieting the disturbance." Then "the gentlemen of the bar became sociable, and the court complaisant."[88]

As soon as the trial was over, Brackenridge returned to Pittsburgh. He had publicly criticised some of General Morgan's officers, and he heard that they were furious; so he thought it best to hasten back and deal with this situation. In Pittsburgh, however, he found conditions greatly changed. Only a few of the military were left in the city, and they did nothing more than talk; no one disturbed him.[89] The insurrection was over.

Thus closed the most distressing period in Brackenridge's life. The difficult rôle which he played in the insurrection was due in the main to his ability to see the legitimate rights of both the national government and the Western farmers and distillers. It probably must be granted, however, that his troubles were partly caused by his nervous desire to avoid both offense to his neighbors and treason to the government. Obviously, in spite of his intellectual comprehension of the situation, he did not care to risk either his person or his popularity by making an open stand for his convictions. There can be no doubt that his broad view of politics was of real service to both sides, but his participation in the events of the insurrection was less creditable than it might have been.

[88] *ibid.,* Vol. III, pp. 35-7.   [89] *ibid.,* Vol. III, p. 38.

CHAPTER XV

THE LITERARY RESULTS OF THE WHISKEY INSURRECTION

BRACKENRIDGE had cleared himself with the courts and the government. After he returned to Pittsburgh he undertook to clear himself with the public. For that purpose he wrote his *Incidents of the Western Insurrection.*[1] In haste to put his account of his conduct before the people, he sent a packet of the manuscript to Philadelphia by each week's post. He did not even take time to correct the manuscript of his copyist, and, still worse, he forwarded some of the sections in his own illegible handwriting. So the book was not only hastily composed, but it was also badly printed.[2] Nevertheless the work was highly valued by at least one contemporary reader of no mean capacity for judgment. William Cobbett said:

Never think that you understand the story of this insurrection, till you read Findley[3] and Brackenridge.

Mr. Brackenridge writes with more ease and vivacity than Mr. Findley. His perspicuity, his simplicity, his picturesque minuteness, conduct his reader into the scene of action. You see, hear, and feel, just as the author actually did; and this itself is a talent of high excellence. Amidst much entertainment, candour will forgive the serious or affected vanity that sometimes peeps through the curtain of his mind. These two writers have been neglected. An estimate of the sales may induce a belief that they have never been perused by more than two or three thousand American Citizens, that is to say, by perhaps a two-hundredth part of the community at large. Without such a perusal, however, it is impossible to comprehend the nature and effects of the western riots. The declamation that fills the Federal gazettes and pamphlets cannot afford a just or luminous conception of this all

---

[1] *Incidents of the Western Insurrection,* Vol. I, p. 5, and Vol. III, p. 142.
[2] *ibid.,* Vol. III, pp. 140, 154.
[3] William Findley also wrote a history of the insurrection.

important subject; which is, therefore, grossly and almost universally misunderstood.[4]

Although Brackenridge was facing the serious problem of retrieving his reputation in the period following the insurrection his characteristic humor was not repressed. The whiskey troubles provided an opportunity for some amusing verse written in Scots. In 1794 David Bruce,[5] a country storekeeper and poet who lived at Burgettstown in Washington County, had written some Scots verse in celebration of whiskey, signing himself "The Scots-Irishman." In "To Whiskey," this unique Scotch-Irishman who not only loved his usquebaugh but *was willing to pay the excise tax on it,*[6] thus addressed the national drink:

> When fou o' thee on Irish groun',
> At fairs I've aft had muckle fun,
> An on my head wi' a guid rung,
>   Gat mony a crack;
> An mony a braw chiel in my turn,
>   Laid on his back.

Then he revealed what whiskey had done for the Scotch-Irishmen on the American frontier:

> Great strength'ning pow'r, without thy aid,
> How cou'd log-heaps be ever made?
> To tell the truth, I'm sair afraid,
>   (Twixt ye and me)
> We'd want a place to lay our head,
>   Hadn't been for thee.

> But when the chiels are fou' o' thee,
> Och? how they gar their axes flee,
> Then God hae mercy on the tree,
>   For they have nane,

[4] William Cobbett, *Porcupine's Works*, Vol. I, p. 312.
[5] For a study of David Bruce see Harry R. Warfel, "David Bruce, Federalist Poet of Western Pennsylvania," *Western Pennsylvania Historical Magazine*, Vol. VIII, pp. 175-89, 215-34.
[6] *Poems of the Scots-Irishman*, p. 11.

Ye'd think (the timber gaes so free)
　　It rase its lane.

　　. . .　　　　. . .　　　　. . .

Then foul befa' the ungratefu' deil
That wou'd begrudge to pay right weel,
For a' the blessings that ye yiel
　　In sic a store;
I'd nae turn round upo' my heel
　　For saxpence more.[7]

Brackenridge, of course, could not accept thus complacently an
excise tax of "saxpence," but he was so charmed by this bit of
good Scots verse that he was willing to overlook the political heresy
of the author. It must have been some time in 1796, soon after
the death of Robert Burns, that, speaking as "Aqua Vitae," he
replied to Bruce:

Your rouse rins glib thro' a' my veins;
I find it at my finger en's:
An' but a gouk that has nae brains,
　　Wa'd it deny,
That many a time, baith wit and sense
　　I can supply,

Far better than the drink ca'd wine;
Wi' me compar'd 'tis wash for swine
Ae gill is just as guid as nine;
　　And fills as fou':
It is nae very long sinsyne,
　　Ye proved it true.

That time ye made sae muckle noise,
About the tax they ca' excise;
And got the name o' *Whiskey-boys,*
　　From laland glakes;
That cam' sae far, nae verra wise,
　　To gie ye pikes.

　　. . .　　　　. . .　　　　. . .

[7] *Poems of the Scots-Irishman,* p. 12.

It was a kittle thing to take
The government sae by the neck,
To thrapple every thing and break
  Down rule and laws;
And make the public ship a wreck,
  Without guid cause.

'Twere safer ye had tulzied here,
Wi' chiels that dinna muckle care
To gouge a wee bit, or pu' hair,
  And no complain;
But a' the tugs and rugings bear,
  Or let alane.

But wha' ist o' ye mak's the verse,
Sae very kittle and sae terse,
That in the Gazzate gies me praise?
  They say 'tis Bruce;
I canna' half sae weel rehearse:
  Tak my excuse.

I'm mair among unlettered jocks
Than well-learn'd doctors wi' their buiks;
Academies and college nuiks
  I dinna ken;
And seldom wi' but kingra folks,
  Hae I been benn.

Ye canna then expect a phrase,
Like them ye get in poets lays;
For where's the man that now-a-days,
  Can sing like Burns;
Whom nature taught her ain strathspeys,
  And now she mourns.[8]

Brackenridge's reference to Burns introduced a literary note which was maintained throughout the rest of the series. Bruce replied to Brackenridge, concluding as follows:

Ye spoke o' Burns, Nature's ain bairn,
Wha rous'd ye aft in merry vein—

8 *Gazette Publications*, pp. 238-40.

Saftly, indeed, flow'd his sweet strain,
And stopt o'er soon;
We'll never see his maik again—
My tears hap down.[9]

Brackenridge's answer gave a fanciful account of the influence
of Allan Ramsay on Bruce:

There was a clerk, i' the neist door,
Cam' to our town; had lear gilore;
And tauk'd about ane Pythagore.
     Wha had a thought,
His saul wad tak, when life was o'er,
     An ither bught:

And lowp into the bodie o' ane,
And in the shape o' a wee wean;
And after shaw the self-same vein,
     O' wit and sense,
He had, before death wi' a stane
     Daug out his grains.

I leught and ca'd him a daft chiel,
And thought his head in a peat creel;
But now I b'lieve him verra weel,
     And gie him faith;
Ye'r Allan Ramsay or the Deil
     Upo' my aith.

His saul has soomit o'er the burn,
To tak in you an ither turn,
And be a while in life's sojourn
     Sic as he was,
Near Frith of Forth where he was born,
     And liv'd his days.

I ken ye Allan verra weel,
Though you may hardly ken your-sel'.
But ah! your sang is nae sae shill,
     Nor pipe sae soft;
The voice ye had, as clear's a bell,
     'S a weething dowff'd.

[9] *Gazette Publications,* p. 242.

But's nae your fau't, my canty Callan,
That ye fa' short o' the Auld Allan;
There's neither Highland man, nor Lallan',
    That's here the same;
But finds him scrimpit o' the talen'
    He had at hame.

What's mair expect'd here i' the west,
Sae near where night taks off his vest
And his gray breeks, and gaes to rest,
    And the lang day
Is dock'd o' several hours at best,
    Sic as on Tay.

I find mysel' degenerate,
And nae sic Aqua as ye gat;
In Clachan horns wi' comrades met,
    To tak a gill;
And though come stacherin hame fu' late;
    Ye did nae ill.

The lads got gumption by their drink;
And Carls could better speak and think;
Tak aff a bonnet wi' a clink,
    And say a grace;
And lug out scripture verra distinc',
    Frae ony place.

But here the drappie that ye need,
Maun ay some wicked brulzie breed;
Gie ane anither's claes a screed,
    An' aften seen,
To gash wi' teeth, or tak in head,
    To stap the een.

Unless it be as folks o' lear,
Say a' things gradually impair,
And human nature wears thread-bare,
    And turns;—Gude help's;
Ae year auld, and twa year war',
    Like the tod's whelps.

Be this as't may, it does me guid,
To meet wi' ane o' my ane bluid,
I was sae glad a'maist ran wud
    To be thegither;
But I maun now, gae chew my cud,
    And haud my blether.[10]

Bruce's good-natured reply closed the argument on this subject:

A'beit we baith ha'e said eneugh,
Yet I maun own, upo' my treuth,
I am sae lifted wi' the seugh
    O'yer sweet chant,
That I maun even stop the pleugh
    To gie ye a rant.

Ware na I sure ye'r nae the same,
I wad hae trow'd ye came frae hame,
Frae Londonderry or Colrain,
    An' that ye'd lickit,
I' yer young days, the *Blarney Stane,*
    Ye are sae sleekit.

Lear'd chiels indeed gie muckle roose
To Pythagore, sae wise and douse,
Wha wadna kill a flea or louse,
    As we are tauld,
For fear he might brack down the house
    O' some poor saul.

But I hae doubts, my canty blade,
The Carle's doctrine winna haud,
In what ye paukily hae said
    'Bout me and Allan:
Ah well-a-day! I'm sair afraid
    I'm nae sic Callan.

His sangs will be the warld's delyte
Till wit and sense gang out o' date;
There's naething I can say or write

[10] *Gazette Publications,* pp. 242-4.

Sic fame will win;
I'm nae mair than a blatherskyte,
Compar'd wi' him.

What ye hae said is right sagacious,
That ilk thing here sae mickle warse is,
An' nae mair like, than trees to rashes,
  To things at hame :—
Foul fa' me, gin the verra lasses
  Be here the same!

Whare's there a Forth, a Tweed, or Tay?
Thro' hills and greens that saftly stray,
Whare shepherds spen' the simmer's day
  Sae peacefulie.
Thir scenes gar'd Allan lilt his lay
  Wi' sic a glee.

What's here to gie the mind a heese?
Deil het ava', but great lang trees,
Nae flowry haughs or bony braes
  To please the een,
Nor bleating flocks upo' the leas
  Are heard or seen.

At morn nae lav'rock tunes his whistle,
Nor i' the bush is heard the throstle,
There's naething but a skreek and rustle
  Amang i' the leaves.—
The musie's sweer her sangs to cuzle,
  She dwines and grieves.[11]

The *Incidents of the Western Insurrection* had been largely personal narrative and apology. The Scots poems were literary byplay. Brackenridge's mature interpretation of the Whiskey Insurrection was presented in a continuation of *Modern Chivalry*, which was published in Philadelphia in 1797.

The third volume of *Modern Chivalry* had ended without concluding anything. Teague O'Regan was simply left in the position

[11] *ibid.*, pp. 245-7.

of a hopeful but undeserving office-seeker. The introduction to the new volume was related directly to this situation. Just when Captain Farrago was getting tired of his game of patronizing Teague as an aspirant to an official appointment, he received a billet from the President asking for an interview so that he could "converse with him relative to the appointment of the young man in his service, of the name of Teague O'Regan, to some office in the government." Captain Farrago felt it to be his duty to warn the President against appointing Teague "to any of the higher offices of government." He found, however, that he need not have worried. Teague was merely made an excise officer, and was assigned to the Western Pennsylvania district.[12] In this position of course he was soon to have enough of office holding.

Having finally lost his servant, Captain Farrago employed a theologically minded young Scotchman, Duncan, to take his place. The Captain and Duncan immediately started for the West. On the way they overtook Teague. When they happened to stop at a crowded inn, the Captain proposed that Teague and Duncan sleep together. Duncan exclaimed: "Guid deliver me frae sik a prophanation o' the name o' Ferguson, as to sleep wi' an excise officer. I am na' o' a great family, but I am come o' a guid family; and it shall never be said that I came to America to disgrace my lineage, by sik contact as that. Gae to bed wi' an excise officer! I wad sooner gae to bed out o' doors, or i' the stable amang the horses."[13] Obviously the tax gatherer will encounter opposition when he begins work in a Scotch and Scotch-Irish community.

As the Captain and Duncan proceeded toward Pittsburgh numerous occasions called forth meditations on American politics. Even the finding of Indian carvings in some caves along the way provided an opportunity for a criticism of the effect of the Federalist financial policies on American culture. Commenting on the incident Brackenridge said:

Happy savage, that could thus amuse himself, and exercise his first preeminence over animals we call Beasts. They can hunt, and devour

12 *Modern Chivalry* (edition of 1797), Vol. IV, pp. 6-7.
13 *ibid.*, Vol. IV, pp. 46-7.

living things for food; but where do you find a wolf, or a fishing hawk, that has any idea of these abstract pleasures, that feed the imagination? Why is it that I am proud and value myself amongst my own species? It is because I think I possess, in some degree, the distinguishing characteristics of a man, a taste for the fine arts; a taste and characteristic too little valued in America, where a system of finance, has introduced the love of unequal wealth; destroyed the spirit of common industry; and planted that of lottery in the human heart; making the mass of the people gamblers; and under the idea of speculation, shrouded engrossing and monopoly everywhere.[14]

Although the Whiskey Insurrection is the main theme of this volume of *Modern Chivalry*, Brackenridge also continued in it his satire on uneducated politicians. In one of the incidents Traddle, the weaver, is represented as having been elected to Congress. When Duncan heard about it he exclaimed: "Guid deliver us! . . . Do they make parliament men o' weavers i' this kintra? In Scotland, it maun be a duke, or a laird, that can hae a seat there." Captain Farrago answered ironically: "This is a republic, Duncan,—and the rights of man are understood, and exercised by the people."[15]

After a few such episodes, the travellers reached the Allegheny Mountains. When Teague came to the pass, he was turned back by two ferocious Western politicians, Orson and Valentine, who were armed with clubs. Captain Farrago and Duncan met him as he was returning on his tracks, and persuaded him to proceed with them. When the party of three reached the pass, the Captain, who considered that Teague was opposed because of the Western feeling against the excise law, attempted to persuade Valentine and Orson that they should not take the law into their own hands:

Gentlemen . . . the law may be exceptionable on general principles, or locally unequal in its operation to you in this district. Nevertheless, it is the law, and has received the sanction of the public voice, made known through the constitutional organ, the representatives of the people. It is the great principle of a republican government,

[14] *ibid.*, Vol. IV, pp. 65-6.
[15] *ibid.*, Vol. IV, pp. 65-9. The narrative at this point is a reworking of a passage in *The Modern Chevalier*. See *Gazette Publications*, p. 314.

that the will of the majority shall govern. The general will has made this a law, and it behoves individual minds to submit.[16]

Duncan was impatient with the argumentative method of pacifying the Westerners; like Alexander Hamilton he favored a strong policy. After hearing the Captain's speech he stepped forward, flourishing his cudgel, and said:

I wad na fleech and prig wi' them. I wad na hae many words about it, but just see at ance whether they will dare to stap the high road. . . . Sae dinna ye tak up time fairlying about the matter; but gae on, and try our rungs o'er the hurdies o' them. I sal gar this stick crack o'er the riggin o' the loons, in a wie while.[17]

The Captain, voicing Brackenridge's policy of conciliation, replied:

Duncan . . . put up your cudgel. Policy oftentimes avails more than force. The law in question may be odious and great allowance ought to be made for the prejudices of the people. By soft measures, and mild words, prejudices may be overcome. These appear to be but young men; and rashness is a concomitant of early life. By expostulation we may probably have the good fortune to be able to pass on, without being under the necessity to attempt battery, or shed blood.[18]

The Captain and his companions were then allowed to pass. When they arrived in the Pittsburgh district, however, Teague was tarred and feathered by a mob. The temper of the people was so violent that the Captain did not dare to attempt reasoning with them, lest he be taken for an accomplice of the exciseman.[19]

To escape from the excited populace Captain Farrago took refuge in a retired spot in the mountains. There he spent several days with the Marquis of Marnessie, an aristocratic French émigré who was living in an isolated cabin.[20]

[16] *Modern Chivalry*, Vol. IV, pp. 90-1.   [17] *ibid.*, Vol. IV, pp. 91-2.
[18] *ibid.*, Vol. IV, p. 92.   [19] *ibid.*, Vol. IV, pp. 106-22.
[20] The "Marquis of Marnessie" is the Marquis Claude François Adrien de Lezay-Marnezia. (See Bernard Faÿ, *L'Esprit Révolutionaire en France et en Amérique*, p. 257.) He was born in Metz in 1735. He early became a moderate Rousseauist. After a short period in the army, he retired to his estate and there showed his liberal tendencies by abolishing the feudal duties. In 1789 he was elected to the Estates General. In the early sessions he revealed sympathy with

"A kind of sympathy was felt by the Marquis towards the Captain, considering him in the light of an emigrant with himself, having been obliged to abscond from *sansculotte* rage, and popular fervour, which, though not of the same height with that in France, yet was of the same nature, and different only in degree."[21]

In their mountain retreat the Pennsylvania farmer and the French nobleman discussed political philosophy. The Marquis maintained that, because of the rights of their elders, members of the younger generation, although they may have the power, have not the right to alter the traditional fabric of the society in which they live, even if the existing system produces injustice to individuals.

Captain Farrago, expressing the author's liberal political philosophy, replied:

I can easily excuse this sally of your mind, and must resolve it into the wounds your feelings have received from the reverse of your fortune, and the dreadful outrages which have taken place, in the course of the revolution, from the fury of the human mind. Nor would I call in question wholly the justness of your position, with regard to the right of changing a mode of government. Nevertheless, it may admit of some discussion in the generality, and be so bounded as to leave some great cases out of the rule. I grant you that the descendant, on the principle of natural right, can claim nothing more of the personal

the Third Estate, but when the assembly became radical he retired. In 1790 he purchased rights in the Scioto Company, which was being promoted in Paris by Joel Barlow, and accompanied the French colony to Gallipolis, on the Ohio. There he planned to develop a French city with a magnificent cathedral. (See Theodore T. Belote, *The Scioto Speculation and the French Settlement at Gallipolis,* p. 63.) Within a year the colony failed, and Lezay-Marnezia found refuge for a time in Pittsburgh. (See "Lettre à M. Audrain, Negociant à Pittsburg," in *Plan de Lecture pour une Jeune Fille,* 2nd ed., pp. 205-7.) There can be little doubt that Brackenridge became acquainted with the Marquis at this time (1791). From Pittsburgh, Lezay-Marnezia addressed to Bernardin de Saint Pierre a long letter in which he presented the American frontier from the point of view of a Rousseauist. (See *Lettres Ecrites des Rives de L'Ohio.*) From America he went to England, and returned to France in 1792.

Since the "Marquis de Marnessie" was not in America at the time of the Whiskey Insurrection, it seems probable that Brackenridge has in *Modern Chivalry* transferred to that period some points of conversations which were actually held in Pittsburgh in 1791.

21 *Modern Chivalry*, Vol. IV, pp. 123 *ff*.

188 HUGH HENRY BRACKENRIDGE

labour of the ancestor, or of his estate than support, until he shall be
of an age which gives strength of mind and body to enable him to
provide for himself. But does he not possess by his birth, a right to so
much of the soil as is necessary for his subsistence? You will say he
may emigrate. But suppose all adjoining known lands already peopled; he cannot emigrate without committing injustice upon others.
He must therefore remain. Now to preclude him from all right to
think or act in affairs of government, with a view to improve, and to
improve is to change, is restraining the mind of man in a particular
capable of the greatest extent, and upon which depends, more than on
all things else, the perfection of our species. I would put it upon this
point; is it conducive to an amelioration of the state of life, and
likely to produce a greater sum of happiness, to innovate upon established forms, or to let them remain? It is true, indeed, that when we
consider the throes and convulsions with which a change in government is usually attended, it ought not to be lightly attempted; and
nothing but an extreme necessity for a reform can justify it. It is
almost as impossible comparing a physical with a moral difficulty, to
change a government from despotism to liberty, without violence as to
dislodge a promontory from its base, by any other means than min-
ing and gunpowder.[22]

While Captain Farrago and the "Marquis of Marnessie" were
thus arguing, "the opposition to the excise law, and disturbance in
the survey, had alarmed the government. . . . The militia had
been called to suppress the insurrection. They had marched, and
were now within a short distance of the survey."

The Captain in the mean time having heard of this . . . left the
Marquis, and came to the village where the outrage had commenced.
He was not wanting in explaining to the people the illegality and great
impolicy of their proceedings, as subversive of the government, and
destructive of the first principle of a republican government.

His conduct, nevertheless, had been otherwise understood by the
administration, and he was greatly obnoxious with the army and
judiciary. When the troops had attained the point of destination, and
the judicial examination had been set on foot with regard to the conduct of individuals, it was always a principal question, What do you
know of Captain Farrago?[23]

[22] *Modern Chivalry*, Vol. IV, pp. 127 ff.   [23] *ibid.*, Vol. IV, pp. 157-8.

Many persons were unfairly treated in the judicial examinations, but Captain Farrago "fell into the hands of an assistant examiner of sense. . . . His account and explanation was understood, and he acquitted from having swerved from the duty of a good citizen."[24] It was thus that Brackenridge himself had been exonerated by Hamilton.

After this Captain Farrago returned home, "having experienced a number of incidents, and some danger in his travels, sufficient for one ramble."[25] Teague, in his garb of tar and feathers, was shipped off to France as a scientific curiosity. By the time he arrived in Nantes the feathers had worn off, and, being taken for a true *sans-culotte*, he was born off in triumph by the *canaille*.

This volume of *Modern Chivalry*, like the preceding ones, is perfectly good-natured satire; it has no Swiftean bitterness. But Brackenridge was far from being carefree when he wrote it. He was still suffering from his experiences in the insurrection. His state of mind is revealed in a passage in which he justifies the light and amusing tone of the book:

It may argue a light airy mind in the writer; and yet these things are sometimes the offspring of a mind far from being at ease; on the contrary, it is to get ease and allay pain. Pain of mind is relieved by an abstraction of solid thought. The early paroxysm of deep grief may be incompatible with playful fancy; but gradually and insensibly, the heart-ache may be cheated of its sensations. What else effect has conversation, or music? Neither of these can assuage great pain, or torture; but will be felt to alleviate more or less the pangs of body, or mind. The mind is prevented from corroding or gnawing upon itself. We use laudanum to allay acute bodily pains; and it gives a pleasing delirium, and insensibility for a time. But in the case of mental suffering it is much safer to attack the imagination by an intellectual paregoric. There is less danger that the use will grow to excess, and induce habit.[26]

This fourth volume of *Modern Chivalry* completed the portion later known as "Part I." The material of these first four volumes was reprinted separately in 1804, 1808, 1815, and 1825. In somewhat bowdlerized form it was republished in 1846, and this text has been followed in all later editions.

The number of editions indicates that Part I of *Modern Chivalry* had a wide circulation. There is little other evidence to show how it was received, but it apparently had admirers both among the intelligentsia of Boston and the frontiersmen of the most remote settlements.

In 1810 Brackenridge's son went to Missouri. At New Madrid he was entertained by a justice of the frontier village. This gentleman, his curiosity aroused by the name of his guest, said:

"From your name, sir, may I ask whether you are related to the author of *Modern Chivalry?*"

Henry Marie Brackenridge, deeply moved and filled with pride, answered, "Sir, I am his son."

"What," replied the justice, in awe and admiration, "the son of the author of *Modern Chivalry!*"[27]

Perhaps the exclamation indicates the popular reputation of the book better than would the formal pronouncement of a critic.

In Boston *Modern Chivalry* was appreciatively read by John Quincy Adams. In 1843 he visited Pittsburgh, where he was entertained by the leading citizens. In the course of the evening's conversation there was considerable discussion of the Whiskey Insurrection. Adams amiably inquired about the descendants of Brackenridge then living in Pittsburgh, and became very animated in speaking of Captain Farrago and Teague O'Regan. A few years later, in 1847, when a new edition of *Modern Chivalry* appeared, Judge Wilson McCandless, who had been present at this conversation, sent Adams a copy of the book. In a letter thanking the judge for the gift, Adams said:

I had read the first part of Modern Chivalry, and formed a pleasant acquaintance with Captain Farrago and his man Teague, at their first appearance, more than half a century since, and they had then excited much of my attention, as illustrations of life and manners peculiar to the times, and localities, not entirely effaced, when I became more familiarly acquainted with them, by this visit to the latter. Captain

[27]*Recollections of Persons and Places in the West* (edition of 1856), pp. 188-9.

Farrago and Teague O'Regan are legitimate descendants on one side, from the Knight of La Mancha and his Squire Sancho, on the other from Sir Hudibras, and his man Ralpho, and if not primitive conceptions, themselves, are at least as lineal, in their descent, as the pious Aeneas, from the impetuous and vindictive son of Peleus. The reappearance of this work, as a second edition since the author's death, more than half a century after the first publication, well warrants a prediction, that it will last beyond the period fixed by the ancient statutes for the canonization of poets, a full century. I shall read it over again, I have no doubt, with a refreshing revival, of the pleasures with which I greeted it on its first appearance.[28]

[28] Wilson McCandless, *Ex-President John Quincy Adams in Pittsburgh in 1843.*

CHAPTER XVI

PRIVATE LIFE

ABOUT 1794 or 1795 Henry Marie Brackenridge, then ten years of age, left Louisiana after spending nearly three years in the village of St. Genevieve. He left the French settlement unwillingly, as he had become fond of the family with which he lived and his "recollections of his father had more in them of terror than of love."[1] Instead of returning to Pittsburgh at once, however, the child stayed for several months in the French village of Gallipolis, on the Ohio. At length Brackenridge sent word that his son should be brought home. General Wilkinson and his staff were leaving Gallipolis for Pittsburgh, and Henry Marie was to go with them.[2] As the party, travelling by river boat, neared Pittsburgh the boy became more and more apprehensive of the severity of his father. In such a state of excitement, he was almost overcome when the artillery of Fort Pitt boomed out a military salute for General Wilkinson. As the thunder of the artillery reverberated among the hills Henry Marie thought of meeting his father and trembled. Brackenridge did not meet the boat, however. Instead, he had sent an urchin named Joe to lead the boy to his office. There Henry Marie found his father sitting "unmoved by the uproar which had disturbed the whole village." To the frightened boy he looked more severe than ever. "Raising his spectacles from his clear and polished forehead, he asked sharply: 'Well, boy, can you read French?' "

Taking down a copy of Fenelon's *Telemachus* he put it into the child's hands. Henry Marie read haltingly. Perhaps his "faculties were benumbed with fear"—then, too, there had been no school at Gallipolis and his French had grown rusty. Brackenridge was not pleased.

[1] H. M. Brackenridge, *Recollections of Persons and Places in the West* (edition of 1856), p. 27.
[2] *ibid.*, p. 28.

"Sir," he said, "your progress does not equal my expectations." Then he turned to the other boy and said, "Joe, take him to Fenemore, the tailor, to get a suit of clothes, and then to Andrew Willcocks, to have his measure for a pair of shoes."[3]

Such was Henry Marie's home-coming.

As soon as the boy was settled in his own home again, Brackenridge set him to a serious course of study. As French master he employed a M. Visinier, who was probably one of the émigrés in Pittsburgh. With this teacher the boy read *Telemachus* and a French prose translation of the *Aeneid*. Brackenridge himself undertook to teach his son English and Latin. Every morning after breakfast they read English literature. First they went through *Robinson Crusoe*. Then they read *Modern Chivalry*. Henry Marie could not restrain his laughter as he read some of the incidents in his father's book. At these moments Brackenridge's severity was relaxed; instead of being displeased he joined in the laughter. In fact, it appeared that the boy's enjoyment of the book confirmed him in his earlier opinion of the brilliance of his son's intellect. After *Modern Chivalry*, they read *Don Quixote, Gil Blas, Tom Jones, The Vicar of Wakefield*, Goldsmith's *Animated Nature*, and some volumes of *The Spectator*.

Brackenridge considered the classics to be the real basis of education. "No person could be esteemed a scholar without them." "According to his estimate, even Franklin had no higher claim than that of a strong-minded, imperfectly educated man, who would have been much greater if he had been bred at a college." He therefore made Latin the most important subject in his young son's course of study. His very zeal for Latin, however, defeated his aims. Instead of using the simple and direct method that he used in Henry Marie's English training, he forced the boy to memorize grammar after grammar: *Ruddiman's Rudiments, The Philadelphia Grammar*, and *Ross's Grammar*. Being of a hasty temper, he often confused his pupil. So this part of the boy's education was disagreeable and discouraging to both father and son. Things went better, however, when they turned to subjects which

[3] *ibid.*, p. 42.

required something more than rote memory. In the classical field Henry Marie enjoyed Tooke's *Pantheon,* and Kennett's and Potter's *Antiquities.* In the modern field he read with pleasure Hume's *History of England,* Bruce's *Travels,* Cook's *Voyages,* and other similar works. Henry Marie's answers to questions on these books and his original observations pleased his father and caused him to "suspend his unfavorable prognostics" on his capacity.

Sometimes Brackenridge ignored routine studies and simply talked to Henry Marie, who later remembered such occasions with pleasure. "In my opinion," he said, "by far the most valuable part of my education consisted in his conversation, or rather lectures, for he spoke to me always as to a man. He was near fifty years of age, had been a remarkable student from his childhood, and was surpassed by few in the depth and variety of his attainments. He appeared to live more in the world of books than of men, and yet his natural genius was of such a high order, that it is questionable whether he would not have been greater by depending more on his native resources. His conversation abounded with wit and eloquence, and original views on every subject, and besides he had a most remarkable faculty of communicating knowledge, perhaps owing to the clearness of his own conceptions."

He was, however, relentless in holding Henry Marie to his tasks. The boy was allowed little play time, and he soon became restless and inattentive as he sat in his father's office and thought of the consolations of marbles and hoops on the village streets. Severe punishment followed. Then, to remove the reluctant student from the distraction of the sounds of play on the streets, Brackenridge sent him to the garret with his books. "Here, unfortunately," said Henry Marie years later, "there was a neglected deposit of old books, which furnished me ample occupation. . . . I ran through, or rather devoured, four folio volumes of the *State Trials* . . . twenty-four of the *European,* and twelve of the *Literary Magazine,* beside an enormous pile of the *Hibernian,* before my occupation was discovered."

When this idling was detected, Henry Marie was taken into the office again. But his father could not keep him at his task even here. The boy secreted a small pocket Bible in the office, and whenever he was not under observation "pored over the sacred volume, but not with the spirit in which it ought to have been read."

This course of education was carried on for three years. In Latin, Henry Marie had got only as far as the fourth book of Virgil, but his general reading was singularly extensive for one of his years. At this time Brackenridge became so discouraged at the slow progress of his pupil that he sent him to the Pittsburgh Academy to pursue the classics and mathematics.[4]

Although the father was solicitous about the intellectual education of his son, he ignored other phases of his training. Henry Marie said later:

My religious and moral principles were left to spring up spontaneously, the cultivation of the intellect being erroneously considered all-sufficient. . . . Vice and impiety may be regarded as follies in the eye of reason, and the mind rightly trained may be supposed to view them in that light; and such was the philosophy of my father, who was a perfectly honest man,—so much so that he scarcely allowed more than a negative merit to mere honesty, but thundered the most terrific denunciations against the opposite quality. He had had the benefit of an education strictly religious from his mother, who was not only a very pious woman, but remarkably intelligent. Common honesty itself is not to be regarded as a mere negative virtue; it ought to be fostered and cultivated by the just reward of praise and approbation. I will relate a trifling circumstance, which will show the propriety of approbation properly bestowed. I once found in the garrett a six-cent piece in the pocket of an old pair of breeches; I ran with it to my father, delighted with the proof of my honesty, but, to my great mortification, he put it in his pocket without saying a word. I instantly resolved to make a different use of the next that should fall in my way, and even to indemnify myself when an opportunity might offer.

The idea he meant to convey was, that honesty is a thing of course, and deserving no praise; for no one despised money, and the lovers and getters of money, more heartily than he did. He was, in fact, continually inveighing against speculators, misers, and avaricious people, and was a perfect example of the philosophy he taught.[5]

[4] *Recollections*, pp. 45-9.   [5] *ibid.*, pp. 51-2.

From the *Recollections* of Henry Marie Brackenridge we may obtain also a glimpse of his father's professional life:

My father's love of letters was such, that he always begrudged the time devoted to the drudgery of business; and nothing so effectually tried his patience as the idle delay of a client after his business was accomplished. Although refined and polished in manners, a gentleman of the old school, he could not contain himself on such occasions, but frequently requested the client to leave him as he had other business to attend to of great importance. As I sat in his study, and not in the outer office with the students, I was present at his conferences with his clients, and had constant occasions to admire his love of justice, his sterling integrity, and perfect disinterestedness. . . . My father always made it a point to discourage litigations. I have often heard him say: "Go away, sir; no man of sense goes to law—did you ever hear of me going to law?" The most lucrative practice at that day, when there were no banks, was the collection of money for the eastern merchants; his strict punctuality and integrity gave him the command of this business. His remarkable eloquence and learning, also, gave him the first practice as an advocate, so that lucrative business was rather forced upon than sought by him.[6]

During this period of tranquillity following the Whiskey Insurrection, Brackenridge had an opportunity to become acquainted with distinguished visitors from revolutionary Europe. One of these emigrants was Harman Blennerhasset, the great Irish liberal. Henry Marie Brackenridge said: "Blennerhasset resided in Pittsburgh a year before he went down the Ohio, and was more intimate with my father than with any other person in America. They thought alike in politics, and the politics of Blennerhasset were such as almost to exclude him from the society of the first families in town, to whom the very name of a United Irishman, at that time, was hellebore."[7]

In 1796 Philippe Égalité and his brothers spent several days in Pittsburgh, mingling freely with people of all classes.[8] Brackenridge entertained them in his house, and evidently made a vivid impression on his royal guests. A half century later, when the

---

[6] *Recollections*, pp. 54-5.   [7] *ibid.*, p. 182.
[8] Christian Birsch, *Ludwig Philipp der Erste*, Vol. I, p. 246.

Prince had become King of France, Henry Marie Brackenridge
sent him a copy of a new edition of *Modern Chivalry* accompanied
by the following note:

Fifty years ago I saw your Majesty at my father's house in Pittsburgh, with your Majesty's estimable brothers. The recollection is as
distinct as if it were yesterday. How wonderful seem to me the ways
of God, when I contrast the modest, wise young man in exile with the
greatest sovereign in the world! I have read that your Majesty some
times speaks of the author of "Modern Chivalry"—will your Majesty
be pleased to accept a copy of that work as a token of remembrance
from his son?[9]

[9] From a Ms. copy of the letter in the Harvard College Library copy of the
1846 edition of *Modern Chivalry*.

CHAPTER XVII

JEFFERSONIAN DEMOCRACY

FOR about four years after the Whiskey Insurrection Brackenridge had lived in retirement, occupied with writing, with the education of his son, and, no doubt, with the reconstruction of his law practice. He had, however, quietly maintained his critical attitude toward the Federalist party during all this time. In 1798 he again entered the political arena and became the founder and leader of the Republican party in Western Pennsylvania,[1] at the period when the Jeffersonian opposition was working toward the national leadership. Since the Whiskey Insurrection the political balance had shifted in Western Pennsylvania. The frontier had become Federalist. "But fifty Democrats could be mustered in Pittsburgh, and not all these were entitled to put a ticket into the ballot-box."[2]

Brackenridge's return to political activity began with the congressional campaign of the summer of 1798. The Pittsburgh district had been represented during the past term by Albert Gallatin, who had offended the Federalists by his French sympathies and Republican sentiments. Furthermore, he was not a resident of the district which he represented. In 1798 he was a candidate for reelection. The Federalists of Allegheny and Washington Counties set up as a rival candidate John Woods, who had long been Brackenridge's political and personal enemy.

Brackenridge thought that Woods, who was already State senator, had received more political preferment than he deserved. He therefore opened the campaign with an attack on him:

Let John Woods reduce his mind within a reasonable compass; let him wait till he is called upon for his services, and then they may be valued. Dropping irony let him occupy the present interval to improve

[1] H. M. Brackenridge, *Sixty Years in the North and Twenty Years in the South*, pp. 11-12.

[2] H. M. Brackenridge, *Recollections of Persons and Places in the West*, p. 70.

himself in books; for most assuredly he is not without the need of this. I am now in the fiftieth year of my age, and have been forty-five a severe student; and yet *because I know something* I should tremble were I to think of a seat in the legislature of the Union, at not knowing more. Perhaps from what we have heard of that house last year, John Woods may think it is but a game of cudgeling to act a part there. Indeed from the half of their speeches, it is pretty evident, that a bear garden would suit some better, than a hall of Philosophers; but ought we not to labor a reform? If there are a number of harsh, haughty, intolerant, and at the same time ignorant young men in that assembly, why carry coals to New-Castle and increase the store from our stock?[8]

This attack on Woods was immediately answered by the Federalists. In Hartford, Connecticut, the authors of *The Echo* published the following ironical version of his article:

> No; let John Woods, instead of all this rumpus,
> Reduce his mind, within some sort of compass,
> Let him take physic, feed awhile on air,
> Or bring himself to water-gruel fare;
> Let him wait patiently until his time—
> In me he has an instance most sublime.
> Have I not lingered on from day to day,
> Have I not loiter'd years and years away,
> In hopes some opportune, some lucky chance,
> To fair promotion might my steps advance?
> Vain hope! for lo! the rays of favour shine,
> On other heads, while shadows fall on mine.
> Ah how unlike this Woods, by most belov'd,
> By all with fond partiality approved;
> In love with peace, yet freedom *he'll defend,*
> Fell faction's foe, of government the friend,
> From school-boy age to manhood's sober hour,
> Has fortune joy'd on him her choicest gifts to shower.
> 'Tis hard that Brackenridge, grown old in toil,
> Should always stumble on some barren soil,
> That he, within whose skull such wisdom floats,
> Can't go to Congress *for the want of votes.*

[8] *The Aurora,* July 28, 1798. This article no doubt appeared first in the *Pittsburgh Gazette*; if so, the issue in which it was published is not extant.

But irony apart—let John Woods read,
Of this most sure, the fellow stands in need.
Let him begin where others have begun,
That is, buy books, and read them one by one.
If to improve's his aim, why let him o'er
Both Young Squire Webster and Tom Dilworth pore;
And he, like me, in time perchance may learn,
That Noah's Ark had neither stem nor stern.
'Tis almost fifty years since I could tell,
The fatal cause why Eve and Adam fell.
How Lot from Sodom ran with visage pale,
And how great Jonah swallow'd up a whale,
How Daniel kept the lions still as mice,
Nor could they Shadrach better burn than ice;
All this I know, and, knowing, can repeat;
And yet, perchance, should I obtain a seat,
By hook or crook, sublime in Congress Hall,
Fear, shivering fear, my senses would appal;
For there, no doubt, some men would meet my eye,
Possess'd of knowledge full as much as I.
And yet, perhaps, from news arrived of late,
Of Griswold's breaking Lyon's leaden pate,
John Woods may think, for empty is his head,
The cudgel's force of sense will stand in stead.
This would be true, if in Creation's round,
Another Matthew Lyon should be found,
Blows in that case would take the place of words,
And reason yield the palm to "Wooden Swords."
If to Newcastle we should carry coals,
The world would call us all a pack of fools.
'Twere nonsense all—we might expect as well
To retail brimstone from a store in hell.
These things just mentioned, let them have their force
And here I'll end my notable discourse;
If John this time should cross the Congress bridge,
'Twould do the job for

                              H. H. Brackenridge.[4]

4 *The Echo*, pp. 159-61.

In Pittsburgh, Brackenridge's criticism of Woods was answered by "A Citizen," who wrote an article for the *Gazette*. In reply to the charge that Woods did not have sufficient knowledge for a congressman, he said, evidently with pointed allusion to Brackenridge, "Learning and talents may be rendered useless by not being accompanied by those qualities which inspire confidence." After expressing his sentiments about choosing a representative from outside the district, he passed to the chief point at issue in the campaign—Gallatin's Republicanism:

Our representative is distinguished by his endeavours to pervert and destroy the principles of that Constitution he was chosen to support. Uniform only in his opposition to as wise and as honest an administration as ever existed in any country, he has constantly set his face against its acts and views. And when the tendency of such opposition became so palpably dangerous as in view of the most ignorant to threaten our very existence, instead of abandoning his system he pursued it with impenitent obstinacy, and has urged and supported measures which would lay us divided and defenceless at the feet of France.

Then he turned to Brackenridge's part in the campaign:

No man knows these things better than Mr. Brackenridge. No man knows better than he, that we owe it to our consciences and our country to choose another representative in the place of Mr. Gallatin. Yet this representative whom I think it as much the duty of the electors of this district to reject as it is the duty of a court before whom an offender is convicted to pass sentence, Mr. Brackenridge endeavours to support not directly but in an indirect way ridiculing the nomination of Mr. Woods who has been set up against Mr. Gallatin. . . .

I am sorry Mr. Brackenridge's discourse seems to proceed from other motives than the interest of those to whom it is addressed—from personal passions, former resentments and rival-ships, suspicion of preference. These are unworthy of the talents of Mr. Brackenridge, they will take away from every discourse which proceeds from them all confidence and credit, and they will be carefully repressed by every man who desirous of fame, recollects that the brightest faculties are sullied by obliquity of conduct.[5]

[5] *Pittsburgh Gazette,* August 4, 1798.

David Bruce also, but with more urbanity, protested against Brackenridge's action:

When Whiskey-Boys sedition sang
An' anarchy strod owre the lan',
When Folly led Rebellion's ban'
    Sae fierce an dowre,
Fo'ks said ye sleely lent a han'
    To mak the stoure.

But ye soon pat it in a beuk,
An' tauld us how, by heuk and cruik,
Ye work't upo' the rabble-rout
    To do your biddin',
An' clear'd yoursel frae ilka doubt,
    As clean's a ribban'.

O! dinna, now, when you're as clean,
An' white, an' clear, as ony thing,
Like the wash'd sow, again begin
    The dubs to plash in
An' gar foul centure's tongue to ring
    Wi' lies an' clashin'.

The clatterin' carlin winna stan'
To say you're naething but a sham—
A selfish, pridefu' kind o' man
    She will you deem
Wi' genious some, an' wit at han',
    But mair o' whim.

To be true-hearted and sincere,
Is better far than wit an' lear,
Or skill to soothe the pop'lar ear
    Wi' words sae bonie.
Plain honesty's rough garb will wear
    The best o' ony.

        . . .   .

It's aye sae simple an' sae neat,
An shows at ance the nat'ral shape.

To tell's o' ilka fauld an' plait
  Needs nae a beuk[6]
We see them a', baith sma' an' great,
  At the first leuk.

But, wi' Dissimulation's sack,
Hangin' sae lowsely on your back,
Fo'ks canna see what ye'd be at,
  Gif you're na canny,
They'll tak ye for a Democrat
  The worst o' any.

I hope in God ye hae mair grace,
Than join that wilfu' obs'nate race,
Wha, 'fore the warl' has rest an' peace,
  Maun a' be driven
To that same dreadfu', red-het place,
  That's far frae Heaven.

Afore I'd join the filthy tribe,
Deil speed me! gif I would na bide,
A Frenchman to rive aff my hide,
  An' mak a purse o't
To carry Talleyran' a bribe
  Wi' my worst curse to't.
. . .   .

Nane doubts it.—But that's nae the thing,—
A story, Lad begins to rin
That you're owre great wi' Gallatin
  The wily Frenchman,
An that again to *put him in*
  Is your intention.

Ye ken, this slee, auld farran knave
Has gi'en the Government a heave,
Wi' intent to throw it i' the grave
  O' mobbish ruin

6 "His conduct in the Whiskey Insurrection was so equivocal as to render him suspected by the Government. He wrote a book to exculpate himself." Bruce's note.

That he an' Willie Thrum[7] might *weave*
A braw *French* new ane.

Ye ken how, wi' ilk art an' shift,
He excus'd French robbery and theft
An', wi' his will, wad let nane lift
    A han' again' 'em,
But rather wad gie them a gift,
    Than strive to restrain 'em.

Gif sic a man be sent again
Whar he can put his plots in train
To which ay has been his aim
    The mob a madding;
What pledge hae honest peacefu' men
    For house or hauding.

Na, na, I'm sure that ye ken better
Than, hae a han' in sic a matter—
I'll think it a' but spitefu' clatter,
    Till I hear mair.—
An sae, to end this great long letter,
    Weel may ye fare.[8]

On August 2, a meeting was held in Pittsburgh to select a candidate to oppose Woods. Brackenridge presided. Presley Neville was nominated as the candidate of the group, and a committee of information and correspondence was appointed with Brackenridge as chairman.[9] The committee immediately prepared an address to the citizens of the district. Although they avowed substantially the same principles as the Federalists in regard to "foreign influences," they were proceeding cautiously toward Jeffersonianism. At any rate they described the Pittsburgh meeting as follows:

We will not conceal that the meeting . . . consisted in greater part of what may be called the mass of the people; but, in that case our coming forward will perhaps, be less invidious, and a ticket will not count the less for being handed by a mechanic or a trader. It is to the farm-

---

[7] *"Mr. Findley."* Bruce's note.
[8] *Poems of the Scots-Irishman*, pp. 46-50.
[9] *Pittsburgh Gazette*, August 4, 1798.

ers, and mechanics that we address ourselves, that have an interest not in offices and honours, but in the labour of their hands, and the industry of their employments.[10]

The Federalists at once began an attack on Brackenridge and his group, who, it was supposed, were merely trying to divide the opposition to Gallatin. Their committee of correspondence and information exclaimed: "The times are critical. The government, liberty and honour of our country are attacked. . . . The man who attempts to divide us cannot be our friend, and his counsels should be heard with jealousy: All personal and factious considerations should be silenced and made to sink under the great object of uniting and defending the country."[11]

In Washington, "A Friend to Union" expressed similar sentiments.

Brackenridge has a private quarrel with Woods and has been abusing him in the newspapers. The public have nothing to do with their quarrel nor ought they to suffer themselves to be divided by the acts and hand-bills of Mr. Brackenridge. . . . Brackenridge and his meeting must only intend to divide us, or serve Mr. Gallatin, or to do both; for everybody who has read in his book about the Insurrection must remember, that he abuses Nevill as much as he does Woods. . . .[12]

The Federalist committee of correspondence of Washington made the same accusation in a communication to the *Gazette*:

We have seen with great pain that from the intrigues of private enmity a division of the federal interest in Pittsburgh has taken place and is likely to be kept up. The consequence must be that the federal interest will be sacrificed and Mr. Gallatin a notorious enemy to our constitution will be rechosen—we are determined that no part of this blame shall lie on us. . . . We are not to take part in the passions of Mr. Brackenridge or any other individual at the expence of our country's interest.[18]

One of the signers of this pronouncement was Judge Alexander Addison, president of the courts of common pleas of the Fifth

[10] *ibid.*, August 11, 1798.   [11] *ibid.*, August 11, 1798.
[12] *ibid.*, August 25, 1798. Reprinted from the *Washington Telegraphe*.
[18] *ibid.*, August 25, 1798.

Judicial District. In putting his name to this document he aroused the lasting enmity of Brackenridge.

Brackenridge's committee issued a vigorous denial of these charges of political machination:

We know of no artifice or management on the part of Mr. Brackenridge; but that his conduct has been delicate; and whatever his motives may have been, or may be, personal or otherwise, we are governed by our own motives, and act for ourselves, and the contrary insinuation or direct allegation, abroad or at home, is an insult upon the freemen of this town and will be resented accordingly.[14]

Brackenridge himself singled out Judge Addison in his reply:

When I took the field against John Woods I had no idea that Judge Addison was at the bottom of his nomination; or at least would be willing to come forward and act the part of Master of Ceremonies in obtruding his name on the public. Whatever may be the right of a branch of the judiciary, to interfere in the elections of the legislature, there is certainly a prudence which it might be well to observe, not to descend upon the sand as a Gladiator lest it disturb his equanimity, when he comes upon the bench, and detract from the impression of his sentiments delivered in his official capacity. . . .[15]

Albert Gallatin had been taking no active part in the campaign, and the Federalists were hoping that he would decline to serve if elected by the district. In August, however, he announced that he would be willing to serve. This was the occasion for further diatribes against Brackenridge. The Federalists of Washington, in an open letter to Presley Neville, said:

What has occasioned this declaration and revived the hopes of Mr. Gallatin can be no secret to you. It is the success of the intrigues of Mr. Brackenridge in sowing divisions among the federal interest by setting you up in opposition to Mr. Woods. . . .

That Mr. Brackenridge is the author of this measure is too evident to bear denial. Indeed he seems to triumph in it himself, as the great juggler, who moves his puppets as he pleases. That he can have been induced to propose you from any motives of respect for you,

<hr />

[14] *Pittsburgh Gazette*, August 25, 1798.
[15] *ibid.*, September 1, 1798; reprinted in *Gazette Publications*, pp. 113 ff.

however willing we may be from our opinion of your character to believe, becomes impossible to reconcile with the most emphatic and explicit declarations of his. Look at his *Incidents [of the Western Insurrection]*. His aim plainly is to mortify Mr. Woods and render you both contemptible, that he may stand out as the only conspicuous character. He has said, that he did not think you would have been so gulled, and he has written to a friend in this town, that he means to kill two dogs with one stone. Who the two dogs are must be plain.[16]

To this charge Brackenridge replied:

What evidence have these men, who signed the paper, of my TRI-UMPHING IN JUGGLING, or MOVING PUPPETS? If they had any it was ex parte; and the maxim must be known at least to the Judge, aude alteram partem. . . . Now the fact is that I have neither INTRIGUED NOR JUGGLED, if it even were exceptionable to out-juggle jugglers, as Moses did the Egyptian Magicians.[17]

Brackenridge's protests should probably not be taken seriously. His opponents were doubtless right in saying that he was merely trying to defeat John Woods and to split the Federalist vote. If so, his "juggling" was successful. At the election in October Gallatin was reelected congressman from the Pittsburgh district by a large plurality.[18]

The congressional election was soon followed by the State elections. Chief Justice Thomas McKean of the State supreme court was the Republican candidate for governor, and James Ross, of Pittsburgh, was the Federalist candidate. Brackenridge supported McKean, but did not contribute any campaign articles to the *Gazette*. He himself was a candidate for the State legislature, but there was no really serious effort made for his election. Only one plea for him was published in the *Gazette*. "A Farmer," at the end of a letter in support of McKean, added the following recommendation of Brackenridge:

But surely if it is necessary to have a good Governor, it is not less so to have a wise and virtuous Legislature. Under this impression, it is with pleasure that I have heard H. H. Brackenridge, esq. nominated

<hr />

[16] *Pittsburgh Gazette*, September 1, 1798.   [17] *ibid.*, September 8, 1798.
[18] *ibid.*, October 20, 1798.

as a proper person to represent the County of Allegheny, in the next legislature.

If a life devoted to study and research; if a thorough knowledge of the history of Governments, and a critical acquaintance with all the rocks and shoals, on which they have split, can render a man adequate to the business, he is certainly among our most proper characters—he has long been our fellow citizen—his interest is here, and he is well acquainted with the difficulties and advantages of our country. . . . I hope he will be unanimously supported.[19]

To this recommendation "A Real Farmer" replied in words that may well have been embarrassing to Brackenridge:

I think it would contribute much towards the object of the person, who, under the signature of the FARMER, recommends Mr. Brackenridge for the Assembly, if the author would indulge the public with his name. The piece discovers so much zeal for Mr. Brackenridge's success, and the stile is so peculiar, that many are wicked enough to ascribe the piece to old Hugh himself. It is an awkward thing for a man to recommend himself, especially where he is so well known— and as talents and information are only to be esteemed, as they may be well employed, why did not the author tell us of Mr. Brackenridge's former services in the legislature? Does he know that Mr. Brackenridge once represented Westmoreland county, that prior to his election he proposed several things for the advantage of the people of the Western Country, which he promised, if elected to effect, and when elected voted against them. . . .[20]

Obviously Brackenridge had not regained the confidence of his neighbors. It is not surprising, then, that he was defeated at the election on October 8, 1799.[21] McKean, the Republican candidate for governor, was, however, elected.[22] After this victory the Republican leaders in Western Pennsylvania organized for further activities, having in mind, no doubt, the coming Presidential election.

On October 26, about forty or fifty "friends of Thomas McKean" met at Smur's Tavern "to see each other and take refreshment." Brackenridge presided at the meeting. The Republi-

[19] *Pittsburgh Gazette*, September 14, 1799.   [20] *ibid.*, October 5, 1799.
[21] *ibid.*, October 19, 1799.   [22] *ibid.*, October 12, 1799.

can sentiments of the group were expressed in the toasts to "our envoys to France, and the adjustment of our differences with that nation," and to "the press, the palladium of liberty." When Brackenridge withdrew at nine o'clock he was toasted as "the friend of his country, of the poor and of the oppressed."

At half past nine the company broke up. In the meantime an armed party had been lingering near Smur's Tavern, and some of the Republicans were accosted by them on their way home. As an excuse for this rudeness it was said that "an alarm had been given to the town" that the friends of McKean had been planning to parade the streets and "assail the houses" that evening.

The Republicans, eager to avoid being branded as disorderly, met two days later with Brackenridge in the chair, and issued the following resolutions:

That we are not sensible on our part of any word, act, or circumstance, that could give rise to the alarm of the citizens on Saturday evening last, and that we must resolve it into strange misrepresentations, or a conspiracy to make a riot, and draw us into an appearance of being concerned in it, and charge it to our account.

That we disapprove of all disorder, in act, provocation in words, or circumstance of insult whatever tending to a breach of the peace.[23]

In the next week's *Gazette* appeared an article in which the Republicans were described as Jacobins.[24] They very naturally objected to the appellation just as they had resented the attempt to make them appear as a disorderly rabble. They replied as follows:

The term *Jacobin,* was originally, and perhaps deservedly popular in France; but by the intemperance and misconduct of the leaders, it became obnoxious, and the credit of it fell with Robespierre. It has since had the same acceptance in that country, and in these states with that of incendiary, disorganizer, &c. To call us therefore Jacobins, and the *greatest liars of all Jacobins,* is provoking and difficult to bear.[25]

At this point in the campaign the Republicans undertook to provide themselves with a party newspaper in Pittsburgh. There can

[23] *ibid.,* November 2, 1799.
[24] This issue of the *Gazette* is not extant. The nature of the charges can be inferred from the reply of the Republicans.
[25] *Pittsburgh Gazette,* November 16, 1799.

be no doubt that the project was conceived by Brackenridge. He had, it appears, long desired to have another press in town for his own convenience as well as for political purposes. His own responsibility in the venture is indicated by a statement which he later made to Jefferson that he had been at considerable expense for the paper. His son later said that he had even purchased the type and set the printer up in business.[26]

At the time, however, the plan for a Republican paper was made to appear as a project of the party. In November 1799, the Pittsburgh Republican group held a meeting at which they made preliminary plans for the new publication and formulated resolutions on the subject. They maintained that recent publications in the *Gazette* had been scurrilous and libellous, and that the printing of such communications relieved them from "all embarrassment on the score of personal considerations in encouraging another Press at this place." A committee, of which Brackenridge was a member, was "appointed to take measures for this purpose."[27]

John Scull, the editor of the *Gazette,* deeply resented this plan to establish another newspaper in the town. He asserted that the Republicans' statement of their grievances against his paper was a mere pretext. He said, "*Another Press* has long been talked of by Mr. Brackenridge. . . . My paper has not teemed with abuse of the government, its officers, and its supporters—on the contrary I discountenanced publications of this kind—in this I have offended —this is the unpardonable sin and for this we are to be vilified with what is modestly termed ANOTHER PRESS."[28]

Brackenridge replied to Scull:

That I may have occasionally talked of another press, is possible though I do not recollect; but it has been often talked of to me. I have talked of a private press, for my own use as a literary man, it not being convenient for you to publish a pamphlet or the like, and being of opinion that the price demanded by you for anything I had done of this kind, was more than I could afford.

[26] H. M. Brackenridge, *Recollections of Persons and Places in the West,* pp. 69-70.
[27] *Pittsburgh Gazette,* November 30, 1799.
[28] *ibid.,* November 30, 1799.

I did say in conversation some time ago that I did not like the general spirit of your paper for some time past: I did not detail the reasons; but they were *not* because *it has not teemed with abuse* of the *government, its officers, and its supporters.* As to my abusing government, *or being in the habit of it,* which seems to be insinuated, you have been upwards of thirteen years a printer, and I have been for that time, a correspondent, and I give you leave to open your files to any one that chooses to inspect, and point out my publications. Indeed after this, as soon as I have leisure, I mean to make a selection of them myself, and publish them, that it may appear whether I have been an advocate of the constitution, and a supporter of the government or the contrary.[29]

Scull responded in the next issue of the *Gazette,* and Brackenridge published another defense in the Washington *Herald of Liberty,* a Republican paper.[30] In reply Scull exclaimed:

How degraded, how fallen must the man be, when he asserts for truth what he knows to be false—I pity him from my soul.—If Captain Farrago is still living, this conduct of his friend will bring a blush into his aged cheeks.[31]

David Bruce, in his turn, thus remonstrated with Brackenridge:

Now, Brackie! ye hae ta'en your side,
Nor longer under covert hide,
But bauldly on, before your tribe,
    In th' open plain,
Ye, like a mighty champion, ride
    And charge amain.

It's nae sma' pity, I maun own,
That ye, wha ance had sic renown,
Shou'd in your auld days, be run down,
    And sae neglected,
That to the mob ye maun turn roun'
    To be respected.

[29] *ibid.,* December 7, 1799. Brackenridge did not prepare his promised volume of newspaper writings until 1806, when he issued *Gazette Publications.*

[30] *The Herald of Liberty* is not extant; hence Brackenridge's contributions to it are not available.

[31] *Pittsburgh Gazette,* December 21, 1799.

Nae doubt, to ye it's unco pleasing,
To sit at night, an' weet your weason,
Wi' Johnston, Baird,[32] an' chiels sic as 'em
  At *Smur's* gill shop
An' pour in grog an' out sarcasm,
  At Federal folk.

It's unco fine to see your wit,
Adorning Israel's filthy sheet;[33]
What's warse, wase me, that I shou'd see't!—
  My *Brackie's* Muse!
Tuning her dainty, winsome reed,
  For sic a use.

When Farmers' dogs upo' the green,
Attack the kie, I've often seen
Ane, 'mang the lave, mair sharp an' keen,
  Snap at the tail;
The ithers, but wi' barking din,
  The beasts assail.

It's sae wi' ye an them ye sit wi';
You're th' only ane, wha's sharp an' witty,
An' on ye come wi' *biting ditty*,
  Before the *pack*
While they but *yelp,* to shaw their spite ay,
  Wi' witless clack.

The opinions ye had ance o' *France*
Ye maun na langer now advance,
Else you'll come aff wi' a toom paunch—
  It is na jest, Sir!—
You'll hardly get the banes to craunch
  Frae your sour Master.[34]
. . .   .

Then ye maun bawl 'bout Liberty,
An' 'gainst the treaty made by *Jay*;[35]

[32] Members of the committee for the "new press."
[33] *"The Herald of Liberty."* Bruce's note.
[34] "The Sovereign People." Bruce's note.
[35] "British Treaty of '94, made by Mr. Jay." Bruce's note.

Wi' mony mair things in that way;
Tho' in your conscience,
Ye b'lieve that ilka word ye say
Is but d——d nonsense.

But, than ambition what's mair sneeking?
Climbing, ye ken, is just but *creeping*;
An', in Republics, he wha's seeking
To sway the mob,
Maun aften do, against his liking,
A dirty job.

Still guided by the pop'lar whim,
Be't right or wrang's, a' ane to him,
Sae he the multitude keep firm
Ay to his side,—
Blaw foul, blaw fair, he still will swim
Lang wi' the tide.

But you're well vers'd in this *fine art*,
An cannilie can play your part.—
I wish ye speed, wi' a' my heart,
An', like *M'Kean*,
Soon may you *Governor* insert
Before your name.[36]

On December 18, 1799, Brackenridge was appointed a justice of the supreme court of Pennsylvania by Governor McKean as a reward for his services to the Republican party.[37] The disgusted Federalists at once addressed a mock petition for mercy to the new judge, greeting him as "President of the Jacobin Society, Protector of Chivalry, Privy Counsellor of the Governor of Bantam, Poet Laureate to the Herald of Sedition, Biographer to the Insurgents, Auctioneer of Divinity, and Haberdasher of Pronouns."[38]

It was the habit of good Federalists to consider Republicans not only as dangerous radicals but also as libertines. The *Western Telegraphe* and the *Pittsburgh Gazette* published a tale of a spree in

[36] *Poems of the Scots-Irishman,* pp. 116-18.
[37] H. Binney, *Pennsylvania Supreme Court Reports,* Vol. I, p. iii.
[38] *Pittsburgh Gazette,* December 21, 1799.

which Brackenridge was supposed to have indulged in the village of Canonsburgh. A correspondent of the *Gazette* expressed his astonishment at the fact that "a Supreme Judge and a sapient Philosopher too, will so far lose sight of the reverence due to himself —to his station—and society, as to be seen almost 'stark naked and nearly stark mad' from too much tipple in the face of open day."[39]

In the summer of 1800 the *Tree of Liberty*, the "new press" of the Republicans, was established under the editorship of John Israel. The first few issues are not extant, but we can study their effect on the Federalists in comments published in the *Gazette*. Pious conservatives professed to be shocked by the religious liberalism of the Republicans. A *Gazette* writer, moved by Brackenridge's relations with John Israel, who was a Jew, said:

Brackenridge of late seems to have a hankering after the *Jews*. . . . Hugh in his younger days affected to be a *Christian*, nay, carried the joke so far as actually to "whip the cat" through the lower counties in the character of a *Tent Preacher* and went by the name of *H. Montgomery Brackenridge*.[40] Like his friend *Jefferson* the philosopher and the *Rogues* in France he has since been accused of *Infidelity*. That he should turn *Jew* in his old days, and build him a *synagogue* in his own ground, surprises nobody. But does it follow of course, that the people about "*the head waters of the Ohio*," are to change their names, their religion, and their politics, as often as he does; or if in one of his crack brained *vagaries* Hugh has submitted to the *knife* of his High Priest, is it expected that man, woman, and child will do the same? Are we all to be circumcised without benefit of clergy?[41]

A country contributor was much disturbed by the "Jacobinism" and "Infidelity" of the Republicans:

What Brackenridge and Israel mean by Republican principles, aristocratic tyranny and power and the rest of that, I know not. I thought we are all republicans. I do not think that it is republican principles to be always in revolutions and insurrections. . . .

---

[39] *Pittsburgh Gazette,* August 16, 1800.
[40] This must be a political opponent's version of Brackenridge's service as a chaplain.
[41] *Pittsburgh Gazette*, August 23, 1800.

I am an old fashioned man. I reverence the Bible, and do not like, nay it shocks me, and I hope it does many others to see the word of God profaned. Messrs. Brackenridge and Israel have taken a motto to their paper from Revelations 22:2 where the Holy Spirit speaking of the Tree of Life says, "And the leaves of the Tree were for the healing of the nations." These sacred words they have profanely applied to their newspaper. I did not expect to see such open profanation in a professing country, and I fear their tree will bring forth very different leaves and fruit . . . for our woe and death and not for our healing. . . . They have published a long justification of this profanation of God's word and mysteries. This makes it worse and shows that they have no regard for religion.

This is the more observable as in the other paper which this lad Israel publishes at Washington, he has taken this motto "Man is Man and who is more?" . . . These words . . . are taken from a French song made in their revolution, when they cast off the belief and worship of God, turned the Churches of God into Temples of Reason, placed Strumpets on Altars, denied a future state, and asserted that man dieth like the beasts. . . . Thus we see that Mr. Brackenridge and Mr. Israel put the Holy Bible on a level with a French ballad. I do not wonder that a Jew who denies the New Testament, or a Deist who denies both Testaments should do so; but better things might have been hoped from a Judge of the Supreme Court than to publish and vindicate profanity. . . .[42]

Another contributor angrily wrote:

Judge Brackenridge, in company with the Herald of Sedition, has set up a press here. . . . For what? What has Mr. Brackenridge been doing ever since he resided here? Fomenting sedition; breaking the peace of families, stirring up strifes and quarrels. He cannot even leave the town in peace, till he kindle this fire-brand; to raise the flame he has always been blowing. He is the Editor—he fills the paper—and he boasts that he has matter prepared for three months to come. It is the Gazette of Judge Brackenridge.[43]

Judge Addison now wrote a letter of protest to Brackenridge, and Brackenridge printed it in the *Tree of Liberty*, with comments. The issue which contained these documents is not extant, but some of the points can be recovered from remarks in the *Gazette*. Brack-

[42] *ibid.*   [43] *ibid.*

enridge evidently denied that he controlled the *Tree of Liberty*, and accused Addison of writing or inspiring the abusive articles in the *Telegraphe* and the *Gazette* and of driving him "from the bar by a systematic series of insults in his official capacity." He also criticized Addison for delivering a defense of the Sedition Law as a charge to a grand jury.[44]

In answer to this a correspondent, alluding to Brackenridge's part in the Whiskey Insurrection, inquired:

Who is best employed—Judge Addison in writing and publishing charges to grand juries to explain and enforce the principles of our government and the laws of the country, or Judge Brackenridge in writing and publishing a *partial* newspaper to persuade the people that their government is tyranny, their officers corrupt, their laws unconstitutional and oppressive, to make people discontented, guilty and miserable, to raise another insurrection, and leave them in the lurch to go down the river with the frogs or bring them before his tribunal for punishment?[45]

An excited Federalist with an ironical turn of mind wrote:

The Judge will oblige a number of his subscribers by stating in his next paper, the names of the persons whose heads he cut off and laid like turnips under his *Tree of Liberty*. We suggest the propriety of adding a Guillotine to the Tree, and a headless trunk or two in the background, together with Judge Marat smiling and enjoying the carnage.—French things should be completely French!!![46]

David Bruce's contribution to the chorus of criticism was a poem "To the Honorable H. H. Brackenridge, Esq., One of the Judges of the Supreme Court of Pennsylvania":

> Nane thinks o' Cox, or sic like wight,
> Wha never had the Bardie gift,
> Tho' he to a' he ance thought right
>   Has twice turned tail;
> But, when a BRACKENRIDGE does *shift*,
>   The Muses wail.

[44] *Pittsburgh Gazette*, August 29, 1800.   [45] *ibid.*, August 23, 1800.
[46] *ibid.*, August 29, 1800.

Nae lang sinsyne, ae bonie day,
Sitting upo' Parnassus brae,—
What think ye did the Musie say?
  "My bairn," quoth she,
"Your brither *Brack* has a gane gley,
  "Alas! wae's me!"

"Goddess," quoth I, "what has he done?
"You ken the Lad's ay making fun,
"We Mortals, aften, are hard run
  "To find him out.
"He canna the Celestials hum,
  "Wi' a' his wit."

"Wit!" quoth she, "Wit's but little worth,
" 'Thout principle to gie it pith.
"He's just as supple as a withe—
  "Alas! Alas!
"Fore interest, whim, or passion's breath
  "He's but a rash.

"The mob, to wham a' pow'r attaches—
"Poor ignorant misguided wretches!
"Has made *'a king o' shreds an' patches,'*
  "O' ane *M'Kean*;
"Him *Brackie* flatters, soothes, an' watches,
  "Like dog for bane.

"O Heavens! but it maks me wud,
"An' gars my tears run in a flood,
"To see ane wi' my powers endu'd,
  "Cringin' for favour
"To the vile puppet o' the crowd—
  "Licking his slaver.

"What did he here, nae lang sinsyne?
"Cause we refused our aid to join
"To please sic chiels as *Burke* ca's swine,
  "The chap grew crusty,
"An' swore in spite o' our teeth he'd rhyme,
  "While he had whiskey.[48]

[48] "Mr. Brackenridge, to gratify the friends of *Thomas M'Kean's* election, when the success of it was known, got drunk with them on whiskey, and wrote silly and abusive ballads on the opposite party." Bruce's note.

"But this is no his whole offence;
"Seizing the *patriot's* stale pretence,
"He urges wi' bold impudence,
    "Against his conscience,
"Opinions which his better sence
"Tells him are nonsense."

This having said, the Musie stopt;
Wi' grief an' rage she maist was chok'd,
While I thus further speech invok'd;
    "Say Muse what fate
"Awaits him, wha thy pow'r has mock'd,
    "Shall he escape?"

"No," she reply'd, wi' stern regard,
"His crimes shall meet their due reward.
"He from Parnassus shall be barr'd,
    "An' doom'd to dabble,
"In Grub-street squibs, and rhymes ill-pair'd,
    "To please the rabble.

"The *Tree*[49] he's rais'd 'gainst honest fame,
"Will be a gallows to his name,
"On which he'll be hung up to shame,
    "Like wicked Haman.
"Wi' *Cox,* wi' *Dallas,* an' *M'Kean,*
    "Will he be hanging.

"Because he has dar'd to scorn our pow'r,
"To *whiskey* we have gi'en him oure;
"He'll tranquil woo the Muse no more,
    "By murm'ring stream.
"His fancy will be wild uproar—
    "A madman's dream."

. . .   .

Thus spake the Musie, wi' a frown,
I hung my head, an looked down,
An', trembling, was as mute an' lown

[49] "The *Tree of Liberty,* a Jacobin paper of that name, published in Pittsburgh, of which *Mr. Brackenridge* is reputed not only the patron, but the conductor." Bruce's note.

As ony mouse;
But she, wi' smiling aspect, soon,
Made me mair crouse.

"Sweet muse," quoth I, "he is my brither,
"Gif he be lost, I've nae sic ither;
"Wha kens, but I might him recover
"By pow'r o' sang;
"Methinks, e'en now I see him swither
"'Twixt right an' wrang."

"Go," she return'd, "go son, wi' speed,
"Blaw up your lang forgotten reed,
"Tell *Brackie* what has been decreed;
"Go, an' alarm him,
"That Vengeance fa' not on his head,
"Without a warning."

The orders o' the heavenly Maid
I readily, wi' joy, obey'd;
Blew up my pipe, an' this hae play'd
To work your guid—
Naething could make me sae glad
Did I succeed.[50]

On September 15, 1800, Brackenridge was to leave Pittsburgh temporarily for duty on his judicial circuit.[51] In anticipation of his departure the *Gazette* devoted almost the whole of the issue of September 12 to vituperation and crude satire against him.

Instead of replying directly to all these charges of the past weeks, Brackenridge, just before his departure, took his revenge by ridiculing the literary productions of his critics:

[50] *Poems of the Scots-Irishman*, pp. 100-3. In reprinting this poem Bruce added the following note: "This was addressed to this gentleman soon after he had risen to high authority. The election of *Thomas M'Kean* to the chief magistracy of Pennsylvania had determined the balance of political parties in that State . . . in favour of the democratic interest, and *Mr. B.* had prudently thrown himself into the preponderating scale.—For the services he had rendered the party, or for what were expected from him, he was appointed one of the supreme Judges of the State. . . ."

[51] *Pittsburgh Gazette*, September 12, 1800.

On the election of Governor McKean, and the appointments under him, much abuse was expected; but, not to the extent that has taken place. It could not escape any one that the pseudo-federalists would be much hurt. But it was expected that they would have had the policy, in great measure, to conceal it. Since the institution of this paper [the *Tree of Liberty*], especially they have shewn themselves in Scull's Gazette, with a rage and lamentation beyond all bounds. The howling has been rather that of beasts than that of men. . . .

As to myself it seemed to me that I was in the situation of a traveller in the Island of Borneo, or other parts of the East Indies, with a thousand monkeys leaping and chattering amongst the trees, and incommoding the Caravan by the fall of excrement.

It is wondered why I have not pointed out some of those by name that call themselves correspondents, or under various signatures come forward through the medium of the press. How is it possible? An individual monkey, ouran-outang, or baboon, may be distinguished while you have your eye upon it; but the colour, the shape,. the jump, and the grin of all being the same, the moment you lose sight of it, there is an end of the identity. So, the style of these creatures being equally ungrammatical, inelegant, indecent and abusive, there is no distinguishing Jacko, one, from Jacko, the other. They are all of the Monkey tribe, and that is all you can say about it. . . .[52]

While he was on circuit he continued his ridicule of the *Gazette* writers:

I am fond of wit, and endure it even at my own expence where there is humour. But mere invective excites contempt and indignation; unless indeed where the charge is serious, accompanied with *name and vouchers.* . . .

There are amongst my personal or political adversaries, Judges, Lawyers, Doctors, Apothecaries, Military men, traders and Tradesmen. Can none be mustered that can write with sense or taste? Must all be stigmatized in public opinion as clumsy satirists and awkward declaimers? It may be thought strange that I should demand such men as could wound me.—A swordsman delights in a swordsman, but is vexed at the vaporing of a Russian who understands neither guards nor passes. I see nothing yet produced by them that is above a scullion, an empiric, or a pettifogger. I cannot say but there are some *inventive faculties*; but they want judgment and discretion. They show nothing

[52] *Tree of Liberty*, September 13, 1800.

but a pert flippant shallow ribaldry. They ought to study models. Let them think of this, & until they are better instructed and more expert, sheath their rapiers. Literary weapons are not for them to use at all. Inhabitants of the country in a ruder state, let them gouge and bite: A mob in the streets, let them throw stones and timber; but Keep away from a Gazette. . . .

I am consumed for the credit of Scull's people; and the only consolation is that their paper is confined chiefly to themselves. It is only a way-faring man that hears of them or it. I hope the liberality of travellers, will make allowance for the dullness of the writers and draw no ultimate conclusion against the capacity or natural intellect of our country. The human mind in this region and climate has not yet had a fair trial. There are two things which money cannot give, instant growth to trees; or *immediate refinement to manners*. These are both, the result of time and cultivation.[53]

His next satire was an ironical proposal of a method to bring out the voters on election day. After hinting that unseemly methods of electioneering had been used at the last election, he said, posing as a Federalist adviser:

Our usual means have been by hand, to lead forward, or to shove along those under our care; but this is a thing of labor and slow operation. The application of mechanics in this as in other employments has been long a desideratum, and appears to me practicable. I would propose that the electioneerer furnish himself with a cord, a common bedcord might be used for the purpose, forming a bite or loop upon it at the one end; this thrown over the votable he might be drawn along by the neck, under pain of strangling by resistance. A strap of leather around a couple of pullies, and fastened to the waist band of the breeches, would facilitate the *pulling* heavy persons; and a block tackle near the windows might be constructed to hoist them up. . . . On the principle of the inclined plane, planks might be placed, so, that when toled along by whiskey and put upon them, such as cannot walk or stand may be gently trundled down to give their suffrages. . . . I am earnestly anxious that the experiment be made. . . . It is the more necessary, on our side, as our friends consist a great deal of the inhabitants of towns, and are young lawyers, and whifflers of one kind and another, and though they have the good will yet not the strength to urge forward the pondrous bodies that come from the country.

53 *Tree of Liberty*, September 20, 1800.

After the last election, which was a busy day, a governor being to be chosen, I have heard many of them complain for a week of aching shoulders, and joints of the limbs, with the sore service of the occasion.

Then he turned to the electioneering activities of Alexander Addison, President of the Court of the Western Pennsylvania district:

The Democratic Jacobins of this country, take exception to the President coming on the ground, and exclaim that a Judge ought to have more *regard to character,* and a more delicate sense of dignity of office, than by mixing in the election bustle, subject himself to be jostled or knocked down; but they do not consider that impudence, not delicacy is the character of the Judge. But even if it were, this is not the time to exercise it. . . . These people are in the habit of resolving all things into first principles.—The rights of man, virtue, fair dealing is their theme. They would have elections conducted on principles of Liberty and Equality. They are the *many,* we are the *few.* Aristocracy is an artificial thing, and it must live by *art.* Strategem, over reaching is necessary for our system. The department assigned to the Judge is to go upon the ground, and by means of his Scotch dialect draw some of his countrymen to our side.[54]

The next week Brackenridge, still on circuit, sent a letter to the *Tree of Liberty* in which he again ridiculed the writing of his critics:

Your town has been said by strangers, to deserve the epithet Kalligunaikae, that is of *beautiful women,* given by Homer to Greece; but to that may now be added, *the village of men of refined wit.* The irony is delicate. It is not just the lepus, or pleasantry of Horace, or the invective of Juvenal; but it is a wit sui generis, of its own kind, truly original. Peter Porcupine[55] made an approach to this species of sarcasm, but fell short in the true salt, that distinguishes this species of writers. Your place has the advantage of a number of men out of office in all senses of the word; that is, who have lost offices, or *have never got them.* They have leisure to cultivate the belles lettres. What a pity it would have been to have oppressed these rare spirits with official appointments. It would have been turning fine barbary horses

[54] *Tree of Liberty,* October 11, 1800.
[55] William Cobbett, editor of *Porcupine's Gazette.*

into beasts of burden. Providence orders all things right. They have nothing now to do but to write epigrams, and pen paragraphs. . . .

These sallies of imagination ought not to be lost. They might be published under the title Pittsburgiana. Subscriptions might be obtained for a neat Octavo Volume, by *Peter Polecat,* gentleman.[56]

At this time Judge Addison imprudently gave Brackenridge another opening for an attack. At the October session of the court in Crawford County, he made the recent election the subject for a charge to the grand jury. "We all know," he said, "what arts were used, by some interested individuals, to promote the election of the present governor. They said, that if McKean were elected governor, he would abolish the excise, the stamp act, the land tax, the standing army and the Alien and Sedition laws. Those who printed and repeated these tales knew them to be false. But they effected their purpose. He was elected."[57]

Brackenridge at once replied to this charge in an open letter to Addison published in the *Tree of Liberty*:

Whether this Charge be INDICTABLE or IMPEACHABLE, I shall leave to the Legislature, or Attorney General of the State. But it certainly cannot be prudent in a Judge, by departing from the subject of his official duty, to subject himself, to have his veracity from the BENCH, with impunity called in question.

After quoting the passage in which the Judge had accused the Republicans of using "arts" and spreading "falsehoods," he continued:

The implication necessarily carries with it two things, 1st. That the election of the present Governor, was the result, not of fair opinion, but of falsehood, and fraud; and 2d. That the people to whom your charge was delivered, were the *accomplices,* or *dupes of the misrepresentation*. In this last point of view, it astonishes me, and is a strong proof of the love of order, and respect for the laws among the people, that under a sense of the groundless and degrading LIBEL, they were not fired with sudden indignation, and did not drag you from your seat, and tread you under foot. . . .

As the district had been long ago surfeited with your Metaphysico-

56 *Tree of Liberty,* October 18, 1800.
57 *ibid.,* November 15, 1800.

politico-theologico-juridico-Charges, so it had thought, that, you were
yourself satiated, with the applause, real or imaginary; which you had
excited: more especially as you had at last, got them in a book, & in a
fair way to travel, by subscription, to some distance. But, not the love
of fame, but a sense of duty, led you to this task. Ah, man, if you
knew the reverse effect of your endeavours! That nothing could be
more calculated to shock the public mind, and disgust, than your
homilies; nothing more likely to bring about an INSURREC-
TION. . . .

But you must lecture, you must declare your sentiments. Have you
not SCULL'S paper in which every *animal* from the buffaloe, to the
civet-cat, has of late been accustomed to EXPRESS itself? Or, if
you must harangue, cannot you do it out of Court? Is there not the
vacation? Must you have the BENCH? Is there not a *stone-step* or
a *horse-block* to stand upon? A *half-barrel* or a keg to put your
legs in? . . .

It is astonishing that your cacoethes dicendi cannot be exhausted.
Does no person tell you how much you expose yourself? But if they
did, what credit would you give! You have no self-examination; no
retro-flexion of mind. You think on one side. I have laboured hard
to get you to know yourself. I have watched over you as a patient, to
see if the inflamation was reduced; if gentle phlebotomy had been
sufficient. The more powerful remedies must come. . . .

You will wonder at the severity of my expressions, and be disposed
to think that something strongly personal, must enter into the composition of my indignation. How far a recollection of personal insult or
injury may inflame a sense of public indignities, unknown and imper-
ceptible to the sensibility, it is impossible to say. But so far as I know
myself and am conscious of the actings of my mind, the present impressions and expressions are the off-spring of a sense of *the wrongs
of society.* As to what relates to myself, I reserve for a more
SOLEMN OCCASION.[58]

The Federalists naturally chose to interpret this letter as an
incitement to revolution. The *Gazette,* in headlines large enough
to announce a major war, exclaimed: "Insurrection. If tumult,
violence, and insurrection do not take place—the failure cannot
be attributed to Hugh H. Brackenridge."[59] "A Citizen" wrote:

[58] *Tree of Liberty,* November 15, 1800.
[59] *Pittsburgh Gazette,* November 28, 1800.

The letter of Judge Brackenridge to Mr. Addison printed in the Tree of Liberty last week, is more censurable and more alarming than any publication which has ever appeared in an American newspaper. . . . If the Legislature do their duty they will put it into the power of the Governor to dismiss Mr. Brackenridge from all further authority in the courts. The Appointment was certainly made without due consideration, and there is now unequivocal evidence that it never ought to have been made.—It is now demonstrated that not only the head is uninformed in point of law, but the heart is envenomed with a poison which must pollute the pure current of Justice, and mortal if it enter into the judiciary system of our State.[60]

Another indignant paragrapher said: "I hope Mr. Addison will scorn to make any reply to the scandalous address of Mr. Brackenridge to him unless it be to issue a warrant against him as a mover of sedition, or have him sent to the Mad-house in Philadelphia, whither the increasing symptoms of insanity will soon lead him."[61]

The Federalists were, of course, either unduly nervous, or they deliberately exaggerated the import of Brackenridge's threat to Addison. His intention was merely to unbench the judge, and he lost no time in starting the proceedings for the accomplishment of his purpose. A few days after his letter was printed petitions to the legislature were in circulation "praying for the IMPEACH-MENT of ALEXANDER ADDISON, Esq."[62]

Meanwhile Brackenridge had been elaborating his satire on his newspaper critics. The conceit in which he had compared his calumniators to apes and skunks had evidently pleased his fancy, and so, as he had previously done with the Traddle theme, he restated it in Hudibrastic verse in the following squib entitled "On the Blackguard Writers in Scull's *Gazette.* In the Course of the Summer."

> The time was when the beasts could speak
> But whether from caprice or pique,
> Or having lost the use of tongue,
> The Devil a word from old or young,
> There has been heard for many a day.

[60] *Pittsburgh Gazette,* November 21, 1800.   [61] *ibid.*
[62] *Tree of Liberty,* December 6, 1800.

But now, it seems, they pay it away,
In writing—Lord! in the Gazette?
Ay faith, just so—The *Marmoset,*
Rhinoceros; and every species,
Or genus, as the learned phrase is,
Of furr, of bristle, or of hair,
Opossum, Ground-hog, or the *Bear,*
Elk or *Racoon*—G—— d——mn their bloods,
The whole of them that come from WOODS;
Pole-cat expressing from his bag,
Or *Monkey* passing for a wag;
All make their mark, or make their water,
And call on us to call it satire.
The scent would make a devil curse,
From these vile creatures on all fours.
Israel take care that none comes near,
Your manufactory, for fear,
The pungent fluid may distil
Upon you, and against our will
There will be a necessity,
I must, my lad, express it t'ye,
To bury you and your whole office,
Under the earth, till it shall suffice,
To take away the smell of vermin,
How long, I cannot now determine.

After interpreting the characters of a number of Pittsburgh
Federalists in terms of animal behavior, he said to himself:

Ah Brackenridge, you must endure
The flood, and excrement impure.
The devil help ye, you must up
To office, and offend the groupe,
And now because they dung, you curse—
Your patience is the best resource—
And, the example of as good,
As you, that have the same withstood
In real history or fable,
When blackguardism has slipt cable

And neither helm of rhyme, or reason,
Can bring it up, and stop its weazon.[63]

This Hudibrastic was reprinted in the *Gazette* with ironical comments. The annotator said, "The following pitiful Poem by 'the Honorable Hugh H. Brackenridge' appeared not only in the *Tree of Liberty,* but was circulated in Hand-Bills by the Judge on his route to Philadelphia." With satirical reference to Brackenridge's preface to *Modern Chivalry,* he said that he was reprinting the poem as a model of style; and he charged Brackenridge with inconsistency in becoming a Republican leader after having ridiculed "the people" in his earlier writings.[64]

Meanwhile the story concerning Brackenridge's spree in July had by December developed enormously in the community imagination, and "An account of the late Mad Circuit of JUDGE BRACKENRIDGE through Washington County" was committed to writing for the Federalist paper. According to this new version of the story the Judge had called on his former friends in Washington, who gave him a cool reception and would not receive him into their houses. "Mortified beyond measure at this treatment, he returned to his tavern, called for brandy to cure his vexation, and after drinking hastily an unusual portion of that fiery liquor rode away to Canonsburgh." With all the precision of village gossip the narrator gave an account of what the judge drank at each tavern, of the number of buckets of water dashed upon him to cool his alcoholic fever, and the exact number of curses heaped upon each landlord who was required to serve him. From his altitude of Federalist rectitude the writer closed his narrative thus:

When these things are done by a magistrate high in office we cannot expect reformation or punishment of the profance and dissolute among us. Office is degraded, Religion dishonoured, and sober virtue wounded by such outrageous behaviour in a Judge. Wise men will see all the mischiefs which must follow the mad career of such an officer in the society, and good men will every where lament the affliction and misfortune which has befallen the state by the appointment

---

[63] *Tree of Liberty,* November 22, 1800.
[64] *Pittsburgh Gazette,* November 28, 1800.

of a man useless in point of industry and sense, and noxious beyond all calculation by his example.[65]

In some verses addressed to Bruce, Brackenridge dealt with this accusation of drunkenness. After reviewing the recent political conflicts he said of himself:

> Auld Brackie spends his time in study,
> And making verses like yoursel,
> I winna say he makes sae well,
> But now and then he casts an eye,
> To look at what is passing by,
> And makes occasional observations;
> But pride is in the way o' his lessons;
> They take their ain gate, let them gang;
> Ye'll see the upshot o't e'er lang.
>
> . . .   .
>
> They canna ca' auld Brackie knave;
> Or say he got his geer or thrave,
> By taking horn, or spoon or pot,
> Or, dispossessing o' his cot,
> The poor man: But they say I think,
> The auld man takes a drop o' drink,
> Ha' got a blatherskite John Scull
> To put it in his prints, the fool,
> That coming hame, O fye upon it,
> He lost his way and lost his bonnet.
> It may be true; but there is BURNS
> Wha gars us laugh and greet by turns,
> Wad tak a drink; alack! o'er muckle;
> But wha e'er gie'd him o'er the knuckle,
> For that which made the bard so canty,
> And gied us a' his sangs sae dainty.
> The water they ca'd Hypocrene,
> Amang the Greeks is long since gane;
> Our water here's no verra guide;
> But Aqua Vitae warms the bluide;
> Is medicine, though an excess,
> Occasionally may take place,

[65] *Pittsburgh Gazette*, December 5, 1800.

When auld folks meet and take a gill.
When ye ha come to go down hill,
And age begins to bind with frost,
And touch the thrapple wi a host[66]
Before ye sing ye'll wet your whistle.
And sae I end my long epistle.[67]

Up to this time Brackenridge's contacts in the Republican party had been limited to the state of Pennsylvania. Early in 1801, however, he entered into correspondence with Thomas Jefferson. His first communication was a note about Jefferson's *Appendix to Notes on Virginia*. Jefferson's reply gave an account of the tie vote for the presidency. Brackenridge was not at home when the letter reached his house, and Mrs. Brackenridge opened it and showed it to a man who was visiting. This seemingly unimportant incident was elevated to the rank of political scandal by Federalist gossip in Pittsburgh, and an account of it even reached the national capital. There the *Washington Federalist* published the following note:

Know ye, that it is rumored about this Federal city, that Thomas Jefferson, Esq. Vice President of the United States, did write a letter, very lately, to one Breckenridge of Pittsburgh, (who has lately received from Governor M'Kean the appointment of Judge of the Supreme Court of Pennsylvania) *that the electors had given an equal number of votes for him (the said Jefferson) and one Aaron Burr: that he (the said Jefferson) did verily believe, or fear; or expect, or doubt, the present House of Representatives, had a most unreasonable leaning, or squinting in favor of him* the said Aaron, &c. &c. and that the wife of the said Judge Breckenridge did receive the same epistle (absente Judice), and having opened it, divulged the contents.

Now if any man knows the character of Judge Breckenridge, and if he does not, he can easily, know it, by applying to Albert Gallatin of Geneva, but last from Pennsylvania, who was very intimate with him about the time of the insurrection in the western counties of Pennsylvania, in 1794—I say, Messrs. Editors, whoever knows Judge Breckenridge, and Mazzei, and Callender, and Duane, and Doct. Reynolds,

[66] "Cough." Brackenridge's note.
[67] *Tree of Liberty*, February 14, 1801. The poem is dated "Jan. 29th, 1801." It was reprinted in the *Tree of Liberty* from the *Herald of Liberty*.

and all the group of *virtuous opposers,* as they call themselves to all government, in this country, from Tom Tinker down to Tom M'Kean, —why then, he will probably know the confidential friends of Tom Jefferson, that's all!

But, what, if they are friends to Mr. Jefferson? Is that Mr. Jefferson's fault? Let candour decide these questions; and while that is doing, let me ask another, could any man believe, that Mr. Jefferson was in habits of friendly and confidential correspondence with such people?[68]

This letter was reprinted in the *Tree of Liberty* with the following note by Brackenridge:

I do not consider it as an absolute priviledge of wives to open letters directed to their husbands. . . . But Mrs. Brackenridge has authority to open all letters to me in my absence, and to forward such as I should receive soon. She did open a letter from Mr. Jefferson to me, and as there was nothing in it of a private nature, permitted a gentleman who was by to read it. It was a letter acknowledging the receipt of one from me on reading the *Appendix to the Notes on Virginia.* To say a single word with regard to the misrepresentation of the *Contents,* would seem to think it possible that any person for a moment could believe it, and would be *an indelicacy towards Mr. Jefferson.* It is a production of the officinae infamiae, or laboratory of slander *at this place,* and unworthy of further notice.[69]

To Jefferson himself Brackenridge wrote on January 18, 1801:

Did not expect an answer to my note, not meaning to draw a person engaged in affairs into a correspondence. . . . But it may be useful to you in your present and approaching responsible situation to have hints, or indicia of the public mind on occasional subjects. With a view to inform and from a zeal for the credit of your administration I may occasionally communicate such hints as do not reach the Gazettes or are proper to be inscribed in them. A drawback upon me is that I do not write myself, but use an amanuensis. My handwriting is not easily legible, and it cramps my fingers, and hurts my nerves to write. Hence it is that I have avoided all correspondence not absolutely necessary: a loss no doubt in the course of my life, both of honour and profit, but it has saved time; I have had leisure to read the more. But

[68] Quoted from a reprint of the letter in the *Tree of Liberty,* January 31, 1801.
[69] *ibid.*

am sensible of the want of that confirmation in actions, or incitement to improvement which communication with philosophic men gives.

After this personal introduction, Brackenridge gave Jefferson several pages of information and advice about the political situation. He said that he had learned in Philadelphia, Carlisle, and Lancaster that the extremists of both the Federalist and Republican parties preferred Burr as President. He also warned Jefferson that there was danger of a political coup—that there seemed to be a scheme to elect a President pro tempore if the deadlock were not soon broken, and that James Ross of Pittsburgh seemed to be designated for this office. He then advised Jefferson to come to a private agreement with Burr, and to announce himself as President on March 4. He closed with some local and personal information:

John Israel printer and editor of the Tree of Liberty at this place informs me that he has occasionally transmitted you some numbers. The patronage of this paper has drawn upon me personally much abuse, and ribaldry in the ex-federalist prints. They are aware of the great importance of the post which has been seized, and have felt the effects of it. But the republicans are poor in this extreme of the state and but for considerable pecuniary assistance on my part, it could not have been set up or supported. The adversary press of John Scull is supported by private contributions from the party, and has the advantage of support from Government by the publication of the laws of the United States—an emolument which we hope to see soon transferred to the Herald and the Tree of Liberty.

Having put this Western house so to speak in order as far as can be done by arrangements and support of mine, I mean to withdraw to a more mid-land situation in the State as necessary to the convenient discharge of the duties of the office which I hold, & my being more in the neighborhood of the sea-coast cities, and the seat of the federal government which I might sometimes incline to visit.

Excuse the trouble I have given in this writing and accept of my gratulation on the testimony which America has given of the high respect they entertain for your talents and virtues, and believe me to be an admirer of your simplicity of manners, your science, political merit and services and irreproachable moral character and liberallity in religious opinions.

In a postscript he informed Jefferson that he was enclosing a poem about him—"I will not say dictated to me by Urania or any other of the Muses, which nightly me revisits, but which I meditated, not altogether in my slumbers, but on my bed in the course of the night."[70]

This poem, entitled *Jefferson, in Imitation of Virgil's Pollio*, was a versified statement of the author's Republican philosophy:

> Begin O muse, begin a loftier strain,
> Than mere bucolic, or the pastoral vein;
> Or, if a pastoral, or bucolic lay,
> Let it be worthy of the rising day;
> A day long look'd for, and late come to pass,
> Changing the course of things from what it was:
> From speculation and acquests by chance
> To gradual riches and a safe advance;
> From love of wealth, to love of patriot fame,
> The joys of Science and the Muses flame;
> From vile hypocrisy affecting zeal,
> For that religion which it does not feel;
> From tinsel form to solid worth and sense
> And value, less of etiquette than brains,
> Now Virgin Justice from her heaven returns,
> And on our continent, once more sojourns.
> Run on the hours, auspicious day be born,
> And blessings pour with Amalthean horn;
> An age of gold in private coffers felt;
> Affection now the Constitution's belt;
> Not forceful energy and iron arms,
> Which treason in a monarchy disarms;
> Provisional armies in an evil hour,
> To pension chieftains and secure in power;
> No Alien Law dishonourable and base;
> Or Act Sedition federal code disgrace.
> But yet some vestige must remain awhile
> Of ancient mischief and our land defile;
> Some strife at home, or public feud abroad,
> To draw our young men from their native sod.

[70] *Thomas Jefferson Papers,* Vol. 109, p. 18645 (Ms. in Library of Congress.)

Not all at once can heavy taxes cease,
These things require a gradual decrease;
Can only hope that boundaries may be set
To national accumulating debt;
That standing troops in larger force no more,
Be deem'd essential to defend our shore,
And in due time our naval thunder sleep,
Adjusting quarrels on the ocean deep,
The soldier quit the camp, marine the sea,
To cultivate the soil and plant his tree.
And there is more of general good which springs,
We trust, from this new dynasty of things.
Ex-Federalists, shall moderation learn,
And those in power the rocks ahead discern,
And boastful triumph and intemperate phrase;
Vain exultation and rude joy repress:
For nothing lasts but what is wise and just,
And arrogance at all times will disgust.
The pure republican is proud in mind.
But casts the form of victory behind;
Is tolerant and gives opinion scope
Free as the air or liquid dews that drop.
O for that time to me not overlate,
But the remains of life outlast the date,
When Truth, immortal daughter of the sky,
The place of vengeful falsehood may supply,
Carnivorous Calumny shall cease to slay,
And Candour be the order of the day:
O may I live to see, if not to sing,
The crystal waters of so pure a spring;
Or if I sing, the subject will inspire
A double portion of the muses fire.
Come on then Jefferson assume the chair—
It is the patriots voice to place you there:
Abroad a statesman, and at home a sage;
An ornament of the existing age.
The western earth rejoices at the event,
By flood and field and the whole heavens extent
As giving philosophy the government.

Columbia views it, and is pleas'd the while;
And you her son will recognize the smile.[71]

In his next letter to Jefferson, written in January, Brackenridge attempted to relieve the embarrassment caused by the paragraph in the *Washington Federalist,* and began with an explanation of the circumstances under which the contents of Jefferson's first letter were divulged. Then he tried to draw Jefferson into further correspondence:

I had said in my last that I did not wish to solicit any thing like a correspondence, though I might on my part give occasional information, yet my wife has been hurt at the use that has been made of opening the letter, and as the malignity of others would be gratified by supposing the object accomplished, it might not be amiss should you think it proper or have leisure, after the matter of presidency is settled to address a letter to me, should it contain but a news paper. It will have the effect of giving me consequence and power to support myself and my friends in this country.

It had been my intention ere this to have removed to a mid-land situation in Pennsylvania. But it is thought that the republican cause in the state requires my residence here some time longer, at least until the next election of Governor. It is a post of danger to me and to my family from active and vigilant calumny, but I feel a fortitude to encounter it. The giving the paper at this place a footing is a great object.[72]

On February 17, after it became evident that Jefferson would be elected President, Brackenridge wrote him a letter giving information about the administration of political patronage in Pennsylvania under Governor McKean, and offering advice about the distribution of Federal appointments. Particularly he urged Jefferson to appoint as Secretary of War a Western general who understood the military needs of the frontier. He also announced that he was about to leave Pittsburgh, and that he would be in Philadelphia and on his circuit until about June 1.[73]

[71] *Tree of Liberty,* January 24, 1801.
[72] *Thomas Jefferson Papers,* Vol. 109, p. 18650 (Ms. in Library of Congress.)
[73] *ibid.,* Vol. 109, p. 18652.

Meanwhile the case against Judge Addison had been growing stronger. At the December session of the court of common pleas for Allegheny County the Federalist judge delivered a characteristic political harangue in which he sketched the spread of revolutionary ideas in Europe and America and gave an alarming account of the work of the radical secret societies, such as the Illuminati. He hinted that the American "Jacobins" were affiliated with these organizations, and that the results of the last election had been due to these sinister influences. Associate Justice John S. B. Lucas, a Frenchman and a friend of Brackenridge, arose to deny Addison's statements.[74]

"Silence, Sir, you have no right to speak here, I am the organ of this court," Addison shouted, according to a Republican report.[75]

For this high-handed conduct, Addison was brought before the supreme court of Pennsylvania for impeachment. Brackenridge did not sit on the case, and the three Federalist judges on the bench merely subjected Addison to sharp censure. At the next session of the court Lucas again attempted to deliver a refutation of Addison's charges, and Addison dismissed the grand jury in order to prevent him. For this offense the Republicans carried impeachment proceedings to the legislature.

By June 1801, Brackenridge was back in Pittsburgh. While he had been absent, Jefferson had been inaugurated, and had announced his policy of conciliation: "We are all Republicans, we are all Federalists." Brackenridge was ready to support the party leader's policy. In the *Tree of Liberty* he presented the doctrine in his usual vein of pleasantry:

Thinking of the means of conciliation of parties, the federal and jacobin, it occurs to me, that intermarriages of young persons, would have a powerful effect to extinguish animosities, by forming a union of interest in the administration of the government, and the population and riches of the country. The Federalists having been in possession of the government for a considerable time, have amassed wealth from

74 *The Trial of Judge Addison*, appendix G, p. 6.
75 *Tree of Liberty*, December 27, 1800.

the offices they have possessed, and the speculations they have had in their power. The jacobins, on the other hand are poor, and many of them, if not literally without breeches which is the meaning of the French words sans culotte, yet at least, not having the best; but they are now of the administration, and heirs apparent of promotion.

After citing possible objections he said:

But why should a discreet and prudent Jacobin, that has felt the pinch of hunger and bad clothing, hesitate at the proposition of marrying a young girl of fortune, provided she is handsome, merely on the score of federal parentage! More especially, if the young lady, as is usually the case, has had a good education; has been taught music, and dancing under the best masters, and may be said to be in all respects well bred and accomplished. Should even an American Republican hang back in the way of matrimony with such offers in view, the numbers of United Irishmen, all of whom are genuine Jacobins, that are expected with considerable influx after the war, will furnish stock from whence to recruit husbands.[76]

He also wrote at this time a good-natured review of his relations with David Bruce. After telling of mistaking a skunk for a "pousie" when he was a boy, and of his vain search for "Dryads, Hamadryads, Muses" among the clearings,[77] he continued:

It was when I cross'd the hills;
Amang these western woods and rills,
Was sitting ae still e'en;
I min't as weel's I do yestreen;
It seemed to me I heard the seugh,
O'ane; I kent the verra air, d'ye see,
Frae the description I had got,
In Latin buke, or Grecian poet.
Ah, hah! thought I, this sang is fine,
It has an inkling of the nine;
It maun be what they call a muse—
What was it but the voice o' Bruce,
O' a Scots Irish origin
And Scotish air sae very fine,

[76] *Tree of Liberty,* June 20, 1801. In the issue of July 11 the facetious argument was continued.
[77] See above, p. 5.

Thought natural, expression saft:
I loupit leke a man ha'f daft;
To think at last, out owre these woods,
Amang the simmer trees and buds,
A bardie should spring up, a musie,
A genuine Parnassus pousie,
In nature real, and in mew,
Of Arcady a *Kitlin' true.*
My wishes led me to caress it;
To stroke the thing and amaist kiss it;
But what my wonder and surprisal,
Without an ill word or devisal,
To find the thing when a' was done,
In verse and sang began to strone,
Wi' Hogo war than assa-fetid,
Or bag o' animal four-fetit:
While Ettison took up the tune,
When wine had made his face a moon,
And sang't to Juries and to Judges,
At tavern where his honour loges.
I thought me o' what happen'd early,
When *Skunkie* pish'd upon me fairly
When I had ta'en it for a rabbit,
And did na think it would grow crabbit.
Sae frae the verra self same things,
Our guid and evil aften springs;
. . .   .

But still the consolation's ta'en;
Hard words, and language break nae bane.
While I can laugh and take a drink,
Ill be to them that evil think.
Here's to the bardie; fill the cogue;
Or send and get another jug:
The best way is to laugh at fools;
It is the wisdom of the schools;
For mirth tak's out the sting o' hurt;
And mental wounds are this way cur'd.[78]

[78] *Tree of Liberty,* June 20, 1801.

Brackenridge's conciliatory mood was expressed again two weeks later at the Fourth of July celebration. "On Grant's hill, under a bower, on the margin of a wood, and near a delightful spring, with the town of Pittsburgh in prospect, a numerous party of *genuine* republicans, convened and partook of a repast, the honourable HUGH H. BRACKENRIDGE President." The following toasts, pronounced by the president, indicate the complexion of his political thought at the time: "The Liberty of the Press without its licentiousness." "Equable industry in trades and professions, and not speculation, the means of happiness." "Conciliation in the federal administration as far as consistent with the support of friends." "Union in private society as far as is consistent with the support of Principle."[79]

Brackenridge also made another peace-offering to David Bruce in this same month. In a dialect poem relating a tale of two rival pipers in Scotland, he closed with the following personal application:

> The same wi' us now canty Bruce,
> Twa pipers that had different views,
> And baith had music in our brain;
> Ye play'd up Ross; I play'd M'Kean.
> And sooth maun a' be Do'phin fish
> That cam' to soom about your dish,
> And a' are turn'd to "*Rooks and Ravens*,"
> And very worst birds o' the heavens,
> That listen to my pipe or spring.
> Now toleration is a thing,
> That's amiable in church and state;
> And why should bardies derogate
> Frae the same licence in their strains?
> While men ha' different heads and brains,
> The same things wil na seem the same;
> And he has the maist sense o' them,
> Wha lets anither think and say,
> And in his turn takes the same way.
> I did na scirl, and clamour out;

[79] *Tree of Liberty*, July 11, 1801.

And ca' ye a fa'se loon and lout;
Or say your pipe had lost its drone,
Because ye play'd up Ettison,
Tho' a' the sense that man can feel,
O' wrang frae that misguided cheal,
I had o' whilk ye nothing knew,
And ought t'ave had still less to do;
Unless like piper to a laird,
At hame in some great castle yard,
Or droupit doup like dog at tether,
Ye blaw'd your cheeks up to a blether,
And play'd a spring just to his liking;
As bardies did to get a picking,
In ault times when the meal was scarce,
Frae failing har'st, or wasting wars.
Ah! no, my canty winsome Bruce,
Ye had nae sic a guid excuse.
It was just thoughtlessness and folly,
Though it strake me wi' melancholy,
To find my bardie take a part,
Against me wi' his tunefu' art,
And though it touch'd me wi' an ach,
Yet, I forgave it for the sake,
O' our relation to the muse.
The mason word has na sic use,
O' brother-hood, as this same charm,
And whilk is got without the harm,
O' raising, or o' laying De'el.
But I maun bid you now fareweel:
I dinna ken I shall say mare:
Am ganging frae this thoroughfare.
May ay the Muse, to you dispense,
The sowth o' sang, and pith o' sense,
And bony art to wale the words,
That make folk friends, and tighten cords.[80]

On August 22, a month after Brackenridge had announced that he was "ganging frae this thoroughfare," the *Tree of Liberty* published its last defense of his conduct, and added, "He leaves this

[80] *ibid.*, July 25, 1801.

place with his family for Carlisle on Monday next." He did not, however, take all his family with him. Henry Marie, aged fifteen, was left in Pittsburgh to study law.[81]

So Brackenridge, after having spent twenty years on the frontier, left the scene of his turbulent career. If he was in a reflective mood as he crossed the Alleghenies, he must have remembered with poignant melancholy the dreams of fame and success which had stirred him years before, as he left Philadelphia to make a name for himself in the West.

[81] H. M. Brackenridge, *Recollections of Persons and Places in the West*, p. 72.

CHAPTER XVIII

THE ATTACK ON THE JUDICIARY AND THE COMMON LAW

FOR about three years after his removal to Carlisle, Bracken-ridge evidently restricted his activities to his judicial duties. No doubt he appreciated an opportunity for peace after the political tumult of 1798-1801. He did not even devote himself strenuously to court business, as he left Philadelphia on account of the spread of yellow fever before the end of the September term, 1802.[1] But while he was thus keeping himself out of con-troversy and political activities, things were happening which af-fected his own reputation and affairs were drifting toward a condi-tion which would again call for the exercise of his satirical pen.

Throughout the nation the early years of Jefferson's adminis-tration were marked by an attack on the judiciary. Pennsylvania had its full share of this particular reform movement.

In January 1803 Judge Alexander Addison was subjected to a second trial—this time before the State assembly—on the charge of having illegally prohibited Judge Lucas from addressing the grand jury of the Allegheny County court in December 1800 and June 1801. In defending himself Addison asked to have the ad-dress which Lucas had tried to deliver read before the assembly. When permission was refused, he said that the whole affair "originated in the malice of a certain individual," and after a few general observations proceeded to make the accusation specific:

The person to whom I alluded I will name; it was Judge Bracken-ridge. And I ask him [Lucas] now, whether Mr. Brackenridge did not advise him to this business, and whether he did not know that Brackenridge wrote petitions, procured signatures, and particularly did he not advise to proceed by way of information to the supreme court in the first instance, and afterwards by impeachment here?

[1] *Modern Chivalry*, Part II, Vol. II, pp. 199-200.

The attorney general objected to this question, and Addison continued:

It is the first time in a criminal court that I ever knew a witness prohibited from answering a question of this kind. The question leads to this. Has the prosecution originated in principles of public good, or did it arise from motives of private malice? And when that is answered I mean to shew that this prosecution did not arise from motives of public good, but from personal malice, not on the part of members of the legislature, but from judge Brackenridge, who has not only a personal enmity to me, but has sworn vengeance against me, and that he set on Mr. Lucas as his instrument; that he assisted him in preparing the charges he wanted him to deliver to the grand juries, and has been the prime mover thro' the whole transaction, till its arrival at the present issue.

At this point Alexander J. Dallas, attorney for the prosecution, interrupted:

If the defendant is permitted to proceed in this mode, it will no longer be the trial of judge Addison, but the trial of judge Brackenridge; for I venture to assert if the assertions thrown out by the defendant can be substantiated, fouler aspersions were never proved on a judge. He asserts that the business has arrived at the present stage under the guidance of motives the most base and malignant that can be imputed. . . . No doubt the understanding of the Senate, although they are not practising lawyers, is sufficiently informed to know, that judge Brackenridge, who is not charged, and who, if he was, is not present to defend himself, cannot by any subterfuge or law fiction, be placed here on his trial in the room of the accused.[2]

Thus prevented from diverting the attention of the legislature to Brackenridge's activities, Judge Addison lost his case. He was removed from office and adjudged incapable of ever holding a judicial appointment in Pennsylvania. This trial was presumably the "more solemn occasion" with which Brackenridge had threatened Addison in the *Tree of Liberty*.

The next attack on the judiciary was directed against the supreme court of Pennsylvania, and grew out of a sentence for

[2] *The trial of Judge Addison*, pp. 50-3.

contempt of court pronounced against Thomas Passmore, a Philadelphia merchant. Passmore had taken out insurance on a ship. During a voyage the vessel sprang a leak, and Passmore abandoned it and applied for the insurance money. This the insurance company refused to pay, maintaining that the vessel had been unseaworthy when it was insured. The case was submitted to arbitrators, under a ruling of the court, and a decision was given in favor of Passmore. The insurance company then filed exceptions with the supreme court, and thus the case was technically continued. Passmore did not understand this; he believed that the underwriters were dishonestly withholding payment of money due him. In rage he posted a scurrilous note about the insurers in a coffee house. Since the case was not yet finally decided, the supreme court construed this action as contempt of court.[3] Brackenridge had been absent from Philadelphia on account of the yellow fever at the first hearing of the case, and at the time of the second hearing he was spending some time at home in Carlisle after holding a special court in Northumberland County. But he was present at the third and final hearing at which Passmore was fined fifty dollars and sentenced to one month in jail. At this session, after asking a few questions about the case and taking part in the discussion, he concurred in the decision.[4]

The court's construction of Passmore's action as contempt aroused public indignation. Impeachment proceedings were at once begun in the legislature against Judges Shippen, Yeates, and Smith—Brackenridge being excepted because of the slight part he had taken in the trial. At once, on March 22, 1804, Brackenridge wrote to the speaker of the house of representatives. After telling why he had been absent from the first hearings of the case, he said:

I was present on the third and last hearing of the case when some additional evidence was given and observations made; the presumption may have been that I did not take a part; I gave the case all the consideration I could at the time, and three-fourths of the court who

[3] *Report of the Trial and Acquittal of Edward Shippen . . . Jasper Yeates, and Thomas Smith,* passim.
[4] *Modern Chivalry,* Part II, Vol. II, pp. 201-3.

had heard all, declaring themselves fully satisfied, I saw no reason to warrant a dissent, but concurred. I cannot therefore distinguish my case in law from that of the other Judges, and in honor I would not: I am far from courting a prosecution, but am unwilling to incur the imputation of screening myself when in strictness equally liable, but I think it absolutely necessary for the credit of the republican administration that I should not be distinguished,[5] as there can be no stronger evidence than a man's own acknowledgment, the house will find no difficulty in a resolution to add my name to the list of impeached officers.[6]

This letter was read before the house on March 24 and was referred to a committee.[7] Two days later the committee reported as follows:

The committee after mature deliberation are of opinion that the name of Mr. Brackenridge cannot with propriety be added to the list of impeached officers, inasmuch as his acknowledgment of concurring in the judgment pronounced against Thomas Passmore, is too equivocal and ambiguous on which to predicate an accusation of high misdemeanor in office. . . . The letter however fully evinces a neglect of his duty by frequently deserting his seat on the bench, which ought not to pass unnoticed by the legislature: But what is more extraordinary (and the committee feel indignant at the idea) it contains evidence of a premeditated insult to the House by insinuating in a manner neither to be mistaken nor palliated, that the House was actuated in their proceedings against other judges by party motives. Such unfounded and unwarrantable insinuations (and more especially by a citizen to whom a trust of administering the laws is confided) must naturally tend to general suspicion amongst our constituents that the laws are the offspring of corruption and caprice, and not framed by the independent and unbiassed will of their Representatives, whereby the confidence of the people in their government might be impaired and the peace and harmony of the citizens destroyed; though the committee are of opinion that there is not sufficient evidence to support an impeachment against him, they believe nevertheless that he is not a proper person to discharge the important functions of a judge; and

[5] All members of the supreme court except Brackenridge were Federalists.
[6] *Modern Chivalry*, Part II, Vol. II, pp. 199-200.
[7] *House Journals*, 1803-04, p. 670.

that a reasonable excuse exists for the constitutional interposition of this House for his removal from office.

The report closed with a resolution calling for a committee to draft an address to the governor to remove Brackenridge from office.[8]

After this report was read a motion to include Brackenridge in the impeachment of the judges was defeated by a vote of 69 to 8, but the report of the committee asking for his removal was adopted by a vote of 54 to 24, and a committee was appointed to draw an address to the governor.[9] The next day, March 27, this committee presented its report to the house. In a petition which included the same points as the report quoted above the governor was requested to remove Brackenridge from office. The report was adopted by the assembly and a committee was appointed to present the petition to Governor McKean.[10]

It happened that the governor was out of Philadelphia at this time, and Brackenridge saw a copy of the petition before the committee had an opportunity to deliver it. As soon as he learned that McKean had returned, Brackenridge wrote him the following letter, dated April 7, 1804:

I have seen the address of two thirds of each house of the legislature, for the purpose of removing me from the bench of the supreme court of the state. I know that by the constitution your excellency is not bound to remove. But I chuse to remove myself and, under these circumstances, decline to hold the commission which I had the honour to receive from your excellency.—I have waited the coming of your excellency to the city to resign it.

The address states it to be in consequence of my letter to the speaker of the house of representatives, relative to a judgment of the supreme court, in the case of Thomas Passmore, for a trespass on the administration of justice; or, in the language of the law, a contempt. My situation was delicate—I had concurred in the judgment, though the evidence of this before the committee and the house was contradictory, and not positive. But it was the fact, and I could not, in honor, stand by, and not submit myself to the consequence. The house have con-

[8] *ibid.*, pp. 676-7.   [9] *ibid.*, pp. 677-8.
[10] *ibid.*, pp. 687-8.

strued it as a *contempt*; but I flatter myself that your excellency will think, that on the part of the house there may have been a misconception of the scope of my letter, or particular expressions. It was in my mind, as I have expressed it, to relieve the administration with the public, whose surmise was, though unjust, that the committee of the house had left me out through favor and affection. For, coming in with the republican administration, I was considered as belonging to it; not in the decisions of the bench, I hope, but in political sentiments.—No contempt was intended.[11]

Brackenridge had a few copies of this letter printed "at a confidential press." "But," he later said, "it was not delivered to the governor, and therefore is not to be considered as a resignation delivered or accepted, though it contains the honest sentiments of my heart on the occasion."[12]

It was provided in the constitution that the governor "might remove" a judge on such a petition as the house presented. The committee, however, rather bluntly told McKean that "may remove" really meant "must remove." But the governor, who was a rather Olympian person, besides being a staunch supporter of the judiciary, "promptly replied that he would have them know that 'may' sometimes meant 'won't.'" A newspaper report at the time said: "We are informed, that the governor has rejected the application made by the legislature, for removing judge Brackenridge, by observing, that the honourable body had 'done many things which they ought not to have done, and left undone those things which they ought to have done.'"[13]

During the period of the offensive against the judiciary, and for a year afterwards, the lawyers and the common law were also attacked. For some time there had been widespread dissatisfaction on account of the delays and expenses of court procedure. In 1802 the legislature passed a bill transferring cases for recovery of debts not exceeding one hundred dollars from the courts to the justices of the peace. Governor McKean promptly vetoed the bill, saying

[11] *Aurora*, March 22, 1805.   [12] *ibid.*
[13] *Pittsburgh Gazette*, April 13, 1804.

that it "would devolve the jurisdiction generally speaking upon persons of incompetent skill in the law."[14]

The next year the legislature received numerous petitions to substitute a system of referees for the regular courts.[15] The inhabitants of Lancaster County, for instance, complained "that a great portion of the time employed in the courts of quarter session are spent in the frivolous disputes of contentious people, to the prevention of a decision on civil actions." Governor McKean warned the legislature against this popular demand. In an address to the assembly on December 9, 1803, he said, "It is not to be disguised, that the defective administration of justice . . . remains a common topic of clamour and reproach." Then, after showing that the enormous increase in population and commerce had produced so much business for the supreme court that the four judges could no longer handle it, he concluded, "The spirit of litigation, the ruin of honest suitors, and the triumph of others equally culpable, can no longer be disingenuously ascribed to the machinations of a profession."[16]

Outside the assembly the attack on the lawyers was waged chiefly through the columns of the *Aurora* which was edited by William Duane, a contentious Irishman who was a leader in the radical wing of the Republican party. During 1804 and 1805 the paper contained many sharp criticisms of the legal profession.

"The time of the court and jury," said one contributor, "is wasted, to no other purpose but to display the ingenuity of the pleader."[17]

A writer who called himself "Sidney" said of the lawyers:

Already the citizens feel the weight of their *hands,* from one extremity of the state to the other, from Philadelphia to Fort Pitt, they form an indissoluble bond of association and union. The slightest shock at one end is instantly felt at the other. Cemented by one common principle, and impelled by the same interest, they have completely realized the fabled idea of the Macedonian phalanx. It is readily

[14] *Pennsylvania Archives,* Series IV, Vol. IV, pp. 496-7. See also *ibid.,* pp. 522 ff.; and *House Journals,* 1803-04, pp. 28-9.
[15] *House Journals,* 1803-04, p. 16.
[16] *ibid.,* pp. 28-9.   [17] *Aurora,* October 20, 1804.

acknowledged, the profession of the law includes in it, a large portion of the most respectable and distinguished men among us; and far be it from the present writer of this, to throw any reflections upon them, in their individual and private capacity. But like all other professions that of the law has its peculiar tendencies and *vices*.

And in defence of truth and liberty I will hazard the observation, that their numbers, their wealth, learning, talents, and general information, joined to their knowledge and experience in business, have already placed them on the *highest* ground in the state, with such a commanding view of the *promised land*, as to afford them a well grounded hope of taking posssession at some future day, of the country itself.[18]

An address to the legislature published in the *Aurora* said of court procedure:

1. The expences are so enormous, as to make lawsuits rather a contest of wealth, than an inquiry into, and establishment of justice.

2. The evasions are so numerous, and by technical forms so established, that the plainest and most incontestible questions stand for years on the records of our courts.

3. Unmeaning forms and absurd modes are so multifarious that a man of the soundest sense, and best judgement, is disqualified from defending his own rights, except through the medium of a hired pleader.[19]

Another plea to the legislature published in the *Aurora* thus sketched the progress of liberation from oppression in America:

Our revolution was promoted in an eminent degree by the existence of causes which after our triumph greatly tended to destroy or to render less fortunate for the people, the acquisition of a national character. After the establishment of our independence, we were endangered by the ambition of particular classes of men—the military soon after the peace of 1783—the *clerical body*—the body of *speculators*—and the *lawyer's corps,* have each severally aimed to obtain exclusive dominion over us. Had either of these corps succeeded, all the perils and sacrifices by which our liberties were acquired would have been as fruitless as the bloodshed in France, where the revolution has terminated after the most splendid events that history has to

[18] *Aurora,* November 9, 1804.   [19] *ibid.*

record only in the change of one family of despots for another—in elevating by means of a *military corps* its fortunate general on the ruins of the popular liberty.

We have been more fortunate than France. The military conspirators, the mercantile body, the clergy, the speculators—have all failed to reduce us to the condition of *vassals* and *villains;* we continue free citizens in despite of their reiterated attacks—but we have yet to bring to a due sense of their equality with the rest of their fellow citizens a corps, which from its peculiar character is at this time both formidable and dangerous to the public prosperity—I mean *lawyer's corps.*[20]

The trial of the judges of the supreme court brought this series of criticisms to a climax. The leading lawyers of Pennsylvania— A. J. Dallas, Jared Ingersoll, and Peter Duponceau—refused to serve the assembly as attorneys for the prosecution.[21] Thereupon the contributors to the *Aurora* became even more bitter.

"It is in vain to disguise it," said one writer, "either the people must determine at once to abandon their liberties, their property and their understandings to the discretion of the *lawyer's corps—* or bring them to a due sense of their equality with the rest of their fellow citizens."[22] Another said, "The spirit of independence of our lawyers is now established beyond all controversy, and the people ought to be congratulated that there has not been one found to aid the commonwealth."[23] An ironist suggested: "We shall . . . learn what the opinions of our lawyers are respecting the common law and our constitutions, and know whether we were 'our own worst enemies' in declaring independence and not remaining under the *protection* of the British *magna charta* and *bill of rights.*"[24]

The judges of the supreme court were acquitted at the trial. Their case was won by an appeal to the principles of the common law. At once the attack of the radicals was shifted from the law-

---

[20] *ibid.,* November 13, 1804.
[21] J. B. McMaster, *History of the People of the United States,* Vol. III, p. 159.
[22] *Aurora,* December 18, 1804.   [23] *ibid.,* December 24, 1804.
[24] *ibid.,* January 22, 1805.

yers to the common law itself. A writer for the *Aurora* made the
following comments on the case:

The actual issue was, whether the constitution established upon the
principles of the revolution of 1776 should remain—or, the dark,
arbitrary, unwritten, incoherent, cruel, inconsistent, and contradictory
maxims of the *common law* of England, should supersede them.

And the sentence on this trial has been such, that the liberty and
safety of the citizens of this commonwealth, hitherto the example of
the union, and the admiration of the ancient nations, are by the
verdict of *eleven senators,* of this commonwealth, put afloat upon
the unbounded and trackless ocean of the common law.[25]

The view was expressed that the puzzling legal terminology,
which the common person could not understand, was formulated
by the priests in the dark ages to mystify the people. "Amicus"
prophesied that resentment against the acquittal of the judges
would "hasten the permanent emancipation of the people from the
only remaining unaltered, imposture of the popish priesthood."[26]

As a substitute for the common law, which was embodied in
usages and in previous decisions of the courts, the radicals proposed a code, which, they thought, could be definite, compact, and
simple enough to be understood by the common man.[27]

This strong current of opposition to the established legal institutions, emanating from the left wing of the Republican party,
produced a situation which called for an ironical protest. Like the
frontiersmen of 1786 and 1794, and the Federalists of 1798, the
extreme democrats had departed from the path of good sense.
So, in the interests of rational democracy and of his own profession, Brackenridge wrote a continuation of *Modern Chivalry* with
specific reference to these topics which had agitated Pennsylvania
politics since 1802.

[25] *Aurora*, January 30, 1805.   [26] *ibid.*, February 9, 1805.
[27] *ibid.*, January 31, 1805.

CHAPTER XIX

"MODERN CHIVALRY, PART II": A DEFENSE OF THE LAW

THE new volume of *Modern Chivalry* was written in the summer of 1804, seven years after the publication of the volume dealing with the Whiskey Insurrection. At the end of the preceding instalment Teague O'Regan had been accepted in France as a genuine *sansculotte*. The continuation therefore began with a summary account of Teague's successful career during the reign of Robespierre. The Captain had been travelling all this time, and Teague at length returned to America and joined him "in the capacity of a pediseque, or foot-boy, as before."[1]

Before dealing with the main subject of the book, Brackenridge treated several other topics. First he satirized Billingsgate journalism. This satire, he said, had been written as far back as 1799 with reference to Cobbett's *Porcupine's Gazette*.[2] He had made Teague an editor because he himself had been subjected to excessive abuse in the newspapers.[3] It seems probable that, in preparing the volume of 1804, he altered and expanded the chapters written about *Peter Porcupine* in order to make them applicable to the writers who had attacked him in the *Pittsburgh Gazette* in 1800-01.

In this section of the narrative Captain Farrago came to a village and saw the clothing of the inhabitants hung out to air. A skunk had recently been brought to town to compete with Peter Porcupine's newspaper which had been annoying the villagers. Now a meeting was called to devise a means of getting rid of the skunk. It was suggested that a rival newspaper be set up in place of the obnoxious animal. The Captain seconded the motion and proposed an editor.

[1] *Modern Chivalry* (edition of 1804), Part II, Vol. I, pp. 3-4.
[2] *ibid.*, pp. 6-8, 24.   [3] *ibid.* (edition of 1815), Vol. IV, pp. 192-5.

"For," said he, "the very Teague O'Regan that you want is at hand; a waiter of mine. . . . The rogue has a low humour, and a sharp tongue; unbounded impudence. . . . He has all the low phrases, cant expressions, illiberal reflections, that could be collected from the company he has kept since he has had the care of my horse. . . . What is more he has been in France, and has a spice of the language, and a tang of Jacobinism in his principles, and conversation, that will match the contrary learning carried to an exhorbitant excess in Peter Porcupine. I do not know that you can do better than contribute to a paper of his setting up. He may call it the Mully-Grub, or some such title as will bespeak the nature of the matter it will usually contain."[4]

The next subject for satire was the economy program of Jefferson and Gallatin. When Captain Farrago came to a certain village in his travels, "it was obvious that little attention had been paid for some time to public works." When he asked the reason, "it was answered that the chief assistant burgesses some time ago had been extravagant; that the works, which, by the charter of incorporation they had power to project, were extensive, and the consequent taxes . . . were thought oppressive." The new administration not only curtailed public expenditure unduly, but also its democratic sentiment worked against efficiency. The Captain was told that "in the works projected, the people insist that no man shall be consulted in his own occupation."[5]

The equalitarian doctrine of the extreme democrats had induced a distrust of everything except the native sagacity of the common man. Hence higher education and professional training were generally suspect. Brackenridge introduced an incident which illustrated this popular attitude. "It came so far," he said at the climax, "that an incendiary proposed to abate or burn down the college. Because, said he, all learning is a nuisance." Captain Farrago persuaded the mob to be content with expelling the schoolmaster. The college building, he said, would be needed for a hospital after learning and law were abolished and anarchy ensued.[6]

---

[4] *Modern Chivalry,* (edition of 1804), pp. 24-6.
[5] *ibid.,* pp. 43-4.   [6] *ibid.,* p. 58.

The next incident showed, with a satirist's exaggeration, what would be the logical result of the popular prejudice against everything English if it were applied in the church. The mob, after being dissuaded from burning the college, was proposing to burn the church instead.

It is not our intention to abolish Christianity, said a grave man amongst them, but to put down the preacher at this place; who is not an American republican, but quotes the English commentators in his sermons. . . . We wish to abolish these, and have nothing but our own commentaries. Are we to be drawing our proofs from under a monarchy, and referring to tracts and essays published in Great Britain? Have we no sense of our own to explain texts of Scripture, and apply doctrines? It is time to emancipate ourselves from these shackles, and every man to be his own expounder, or at least to confine our clergy to the Bible and the Psalm book, or such of our divines, as have written amongst ourselves, and are of our own manufacture in a republican government.

Captain Farrago replied to this republican nationalist:

Religion is of no government. Wines are the better for being brought over seas, and our best brandies are from Monarchies. Where was the cloth of that coat made? Will you reject a good piece of stuff because it came through the hands of an aristocratic weaver? These are false ideas of what is right and useful to mankind. The common law is not the worse for having been the common law of England, and our property and birth right which our ancestors brought with them; nor is our Bible the worse for having been translated under James the first of England. . . .[7]

In his comment on these scenes Brackenridge said:

It will be natural for a reader to apply in his own mind, the history of the Village and its agitations, to the state where we live; and it will be asked, what ground is there for the idea, that we talk of pulling down Churches, or burning Colleges. There is no ground so far as respects churches; but it is introduced by way of illustration. . . . Give us the gospel in a narrow compass, and have no more preaching about it. This would be no more than is said of the law.

[7] *ibid.*, p. 61.

Why cannot we have it in a pocket-book, and let every man be his own lawyer? . . .

I will not say that people talk of burning colleges; but they do not talk much of building them up. . . . It is not the want of learning that I consider a defect; but the *contempt of it.*[8]

In this volume of *Modern Chivalry* Brackenridge also satirized again the people's preference for uneducated politicians. When the Captain was engaged in conversation at a fair, the discussion was interrupted by the following vociferous soliloquy of a man who was clenching his fists in extreme agitation:

I a scholar! I a learned man! It is a falsehood. See me reading! He never saw me read. I do not know a B from a bull's foot. But this is the way to injure a man in his election. They report of me that I am a scholar! It is a malicious fabrication. I can prove it false. It is a groundless insinuation. What a wicked world is this in which we live. I a scholar! I am a son of a whore if I ever opened a book in my life. O! The calumny; the malice of the report. All to destroy my election.

A bystander interrupted and asked, "Were you not seen carrying books?" The distressed candidate answered:

Aye, two books that a student had borrowed from a clergyman. But did I look into them? I will take my Bible oath I never looked into them. . . . I am an illiterate man, God be praised, and free from the sin of learning, or any wicked art, as I hope to be saved; but here a report is raised up, that I have dealings with books, that I can read. O the wickedness of this world! Is there no protection from slander, and bad report? God help me! Here I am, *an honest republican; a good citizen,* and yet it is reported of me that I read books. . . . I am ruined; I am undone; I shall lose my election; and the good will of all my neighbours, and the confidence of posterity.

Captain Farrago, overhearing this monologue, thought to himself, "It is a strange thing that *we admire learning in a pig; and undervalue it in a man.*"[9]

Together with this popular distrust of learning and professional training Brackenridge presented a view of the prevailing

[8] *Modern Chivalry,* pp. 184-7.   [9] *ibid.,* pp. 141-2.

radical spirit. His conception of the temper of the time comes out most clearly in an account of a discussion at a public meeting which Captain Farrago attended. The orator of the occasion said:

"A madness prevails at present. It will be but a fortnight's continuance. When the people get a thing into their heads, the best way is to let them go on. They will come to themselves by and by."

"But in the mean time they will do a great deal of harm," Captain Farrago observed.

"It is in the atmosphere," continued the orator.

"Is it imported, or of domestic origin?" inquired a man in the crowd.

A bystander replied:

"It may be imported, or it may be of domestic origin; for both abroad and at home, we have examples of such madness occasionally breaking out, owing to some subtil gas in the holds of vessels, or that breeds in our own streets. It may come from France or Ireland: but what is there to hinder it of springing up here, where there are as good materials to work upon, as on the other side of the water. Human nature is the same everywhere."[10]

Against this background of opposition to the established order in education, church, and state, Brackenridge sketched his view of the law. His mouthpiece is a blind lawyer, to whom Captain Farrago appeals for legal information on several occasions. In a typical scene the Captain stated the popular view as follows:

What is this common law which you speak of, and why cannot it be abolished? The common law of England! Why not a common law of our own; now that we have an independent government?

The blind lawyer, speaking for Brackenridge, answered:

It is our common law. We derive it from a common source with the inhabitants of Britain. Shall the people on that side of the water alone possess this jurisprudence, which our common ancestors possessed, just because we have left the island? It was because our birthright to this law was questioned that we resisted in war, and declared our independence. The representation is a principle of the common

10 *ibid.*, pp. 70-1.

law, and this right was denied to the colonies. The right of trial by jury is a principle of the common law, and this in some cases, was abridged, in others, taken away altogether. On what ground were these defended? On the ground that they were our inheritance by the common law. . . . Abolish the common law? Why not abolish the art of medicine, because it has been cultivated in Great Britain?[11]

The opposition to the judiciary is also portrayed. "The clamour became general, down with the judges." The people of "the village" demanded that Teague O'Regan be put on the bench. They felt that he, being ignorant of "Hooks' and Crooks' reports," would apply plain common sense to his duties.[12]

The prejudice against learning and the revolt against law are most sharply satirized in a song which was sung by a crowd following "O'Dell the revolutionist"—a song which Brackenridge ironically composed as the "Ça Ira, or Marseilles hymn" of the American radicals:

> Down with the sessions, and down with the laws
> They put me in mind of the schoolmaster's taws.
> There's nothing in nature that gives such disgust,
> As force and compulsion to make a man just.
> Hillelu; Billelu, set me down aisy. Etc.
>
> A lawyer's a liar; old Sooty his father;
> He talks all day long, a mere jack-a-blather.
> His books, and his papers may all go to hell,
> And make's speech there, sings Lary O'Dell.
> Hillelu, &c.
>
> The state is a vessel, and hoop'd like a tub;
> And the adze of the cooper it goes dub, a dub.
> But hooping and coopering, is fitting for fools;
> *Away wid all learning,* and shut up the *schools.*
> Hillelu, &c.[13]

In his comment on this American *Marseillaise* Brackenridge said:

The popular mind does not easily avert itself when descending an inclined plain of opinion. Popular ballads are an index of the public

[11] *Modern Chivalry,* pp. 66-7.   [12] *ibid.,* pp. 92-3.   [13] *ibid.,* pp. 146-7.

mind. Hence we see that an antipathy to laws, lawyers and judges, is the *ton* at present; and also that œconomy is the ruling passion of the time. Yet in all things, there may be an excess. *For the people are not always right.*[14]

Also, later in the volume, he reverted to this ballad and said:

In the song which I put into the mouth of O'Dell, I have nothing else in view but to give a picture of the excess of the spirit of reform. It is taken from the life; for though not in verse, yet I have heard similar sentiments expressed by the uninformed.[15]

To counteract this disintegrating radical movement Brackenridge proposed a humanistic antidote. "Political studies," he said, "ought to be the great object with the generous youth of a republic; not for the sake of profit; but for the sake of judging right, and preserving the constitution inviolate. *Plutarch's Lives is an admirable book for this purpose.* I should like to see an edition of 10,000 volumes bought up in every State."[16]

Besides recommending Plutarch, he offered his own book as a contribution to the political education of the people. In concluding the volume he said:

In what is hinted at, in several pages of the preceding chapters, of hostility to laws and a disposition to overthrow establishments, and judges, I have in view, not the proceedings of a public body, but the prejudices of the people. It is the talk out of doors that I respect. And this is the fountain which is to be corrected. Representatives must yield to the prejudices of their constituents even contrary to their own judgment. It is therefore into this pool *that I cast my salt. It is to correct these waters that I write this book.*[17]

After he had completed this volume, he wrote the following personal confession with reference to it:

These concluding pages I had written, and had printed off, to this point of the game, if I may so express myself this 19th of November 1804; and had intended to publish; but it struck me that it might give offence to the legislature, and it might be as well to let it rest

14 *ibid.*, p. 147. 15 *ibid.*, p. 191.
16 *ibid.*, p. 162. 17 *ibid.*, p. 191.

until next spring after they had risen; and if any thing should give umbrage; though I cannot possibly see what, they might have a summer to think of it before they met again, and so could do nothing hastily. I asked the printer boys what they thought of it. For I could communicate to no one else lest it should get out. In the language of John Bunyan; in the preface in verse to his Pilgrim's Progress; which I remember something of, having read it 30 years ago,

> Some said John print it; others said no.
> —And I said not so.

It is said of Molière, that he recited his comedies to an old woman in his house; and when she smiled the audience never failed to smile also. This is an appeal to simple nature. On that ground I took the opinion of an old man about the shop, that wore spectacles. It was his opinion "that it might be thought *I was making a dash at somebody.*" He thought the lawyers[18] and the Irish might take offence; and perhaps the legislature themselves for any thing he knew. This last was the most delicate consideration, and at the present time, I would not think it advisable to add the bar and the Irish to the weight against me. For that reason, nonum prematur, say in mensem. Six or nine months hence, it may be safer to let it come forth. . . .

This book then rests for a period; lest the publication should *do myself harm.* It will depend on circumstances whether I do not burn it altogether; or put it off at the book fair, with some New-England man, who will give it a circulation in the Northern States; and keep it away from Pennsylvania.

How a man feels himself cramped in such a fear, and trembling of mind! I am positively more afraid at this moment of the mistake of the honest, than I was of the resentment of the *knave* at a former period. During the reign of terror my strictures were very free; but I begin almost to call this a reign of fear, which is the same thing with the former reign.

A word to the critic seems necessary in some part of a book. It happens to come here at the end of it. It is now ten years since I last put pen to paper in anything above dissertation in the gazette or a newspaper paragraph. I am well aware that there will be found a

---

[18] Although Brackenridge was defending his profession, he agreed with the reformers in thinking that the lawyers were too much given to long speeches to display their eloquence. See *Modern Chivalry* (edition of 1819), Vol. II, pp. 95-6.

great falling off since my last about that time. I am not conscious to myself that the vigour of my mind has abated in matters of judgment; for as would seem from the story in Gill Blass [*sic*], I shall not be the first to discover that. But I must acknowledge that I am not sensible of the same powers of imagination in that respect.

Non sum qualis eram.

No wonder; for the snow of age has come upon my head; and winter has taken possession of my brow. My fancy is as cold as it was once warm. My inclination leads me to metaphysics, chiefly. But that subject is exhausted; or, so many have written well, that it is discouraging to come after them.

It is on account of the decline of fancy, that I have confined myself in this volume to mere narrative, which is the province of old age. . . . There is some attempt at humour; but seldom have I been able to reach it. . . . Nevertheless it may serve to let people know that I am alive. . . .

It will be observable that Latin quotations abound more than a reader of English may be disposed to relish. But the fact is, that I have forgot almost all the reading of my middle age; and recollect chiefly my academic studies. Hence it is that the classics are more in my head, than Shakespeare or Milton.[19]

Although he had decided not to issue the volume that had just been printed, Brackenridge proceeded to write another one dealing with the same topics. In this book, which contains a miscellany of incidents and comments, he took particular pains to explain his conception of a rational democracy equally removed from aristocracy and radical democracy. Early in the book he shows how the two extremes had alternated in Pennsylvania since the Declaration of Independence.

It would be a gratification to myself, and it might be of use to others, to give some notes of *political history in this state*. Those *just grown up*, or lately come amongst us, from abroad, would better understand, why it is that *democracy* has been occasionally the order of the day, and again put down. It has always had numbers on its side, and yet has not always possessed the administration. I use the term democracy as contradistinguished from the aristocracy; that is, a union of men of wealth, and influence.

19 *ibid.*, pp. 213-16.

In the state constitution of 1776, the democracy prevailed in carrying a *single legislature;* but this laid the foundation of their overthrow; because experience proved that it was a wrong. . . .

The constitution of 1776, gave way to that of 1790, and the aristocracy obtained the ascendancy; or rather having obtained it, they brought about a convention and carried the constitution of 1790; *which is the present.*

But connecting themselves with the errors of the administration of the federal government, in 1797, 1798, they lost the state administration, and the *democracy prevailed.*

Five years has it retained the administration; and will an interminable time, provided *that wise measures are pursued,* and justice done.

This, I am not addressing to the legislative or executive power of the government; but *to the people.* It is for them my book is intended. Not for the representatives of a year, *but for themselves.* It is Tom, Dick, and Harry in the woods that I want to read my book. I do not care though the delegated authorities never see it.[20]

Being a member of the Republican party and believing that this party would retain control if wise measures were pursued, Brackenridge was trying to recall the people to a reasonable democratic philosophy.

In this volume he again used the blind lawyer as an oracle. Captain Farrago, visiting the lawyer, "ventured to put the question, whence the rage against the Judges? Had it always been the case or was it a late matter that had broken out? Did it depend upon moral causes; or was it a matter of accident unaccountable for by man?"

The blind lawyer replied:

There is in the human mind, at all times, a disposition to throw off shackles and revert to the natural simplicity of early ages. . . . Down with the lawyers, has been the language of the human heart ever since the first institution of society. It breaks out into action, some times, as the history of Jack Cade informs us.

A spirit of reform is, unquestionably, a salutary temper of the times; because there is at all times, need of reformation. This is the angel

[20] *Modern Chivalry* (edition of 1805), Part II, Vol. II, pp. 9-10.

that descends into the pool, and troubles the waters; so that 'he who slippeth in afterwards, is made whole. But troubling does not mean muddying the waters; but giving them motion, and exciting a current. . . .[21]

In further conversation he continued:

The idea of reform delights the imagination. Hence reformers are prone to reform too much. . . . A great enemy to a judicious reform is a distrust of those skilled in the subject of reform; and yet there is ground of distrust where those skilled in the subject, have any possible interest in the reform itself. One would suppose that an old lawyer out of practice, one who had been a judge, and no longer on the bench, might be trusted in all questions of amendment of the judicial system. But the legislative body is the organ of amendments; and it is natural for one branch to endeavour to absorb the independence of another, or to be suspected of it. Hence jealousy and distrust, which an enlightened policy can alone dissipate.

Captain Farrago replied:

But the present idea of reform seems to be to pull down altogether. I do not know that you will see *down with judges* just written upon fence rails; or scored on tavern windows; but it is a very common language, among the more uninformed of the community. The danger is that it may be mistaken *for the voice of the people,* and under that idea, influence the constituted authorities.[22]

After writing such a criticism of the extremists Brackenridge took pains to give assurance that he himself was a genuine democrat.

But if justice cannot find a *certain residence in a democratic government, she must leave the earth.* I despair of finding it anywhere else. But I have felt tyranny, or have thought to have felt it, even in the courts of justice. I had thought that I felt it, and left a certain bar prematurely on that account[23]: so that I am not one of those who lean against *the investigation of judicial conduct.* It is my object only to assist the democracy, I mean not so much the tribunals that are to judge, as the *people that delegate the judgment.*[24]

[21] *ibid.,* p. 34.   [22] *ibid.,* pp. 36-7.
[23] This evidently refers to Brackenridge's trouble with Judge Addison.
[24] *Modern Chivalry,* Part II, Vol. II, p. 55.

In this part of *Modern Chivalry,* as in the early volumes, Teague
O'Regan is presented as a favored aspirant to important positions.
Having been annoyed by crude journalism and by the public demand for arbitrators without legal training, Brackenridge showed
Teague as a candidate for an editorship and for a judicial appointment. In this episode Captain Farrago is thus reprimanded by "a
man in leather breeches":

Captain, is it fair to attempt a burlesque on the democracy, by intrud-
ing your servant on the public mind, for a post of profit or of honour?
It is true, the greater part of us, are but plain men, and illiterate,
if you chuse to have it so; but yet, it is to be hoped, we are not just so
hard run for persons capable of civil employments among ourselves,
as to be under the necessity of recurring to your bog trotter.

The Captain, rather angry, replied:

Heavens! Has it not been yourselves, that have proposed the matter, and brought all the trouble on my head respecting it? I did, it is
true, in the first instance, suggest the idea of putting him at the head
of a paper; but it was without consideration; and I retracted it, both
in my own judgment, and in my words, to you, immediately after. For
though the press has been degraded *by such as he is, in that capacity,*
yet I was not willing to contribute to the evil. The making him a
judge came from yourselves; it was an idea that never started in
my brains. It was your own burlesque, not mine.

Then, uttering Brackenridge's conception of his own career, the
Captain continued:

Why should I undervalue democracy; or be thought to cast a
slur upon it, I that am a democrat myself. What proof have I given
you of this? *My works shew my faith.* It is true that I have not undervalued learning, or exclaimed against lawyers, or joined in the cry
of down with judges; but, take the tenore of my life and conversation,
since the foundation of the village. I was at the first settlement of it.
Did I engross lots of ground? Has there been a necessity of an agrarian law in my case? Have I speculated on the wants of men, by fore-
stalling, or regrating? Have I made haste to be rich? . . . Who has
heard me call out against foreigners; or fixing a prejudice against
emigrants?

Brackenridge understood that his presentation of Teague might offend not only the people in general but the Irish immigrants in particular. Just as Captain Farrago finished his affirmation of democracy an Irishman came forward and said:

Captain, all dis, dat you tell us, is very well. But is it a gentle ting, to trow a ridicule upon de whole Irish nation, by carrying about wid you, a bog-trotter, just as you would an allegator, or some wild cratur dat you had catched upon de mountains, to make your game of paple dat have de same brogue upon deir speech; and de same dialect upon deir tongues, as he has? By de holy faders, it is too much in a free country, not to be suffered. . . .

The Captain replied, perhaps rather speciously:

Far be it from me to undervalue Ireland, or to mean disrespect to the nation. On the contrary, it was from good will to the people, that I have taken the notice of this young man that I have. Much less have I intended a reflection upon a democratic government, in the countenance I have given to the proposition of advancing him in grades, and occupations.[25]

In this volume Brackenridge also continued to defend the Anglo-American common law against the reformers who demanded a new and simple code based on reason rather than on tradition:

Common sense, or reason, doubtless, is a ground of the common law, and the great cases that occur in the relations and transactions of men; but it is more than common sense, otherwise, the knowledge of it would be possessed by all men in proportion as they had common sense. It is not an easy thing to explain to the common mind, what the common law is; nor does it seem to be understood, even by literary men who have not made it a particular study. I observe that even journalists of great acuteness of mind hold it out as a grievance in these commonwealths;[26] whereas it is considered by sages of other countries, as the best system of jurisprudence the world ever saw. ·. . .

Where is the common law to be found? You will get a pretty good view of it in Blackstone's Commentaries; but could we not employ a few wise men, such as perhaps we might find in the state of Pennsylvania,

25 Modern Chivalry, pp. 68-71.
26 Brackenridge is here referring to such journalistic writings as have been quoted from the Aurora above, pp. 247 ff.

to make a code entirely new, and by an act of the legislature declare it law. Thus laying aside the common law, just as if no system had ever existed. The thing is impossible. *For it is the experience of man that has begot it.* . . .

The common law, is a system of reason and justice, and a most valuable possession. The abridging it or changing a principle is dangerous. It requires the hand of a workman who knows every pin in the building, and can tell what to substitute in the place of what is taken away.[27]

Part of this volume also is devoted to an ironical treatment of the popular distrust of learning. The following episode in Captain Farrago's travels presents his satirical version of the situation:

They were now entering the Lack-learning settlement, where a great uproar had been made on account of their coming. It had been given out that their company consisted of *Scholars* and *Lawyers*. This, either from mistake, or the design of wags, who liked to see misconception, even though it occasioned mischief. A multitude had got together, with sticks and stones, to obstruct the march into their country.

It was at the opening of a defile they were met, and could proceed no farther. The Captain himself, advanced with a flag, and with great difficulty obtained a parley, and a conference. "Friends, and countrymen," said he, "what do you mean? There are no scholars among us, save a Latin schoolmaster, and he is going to become an honest man, in a new country. We have no lawyers: not a soul that has ever been in a court, unless indeed as culprits, and to be tried for misdemeanours; and that, I take it, is not likely to give them a strong prejudice in favour of the administration of justice. Here is Tom the Tinker; Will Watlin; Harum Scarum the duelist; O'Fin, the Irishman, and several others, that have no predeliction for scholarship. It will be but little learning they will introduce among you.

In a discussion which followed, a German farmer expressed the backwoods opinion of educated preachers and lawyers:

De clergy are de biggest rogues of de two. An honest Sherman minister widout larning, ish better. But de lawyers are de tyvil wid deir pooks, and deir talks in de courts; and sheats people for de money. I sticks to de blantation, and makes my fence. Learning ish good for

27 *Modern Chivalry* (edition of 1805), Part II, Vol. II, pp. 197-9.

noting; but to make men rogues. It is all a contrivance to sheat people.[28]

The journalistic organ of the extreme democrats was, as has been seen, the Philadelphia *Aurora*. In the following passage, Brackenridge dealt with this paper:

Under this idea of the effect of a journal to guide, or mislead, the public mind, the governor solicited an interview with the editor of the *Twilight*. After such introductory compliments and observations as may be presumed on the occasion, the governor insensibly drew him into a conversation on the subject of the press, and his gazette in particular. "Editor," said he, "your good sense I know, and your patriotism; but I am afraid of your being a little too much carried away with the spirit of the times, oeconomies; dissolution of the courts, disuse of codes of law, and invectives against lawyers. There is a medium in all things. This may be carried too far. Would you not think it prudent to restrain this down-hill speed a little? As to attacks on the administration, or the policy of measures merely executive, or even the constitutionality, or expediency of a law, I should think the greatest freedom may be used; or the public conduct of men in office may be canvassed; though, by the bye, I should not think the public had any interest in their amours, their costume, as for instance the art of their pantaloons, or the color of their breeches; or pecadilloes, even in the breaches of decorum."[29]

As Brackenridge neared the end of this volume of *Modern Chivalry* he again realized that his work would offend a large and excitable portion of the public. He was more courageous now, however, than he had been a few months earlier when he finished the first volume of the continuation. He now wrote:

When I had written and printed off the first volume of this second part, which was in the course of last summer, looking over it, at some distance of time, I concluded to burn the impression. But not being near a fire, it escaped; and in the mean time, I began to consider, that it was paying but a bad compliment to the understanding of a democratic people, who are in the habit of freedom of speech, among themselves, and allow great liberties, not to say licentiousness to the press,

[28] *ibid.*, pp. 97-9.   [29] *ibid.*, p. 162.

to suspect them of being so intolerant, and so ready to take offence, when it was not meant. Hence it was that I have taken courage to write on, and thought that if it did give offence, I might as well be hanged for an old sheep as a lamb.[30]

So the book was issued at Carlisle in 1805. The two volumes were bound together, the first bearing the date 1804 on the title page and the second the date 1805.

On January 29, just before the publication of the book, Brackenridge received word that the judges of the supreme court had been acquitted.[31] He added an "epilogomina" relating to the case. In the course of his remarks he inquired, "What is it produces a third party, but the excesses of that to which the individuals belonged?"[32] The question was pertinent to the condition of Pennsylvania politics in 1805. The extremes of the reformers had by this time produced a division in the Republican party. It was with this situation that Brackenridge was to be concerned during the next few months.

[30] *Modern Chivalry*, p. 188.   [31] *ibid.*, p. 215.   [32] *ibid.*, p. 224.

CHAPTER XX

THE CAMPAIGN OF 1805

SINCE the radicals had failed in their attack on the supreme court and since their projects for reforming the legal system encountered the determined resistance of Governor McKean, they next made an effort to fill the State offices with men of their own choice. They appeared to be in control of the Republican party of the State, and the Federalists were too weak to offer serious opposition; therefore the moderate Republicans withdrew and formed a third party which was contemptuously called the Tertium Quid by the extremists. In the campaign of 1805 the radical reformers were especially eager to elect a sympathetic governor and to secure a revision of the State constitution. These political rearrangements would, they hoped, assure the success of their next attempt to overhaul the legal machinery of the State. The plans for the campaign were formulated, according to the custom of the time, by a party caucus of State legislators.

The radical Republicans nominated Simon Snyder, a man of the people, to succeed the haughty McKean. They also proposed that a convention be called to revise the State constitution. The Quids nominated McKean and opposed the convention. Brackenridge allied himself with the Quids, and, in the course of the campaign, contributed several articles to their newspaper—the *Freeman's Journal.*

His first effort was to defend McKean against the popular prejudice. Unfortunately the governor had lately offended the radicals and the populace by a very impolitic remark. He had been in conference with a group of Republican legislators, and, wishing to change the subject of conversation, had commented on an item in a Yorktown newspaper which he happened to have in his hand. The article was an address to the people by a former member of congress who had failed to be reelected. "I am now returned to the plow," the ex-congressman had said, "but I shall do my utmost at elections to prevent all men of talents, lawyers, or rich men from being elected." Referring to the author of this sentiment, McKean said, "As he is no longer a member of congress I suppose we shall have him and other such clodpoles of the same pernicious sentiments, returned as delegates to the projected convention."[1]

The Republican assemblymen immediately published the remark. Soon the public was hearing and reading in the Democratic press that Governor McKean had called the people clodhoppers.

On July 16, 17, and 18 Brackenridge published a defense of McKean, entitled "The Standard of Liberty," in the *Freeman's Journal*. He referred only lightly and warily to the governor's remark about clodpoles, although, in view of his own experiences in the Pennsylvania assembly, he must have agreed secretly that the epithet was deserved. He chose rather to defend McKean's platform. Especially he argued for the governor's declared policy of maintaining the legal system of juries, judges, and lawyers against the popular demand for non-professional arbitrators. He also supported his proposal to eliminate the admitted inefficiency of the courts by increasing the number of judges. Summarizing his views on these points, he said:

An administration of justice by men ignorant of law, produces timidity in them; gives rise to illiberal, and enduces dishonest practice in the profession. This aided by the incompetency of prothonotaries; or collusion with sheriffs, and their deputies, invites and supports craft, and that species of talent that is not derived from books or a good education. Muddy waters produce ignoble fish; the trout and salmon love the clear stream; so that Governor McKean looks to an administration of justice in his idea of improving *the judicial system*, that would give able judges, and a competent number of them, which would in fact lessen controversy by the greater certainty of law,

[1] *Aurora*, June 3, 1805.

and dispatch of trial, and would, at the same time, reduce the number, but increase the talents, and the reputation of the lawyers.[2]

Even in this campaign document Brackenridge did not hesitate to state frankly his view of the people:

Certain it is that the whole body politic have not the means of information upon a great scale. It is in contemplation of law only that they are infallible, and whatever the people do is right. Individuals in their respective occupations have not the opportunity to investigate great questions. It is the part of a faithful representative *to respect the rights, but to distrust the impulses of the people.*[3]

After supporting the governor by serious argument in this long article, Brackenridge turned to his habitual pleasantry. On July 29 he published in the *Freeman's Journal* "Ironical Reasons for a New Governor and Constitution." In a representative passage of this piece he makes the radical democrats say with reference to the democratic victories of 1799-1802:

What have we got by an election struggle, a number of us? There are no proscriptions as in other wars; no estates forfeited; none to be sold for a song as in France. The rich keep their estates as in a time of peace and security. What is it to them to be kept out of representative bodies. They stay at home and mind their farms, or their occupations, and get richer, under all the reforms we have brought about. Some of them go so far as to say they are not dissatisfied with the administration of McKean. Nor, is this to be wondered at; for his object is a stable government, and a settled order of things, which coincides precisely with what they want. No wonder they are coming over to him, because he has gone over to them, or at least met them half-way. What use is there in a revolution unless there is something to be gained by people that do not like to work; and this is the case while the government remains in the hands of those who are opposed to an equable division of property, and to the

2 *The Standard of Liberty*, p. 21. The references in this chapter are to an undated reprint of these articles in book form under the title *The Standard of Liberty*. C. F. Heartman's *Bibliography of the Writings of Hugh Henry Brackenridge* gives the date of this volume as 1802. That date is impossible, as the articles were first published in the *Freeman's Journal* in the summer of 1805.

3 *The Standard of Liberty*, p. 24.

taking what another has to spare, because he has more than enough. . . .

It is not all at once that we can get to the true spirit of democracy. What we have amongst us, yet, must undergo another process. We have seen in France, that whatever numbers they had, and however rapidly they wrought, it was a length of time, and a work of several revolutions before they brought the fermentation to a proper height, and produced the real jacobinical stuff, that has made so much noise in Europe since. There is a squeamishness in our people yet, that must go before they can be said to have proper stomachs for a government without moderation.[4]

On August 1 and 2 the *Freeman's Journal* published a campaign article by Brackenridge entitled "Amicus Amicorum, or a Friend of the Friends of the People." It added nothing material to the political argument of the series.

His last campaign article, published on August 3, was an attempt to win Federalists over to the Tertium Quid. In order to show that he and his party were reasonable people he gave a sketch of his own relations to the Federalists since 1787. He had, he said, been with them on the question of adopting the Federal Constitution, but he had disagreed with them in their financial policies and on their attitudes toward France and England. In State politics he had opposed the alteration of the old constitution of 1776, but when the constitution of 1790 was once adopted he had approved and supported it. Now he called upon the Federalists to join with the Quids in order to protect that constitution against the radical Republicans.[5]

The result of this campaign was a victory for the Quids. Governor McKean was reelected by a majority of 4766. Since the moderate party was now in power, the revision of the legal institutions of Pennsylvania was to be accomplished by men of law rather than by radical reformers.

[4] *The Standard of Liberty*, pp. 34-5.   [5] *ibid.*, p. 52.

CHAPTER XXI

AT HOME AND ON CIRCUIT

AFTER the period of conflict with the extreme democrats Brackenridge appears to have enjoyed a period of leisure. From this time we have glimpses of his personal life in his own confessions and in the reminiscences of his son.

In 1806 he published a collection of his journalistic and other minor compositions in a volume entitled *Gazette Publications*. In the introduction to the book he commented on his literary accomplishments as follows:

But I do not flatter myself that my memory will survive me long. It is sufficient; at least it is the utmost that I can expect, that it can survive a few years. And even this not without some pains to make it live. For I do not conceive myself to be, what I will acknowledge, I was once disposed to think myself, a thing endued with faculties above the capacities of ordinary mortals. But had it not been that I had some idea of this kind, I would not have made the exertions that I have made. For since the discovery of my mistake, I feel myself sinking into indolence; and considering only how I shall get through the world, the small remainder of it that lies on my hands.

It is of little consequence to me what mankind think of my talents provided I can get ease, and quiet living. It may seem then strange that I should collect this trash, and put it together in a volume. It is not with a view to a long period of posthumus existence, but that of a few years amongst my immediate descendants, who may take some little pride in preserving the memory of a literary man, and this for their own sakes; for though my fame must fall short of giving luster to a country, yet it may throw a little light on a small circle of immediate descendants; and endure, perhaps, for a generation after I am gone. By a generation I do not mean any determinate number of years; but the age of a child who may preserve a volume of these publications. For as to grandchildren, I give it up. I shall not be remembered by them. So far am I from anticipating immortality, in the language of Poets, that I think 20 years will about do; and I am resigned to this, finding that with all the pains I have taken, I can make no better of it. But who could know unless he had tried? But I am willing to give myself the best chance, even for the few years of recollection that may be in my power to add to my name. Memoriam nostri quam maximo longam efficere.

I feel some regret that I have lost many things occasionally written, and thrown by in manuscript, or appearing in fugitive pamphlets in print. Some of them, which is not saying much, probably better than any thing which is preserved. I have no idea that this volume or any part of it will be republished, but it is something to have seen the light at all, or to have born [sic] to be collected; this I do not believe it will do, so as to defray the expences of printing; but it may go a certain length towards it; and the self-love of the author must supply the rest. Who knows after all but that even an hundred years hence a copy of this impression may be found in an old library among scarce books, and be valued because it is the only one remaining. It has been always a matter of amusement to me to be rummaging amongst old and scarce books, to see in what manner the human mind had employed itself in times past. It is astonishing to think on what a variety of subjects books have been published since the art of printing has been invented. I remember to have heard old Doctor John Witherspoon, Principal of the New Jersey College, make this remark, and say that he was particularly struck with this in looking over an old library in Britain, and finding a Treatise in Latin "De humani capitis Caesarie."

It is true, what I have collected here consists of nothing but shreds; but I have been always fond of miscellanies, and it was not so much the value as the variety that pleased me. Hence it is that I have supposed these scraps may afford some amusement; especially if they are accompanied with observations, as they occasionally will be, which will throw some light upon the affairs of men and the history of the time.

In concluding the volume Brackenridge again commented on his career as follows:

In looking over this book, there is no part with which I am less pleased than the Introduction. There would seem to be vanity under the guise of humility. By the word "exertions" in that preface, I do not mean the labours of my composition, but my efforts in life which have been successful to a certain extent. But even with regard to my literary attempts, though I cannot apply to myself the gratulation of the Poet,

"Exegi monumentum aere perennius."

Yet the selections here made, may be considered as remembrances of some short duration. True it is, that having had perhaps too great a desire of distinction in early life, I may have less now than is necessary to application; but my ambition was never for place or office; nevertheless, I begin to think it had been better to have set less store by the opinion of the world as to my flight or song, and to have made my nest with more care like the other birds of the grove.

Be that as it may it has been my ambition to write; and I have set a greater value on the praise of genius, than on all else that is obtainable amongst men. A man of very moderate parts can fill an office; perhaps the better for being moderate; but it is but one in many that can shew a single spark of the celestial fire that distinguishes the orator, the philosopher, or the rapt poet. I have always considered every hour, in a sense, lost, that was not employed in the cultivation of the intellect; with a view either to the virtues of humanity, or the delights of the fancy; for I give the virtues of humanity the first place. But when a man of taste considers how much more he owes to those who have increased the store of literature, than to such as have amassed wealth for themselves and others, he will certainly consider the productions of the mind as more deserving his respect, than the acquisitions of the purse-proud; even though there may appear a little vanity in the publications of the author, which he has not had the self denial to suppress, or the prudence to conceal. . . .

One thing I will add in excuse of employing so much of my time, and whatever talents I may possess, in what may seem to be of too light a nature for a serious mind, that the taste for playful humour, and the habit of versifying, was contracted in early life, from the want of a monitor to direct resistance to the propensity; and at the same time that I present the result to the public, I must caution others to beware of the indulgence. It is not an age or country, that will make it the means of emolument, or the way to honour. And though I would rather be the poet than the Maecenas as to after-fame, yet it is better to be the Maecenas as to present enjoyment. I would warn therefore a son of mine against too much attention to some parts of what may be called polite literature, as not fashionable in our present state of society, and as a seducing syren from the more profitable pursuits of life. . . . [1]

About a year after the publication of this volume, Henry Marie Brackenridge, who had been reading law in Pittsburgh, joined his father in Carlisle. For two or three years Braçkenridge had been uneasy about his son's conduct. About 1805 some young men of Pittsburgh had organized an amateur dramatic company and Henry Marie had taken a leading part in their performances. "My father," he later wrote, "who had the greatest contempt for village play-acting, and no great respect for actors on any stage (although he possessed the talents to be one of the greatest both in tragedy and comedy), was distressed with hearing of my performance, no doubt exaggerated by some who thought they were giving him agreeable news. In consequence of this I received a very strict injunction to attend to my law books, 'as the law is a jealous mistress and will not abide a rival.' Shortly after, he gave me orders to repair to Jefferson College, and to remain there six months, in order to place myself under the instruction of a celebrated mathematician and philosopher (that is, natural philosopher), Mr. Miller; and at the same time, to join the other college exercises."[2]

A more serious cause for worry than amateur theatricals soon developed. In 1807 Aaron Burr spent some time in Pittsburgh while he was organizing his expedition to liberate Mexico. He found eager followers among the young men of the village. One day when he was walking along the street with some of his recruits he saw Henry Marie Brackenridge and said, "He must be one of us."[3] Instead, Henry Marie went to Carlisle to join his father.

"On my arrival at Carlisle," he says, "I found my father very uneasy about me. He had heard of the movements of Aaron Burr at Pittsburgh, and was apprehensive that I had joined the expedition with the other young men of the place."[4]

Within a few days after his son had come home, Brackenridge

[1] *Gazette Publications*, pp. 3-5, 345-8.
[2] *Recollections of Persons and Places in the West*, pp. 88-90.
[3] *ibid.*, p. 103.   [4] *ibid.*, p. 109.

suggested a plan for his professional future. He advised him to go to Baltimore after he had finished his legal reading. The Maryland city was, he observed, rapidly growing and would soon be one of the leading commercial centers in the country. It therefore offered the best opportunities in America for a young lawyer. He had himself, he admitted, "committed an error in going to a new country, and regretted not having remained in the city." With unpleasant memories of his twenty years in Pittsburgh, "he painted the unfavorable side of the society and the profession in villages and country courts."

"If you have but a pig," he said, "carry it to the middle of the market. The vicinity of Baltimore to Washington must open a great theater for the display of forensic talents. If it should be your lot to become eminent, here is a prospect worthy of ambition. But you are not yet prepared to appear upon a stage; although you have gone through the usual course of legal education, there are particular branches of the law which are indispensable for city practice, and with which a general acquaintance will not suffice."[5]

So Henry Marie settled down to serious study, devoting thirteen or fourteen hours a day to his books. His father assisted him with his instruction whenever his circuit duties permitted him to remain at home. The Brackenridge household at this time was a perfect place for study. Mrs. Brackenridge attended to all the wants of her stepson, leaving him nothing to think about but his books. The younger children, of whom there were three, were busy with their studies. A little girl, three years old, was already reading newspapers. The youngest boy, aged six, was learning Latin and French. The other boy, fourteen years old, was translating Longinus and Xenophon into English. Brackenridge was trying to make this Greek study a practical course in rhetoric. First he had the boy make a literal translation. Then he helped him to turn it into idiomatic English, and supplemented this exercise by lectures.

This studious family was little disturbed by visitors. Brackenridge himself never dined out nor invited guests to dinner, and was unwilling to see company or say a word except on business

5 ibid., pp. 109-10.

during the day. After tea, however, a few friends with literary interests were accustomed to drop in to hear Brackenridge's conversation. Of his father's talk on these occasions Henry Marie said: "It was indeed a treat to hear him speak when he chose to unbend. He was an improvisateur of the first order. I have heard him relate a story, when the illusion was so perfect that the hearer would suppose there were half a dozen characters on the stage. Jeffrey, in one of the numbers of the *Edinburgh Review,* says that Mathews was inferior to him in relating a story.[6] He was entirely different; there was no buffoonery or broad humour, either in the choice of his subjects or in his manner. Compared to the stories of Mathews, it was genteel comedy or tragedy compared to broad farce. He generally walked about, and seemed to require this, in order to give full play to his powers. It is remarkable that what he said on the bench while seated had nothing of his usual eloquence; and when he was eloquent there, which was but seldom, he rose to his feet."

While Henry Marie was living at home he assisted his father in his literary work. Brackenridge's handwriting was virtually illegible and he frequently dictated to his son, sometimes articles for the newspapers and sometimes chapters of *Modern Chivalry.*[7] He dictated so rapidly that it was difficult for his amanuensis to keep pace with him, and he directed the punctuation as he went along.[8]

After about a year of study at home Henry Marie became very impatient; he was eager to begin his law practice immediately. His father wished him to continue his reading longer, and put into his hands an English legal treatise which counselled young men not to come to the bar before the age of thirty. But Henry Marie, who

[6] I have not found this description of Brackenridge in the *Edinburgh Review.* It is probable, however, that Jeffrey had heard Brackenridge "improvise" when he visited America in 1813. It is quite possible that in conversation he made some comparison between Brackenridge and the English comedian, Mathews, and that Henry Marie Brackenridge erroneously remembered it as having appeared in an *Edinburgh Review* article.

[7] These were evidently some of the new chapters included in the 1815 edition of *Modern Chivalry.*

[8] *Recollections of Persons and Places,* p. 111.

was just past twenty-one, could not tolerate the prospect of nine years' more preparation. It might be proper in England, he thought, but not in America. So his father yielded to his impatience. Before the youth set out for Baltimore, Brackenridge said to him:

The profession of the law is the road to honor and preferment in this country; but in a city you cannot expect to succeed without the utmost application to business. You must always be in your office; and until you are enabled to lay up something let that be the *only office* you will seek; at least avoid everything connected with politics. When you shall attain the age of forty-five or fifty, and have secured a moderate competence, you may amuse yourself with politics, or in any other lawful way; but until then your attention must be constantly directed to your business. I will make you up a small library and a purse of a hundred dollars or so. As my salary is almost my only dependence, for I have committed a great error in not attending sufficiently to the main chance, you must now swim without a cork jacket.[9]

We are not dependent entirely on the words of Henry Marie Brackenridge for a description of his father during this period. But Brackenridge was obviously the kind of person about whom legends develop, and the accounts of his contemporaries are often so contradictory and so evidently colored by personal bias that it is not easy to see where the truth really lies. David Paul Brown, who was studying law in Philadelphia while Brackenridge was on the bench, and Horace Binney, who wrote reports on the cases that came before the supreme court from 1807 to 1814, have left descriptions of his appearance and conduct during the time of his service as judge.

As David Paul Brown remembered him, Brackenridge was tall, but "bent in the shoulders." His complexion was dark and sallow, and his eyes were small, black, deep-set, and penetrating. His face was wrinkled, and his mouth was sunken from the loss of teeth. His hair was "sable-silvered." Of his dress he was extremely careless. He wore a rusty black coat and waistcoat and a shirt of almost the same color. "In the coldest weather he sat with his

9 *ibid.*, p. 112.

breast entirely open; his small clothes without suspenders, and neither exactly on, nor off; his beard unshaven, and his hair undressed; with large ungainly boots; cravat twisted like a rope, and his whole demeanour anything but attentive to the business of the court." "He has been known," Brown said, "to sit upon a trial, at a case of Nisi Prius, with coat and jacket both off, boots drawn, and feet propped up against the desk; and this too while surrounded by the most polished and distinguished men that ever graced a judicial tribunal."[10] Horace Binney said, "I once saw him charge a jury with his coat and jacket off, standing in his bare feet, with his boots beside him, for he had no stockings at that time. . . ."[11]

Although extremely careless in his dress and bearing, he was "a great devotee to shower baths, which he regularly continued the year through. . . . Upon some occasions, when the luxury of a regular bath could not be obtained, he would place himself behind the grating of a basement window, or some similar contrivance, and employ some sturdy servant from the outside, to dash a bucket of water upon him through the grating."

It is reported that once, while he was on circuit in western Pennsylvania, "a prodigious storm of wind and rain" arose. A friend of his, riding in a carriage, "saw a figure approaching, which resembled, what might be conceived of Don Quixote, in one of his wildest moods: a man with nothing on but his hat and boots, mounted upon a tall, raw-boned Rosenant, and riding deliberately through the tempest." On nearer approach the traveller found the strange figure to be Judge Brackenridge, who, seeing the approach of the storm, had stripped himself and put his clothes under the saddle.

"Although I am a *judge*," he explained, "I have but one suit, and the storm, you know, would spoil the clothes; but it couldn't spoil me."[12]

Brackenridge, it is clear, was not wholeheartedly devoted to court business, just as he had not given himself completely to his

[10] David Paul Brown, The Forum, Vol. I, p. 396.
[11] C. C. Binney, Life of Horace Binney, p. 41.
[12] David Paul Brown, op. cit., pp. 404-5.

law practice at an earlier period. Horace Binney, who seems to have been by nature incapable of understanding a humorist, said: "He despised the law, because he was utterly ignorant of it, and affected to value himself solely upon his genius and taste for literature, both of which were less valued by everyone else. He once said to me, as I was standing by his chair on the bench, 'Talk of your Cokes and Littletons, I had rather have one spark of the ethereal fire of Milton than all the learning of all the Cokes and Littletons that ever lived.' The misfortune was that he had not a grain of the learning that he undervalued, and that his fire, such as it was, was not ethereal."[13] David Paul Brown, on the other hand, remembered him as "a man of considerable genius and humor, as his *Modern Chivalry* and *Law Miscellany* abundantly prove. . . ."[14]

"Although a ripe scholar, and by no means deficient in legal lore, he took but little pains to exhibit his knowledge in his written opinions; and, as has been justly said of him, in the most of his discussions even of the gravest subjects, intermingled some facetious story, or a quotation from ancient or modern poets, either in the way of merriment or ridicule."[15]

Regarding Brackenridge's professional ethics these two witnesses also give conflicting testimony. Binney said of a certain trial before Brackenridge: "In this cause, in which I was of counsel, and his charge was in favour of my client, who succeeded, I saw what satisfied me that his honesty as a judge was no greater than his learning."[16] Brown, on the other hand, reported that he was "a man of undoubted integrity, and by no means deficient in intellectual power."[17]

On the bench there was a decided want of harmony between Brackenridge and his colleague Yeates. Binney says: "He hated Judge Yeates to absolute loathing. If Chief Justice Tilghman had not sat between them, I think that Brackenridge would sometimes, at a later period of his life, have spit in Yeates's face, from mere detestation. Yet this is proof of his own brutality, for Yeates was

---

13 C. C. Binney, *op. cit.*, pp. 40-1.   14 David Paul Brown, *op. cit.*, p. 399.
15 *ibid.*, p. 400.   16 C. C. Binney, *op. cit.*, p. 41.
17 David Paul Brown, *op. cit.*, p. 400.

vastly his superior in everything that deserves praise among men, and never, that I heard of, gave him any cause of offence."[18]

On one occasion, the story goes, Brackenridge and Yeates had as usual taken their seats at opposite ends of the bench, before the arrival of the chief justice. "Judge Yeates was employed eating an apple, and probably, from the difficulty in masticating, making more noise than was agreeable." Brackenridge, who was very nervous, bore it for a long time, with some signs of impatience, until at length, being unable to endure it any longer, he turned petulantly to his learned brother, and exclaimed:

"I think, sir, you once informed me that you had been to London, visited Westminster Hall, and saw Lord Mansfield on the bench."

"Yes, sir, I had that honor," replied Yeates.

"Pray, sir," Brackenridge asked tartly, "did you ever see his lordship munch a pippin on the bench?"[19]

Brackenridge's peculiar independence of character and striking individualism naturally made a deep impression on his contemporaries. Of his personality, Brown said:

"Judge Brackenridge . . . was reserved and misanthropic. He resolved never to dine out, for fear his host might some day be a suitor in his court. He seemed to shun social or convivial scenes, and to hold communion only with himself. . . . [He] created a world of his own. . . .[20] To look at Judge Brackenridge, you would have supposed him to be an ascetic. Not at all; on the contrary, he was always mentally engaged either in some amusing fancy, or in reflecting upon the fantastical fashions, or ridiculous pretensions or extravagances of the day."[21]

Not all of Brackenridge's contemporaries, however, remembered him as an eccentric. When Henry Marie Brackenridge was just beginning the practice of law he once examined a witness, who had descended from respectability to drunkenness, very bluntly and rudely. This witness, after the trial, reproved him very effec-

---

[18] C. C. Binney, *op. cit.*, p. 41.
[19] David Paul Brown, *op. cit.*, p. 398.
[20] *ibid.*, p. 400.   [21] *ibid.*, p. 409.

tively by saying: "Young man, I knew your father well, he was a gentleman."[22]

Indeed, it is as a wit and gentleman of the eighteenth century school that Brackenridge appears in the portrait of him painted by Gilbert Stuart in 1810.

[22] H. M. Brackenridge, *Recollections of Persons and Places*, p. 157.

CHAPTER XXII

ENGLISH LAW AND AMERICAN SOCIETY

AFTER the survival of the common law in Pennsylvania had been made certain by the victory of the moderate party in 1805, there remained the problem of excising archaic features of the system which were not adapted to a democratic society. Brackenridge's participation in this process of adjustment provided the occasions for some of the most important writings of his later years. His position as associate justice in the State supreme court naturally gave him opportunities to make practical applications of his legal philosophy.

One of the most important problems with which he had to deal was that of determining the status of English statute law in Pennsylvania. An act of assembly of April 7, 1807, provided: "That the Judges of the Supreme Court are hereby required to examine and report to the next legislature which of the English statutes are in force in this commonwealth, and which of those statutes in their opinion ought to be incorporated into the statute laws of the commonwealth."[1] In the accomplishment of this assignment, each of the judges made an independent study of the problem. A letter which Brackenridge wrote to accompany his own report to Chief Justice Tilghman stated his conception of the situation and indicated the point of view from which he approached the task of adapting English law to American society.

Considering the subject historically, he stated that an act of January 28, 1777, had provided that the principles of the common law should be adopted in usage and also, with certain exceptions, such of the statute laws of England as had hitherto been in force. One part of the problem, then, was to discover which of the English statute laws had been in force in the province and the State

[1] Frank M. Eastman, *Courts and Lawyers of Pennsylvania*, Vol. II, p. 302.

of Pennsylvania. Carrying the investigation back to the colonial period, Brackenridge found that originally acts of Parliament were binding on the colonies only when the colonies were specifically named in them. The British legislative authority over the colonies had, however, not been exerted until the sixth year of the reign of George III, when an act of Parliament declared that the Crown and Parliament had full power to pass laws binding the American colonists in all cases whatsoever. "The attempt to carry this power and authority into effect, gave rise to the revolution," said Brackenridge, "and solved the question that no English statute was in force, in a colony, plantation, or province even by *particularly naming it.*"

But, although the Revolution had put an end to the authority of acts of Parliament as such, many English laws had been ineradicably incorporated into the colonial juristic systems.

In Pennsylvania the original charter had provided that the English laws governing property, laws of inheritance, and criminal laws should be in force until altered by the proprietors and freemen of the province. It was understood, however, that, on account of the very nature of colonies, only such laws could be applied as were not excluded by the nature of the new situation. Thus the principle of adaptation had been recognized from the beginning of the province. A body of precedents had grown out of the application of English statutes to colonial conditions, but, since there were almost no records of decisions during the colonial period, later jurists had to depend on the legal traditions of the State for their knowledge of the usual application of certain English laws. Although there were judicial memoranda for some cases, and the recollection of persons present for others, many principles had been handed down like the laws of a school game. From such miscellaneous and sometimes intangible evidence Brackenridge and his colleagues were to compile a report on the English statutes still in force in the commonwealth of Pennsylvania.[2]

The judges submitted their report to the legislature on Decem-

[2] *Law Miscellanies,* pp. 39-48.

284   HUGH HENRY BRACKENRIDGE

ber 14, 1808.[3] Although their recommendations were not incorporated into the body of Pennsylvania law by act of legislature,[4]
they were considered to be important. Horace Binney, who was
writing the supreme court reports at the time, said of this important document: "In many respects it deserves to be placed by the
side of judicial decisions being the result of very great research
and deliberation by the judges, and of their united opinion. It may
perhaps not be considered as authoritative as judicial precedent;
but it approaches so nearly to it, that a safer guide in practice, or
a more respectable, not to say decisive authority in argument, cannot be wanted by the profession."[5]

Although the legislature had shown a judicious attitude toward
English statute law in calling for this report, other acts showed a
continuance of prejudice against English legal tradition. In 1807
the legislature passed a resolution to prohibit attorneys from reading in court any precedent or case decided in any other country
than the United States. Governor McKean at once vetoed the resolution and stated that the prohibition would exclude judge, jury,
and counsellor from the usual sources of legal information.[6] Three
years later, in 1810, a similar but more limited prohibition was
attempted in an act which provided that it would be unlawful to
quote in court any British precedent or ajudication made since the
Declaration of Independence, except in cases of maritime law or
international law.[7] While this bill was being considered, Brackenridge drew up an argument against it for the instruction of a
member of the assembly.[8]

His view was that, although English decisions since the Declaration of Independence would not govern as precedent, they might
"guide as reason." Since the separation, light had been thrown
upon many points of law in England. "The science is improving
there," he said. Then he asked, "Shall we refuse the advantage of

[3] Horace Binney, *Reports of Cases Adjudged in the Supreme Court of Pennsylvania*, Vol. III, p. 625.
[4] *Law Miscellanies*, p. 48.   [5] Horace Binney, *op. cit.*, p. 596.
[6] *Pennsylvania Archives*, Fourth Series, Vol. IV, p. 613.
[7] Frank M. Eastman, *Courts and Lawyers of Pennsylvania*, Vol. II, p. 304.
[8] *Law Miscellanies*, p. 49.

any help?" He admitted that there had been abuses in the use of English precedents: some jurists were too servile, and same lawyers took up too much time in court in citing English decisions at great length. These decisions could be very useful, however, if they were used with sufficient independence of judgment. In conclusion he said:

My idea of decisions posterior to the revolution is this; that they are the comments of men upon the same subject with that which we have to consider. It is as if men who had set out from the same place and having travelled together a certain distance had parted; but having occasion to refer to the point at which they had set out, and the part of the ground they had travelled together, they should compare notes and correct their journals, as well as to notice improvements that might be made or to co-operate in making them.[9]

Although Brackenridge had shown himself attached to the traditional English legal system, he did not hesitate to disagree with English precedent in an important aspect of maritime law. France and England were at this time in contest for the mastery of the seas, and many American cargoes were being confiscated as contraband by both nations. Since Philadelphia was one of the centers of the marine insurance business, this confiscation of American cargoes brought many cases before the supreme court of Pennsylvania. In such cases the English courts had habitually refused to accept the decisions of foreign courts as to the contraband nature of cargoes. Brackenridge did not assent to this doctrine. In an article published in *Poulson's Advertiser* (Philadelphia) on January 6, 1808, he maintained that decisions of foreign courts of admiralty as to the contraband nature of cargoes should be considered as conclusive by American courts in adjudicating marine insurance cases.[10]

In domestic politics there was at this period a dispute regarding the jurisdiction of the State and the Federal courts. Brackenridge thought that the Federal courts were encroaching on the province of the State courts. In an article published in the *Democratic Press* on March 15, 1810, he urged that Pennsylvania "resist the begin-

---

[9] *ibid.*, pp. 49-53.   [10] *ibid.*, pp. 345 ff.

ning of usurpation." He believed that the Federal government was beginning to dominate the States as the British government had dominated the colonies before the Revolution. Fearing serious consequences from this conflict, he proposed that the United States Senate be designated as arbitrator to decide in cases of contested jurisdiction.[11, 12]

[11] *Law Miscellanies*, pp. 362-74.

[12] To this period belongs a pamphlet entitled *Considerations on the Jurisprudence of the State of Pennsylvania* (Philadelphia, 1808), which is assigned to Brackenridge by a manuscript note on the title page of the copy in the Library of Congress and by C. F. Heartman in his *Bibliography of the Writings of Hugh Henry Brackenridge*. I cannot accept it as his work. It is a serious indictment of the English common law, and therefore represents the point of view which Brackenridge was opposing at the time. Also its style is absolutely different from that of Brackenridge.

CHAPTER XXIII

"AN EPISTLE TO WALTER SCOTT"

IN THE autumn of 1811 Brackenridge's duties as justice on circuit took him back to Pittsburgh. There, on September 9, he took up by chance Scott's *Lady of the Lake*.[1] As he read the Scottish tale, memories of his boyhood were awakened, and he hastily wrote a versified epistle to Scott to express his gratitude for the poetic glorification of his native land. After describing briefly his own childhood in Scotland he said:

> For most the ballad and the rhyme
> Imparts a charm to every clime;
> And not the deeds that men have done
> So much the listening ear has won,
> As magic of that art divine,
> Which springs from the harmonious nine.
> Oh give me Burns; or give me Scott;
> I want no more when these I've got,
> To make a rock of any sea
> Immortal by such minstrelsy.
>
> . . .   .
>
> These fairy footsteps here I trace
> Here heights are sung, unknown before,
> But by traditionary lore.
> Who would have thought that Thule's isle
> Would be the seat of song erewhile;
> And lyric fire and epic swell
> Come with Apollo here to dwell.[2]

Then he lamented his separation from the enchanted ground of Scotland, and his want of genius:

> Ah me that cannot nearer be
> To hear such native melody!

[1] *An Epistle to Walter Scott*, p. 1.   [2] *ibid.*, p. 2.

Here by Ohio's stream my pen
Gives image to a sort of strain
Which feeling prompts but Genius none,
So gifted to a native son.
My gift is only to admire;
In madness I attempt the lyre,
At hearing this celestial sound
From Scotia's hills and distant bound
Of this I dream and when awake,
I read the Lady of the Lake.[3]

Then he showed how the Western American landscape was also
calling for a poet to glorify its beauties. He represented the "silly
hills," the "untaught wood," and "the lonely weeping wilderness"
as asking him:

Have you not something of that vein,
A little of that minstrel strain,
To give us also here a name,
And taste of an immortal fame?

He replied:

Ah! lovely bowers you gave me shade,
But such return cannot be made;
Sweet waters, you must trickle on
Till some more favour'd muse's son
Shall sing of you like Walter Scott
And to immortal change your lot!
. . .   .

Who knows but this epistle may
To you attract a poet's lay;
To put in verse some height, some stream
Just incidental to his theme.
Oh! might my name of Bracken born
Some ridge where infant lay forlorn
Or peasant built his hamlet drear
Attain the sanctity to hear
It named in one immortal line,

[3] *An Epistle to Walter Scott*, pp. 2-3.

Which turns a harsh word to divine!
But this too much; I cannot claim
The meed of such advance to fame,
So far secluded from my race,
And cut off from romantick base.
It can't be said that such a dale
Where deeds were done, is where I dwell;
Or that I vegetate among
The hills which once were hills of song.
Here neighboring to the savage tread
Inglorious I must bend my head,
And think of something else than fame;
Though in my bosom burns the flame
That in a happier age and clime
Might have attempted lofty rhyme.[4]

After thus apologizing for his own lack of skill he addressed Scott directly as follows:

But thou, celestial take thy course
With fancy's pinion, reason's force;
Go on; enjoy increasing fame,
Now equal with a Milton's name;
Or him that sang the fairy-queen;
Or other Southron that has been.
Not Shakespeare would himself disdain
The rivalship of such a strain.

Oh! for a theme of ampler space,
Whereon eternal lines to trace;
Embracing sea and continent,
And not within an island pent;
A stage commensurate with power
Of bard and sacred orator!
But this would kind of treason be
To isle of my nativity,
Which claims. and has a right to claim
Her bard for her own sep'rate fame;
Since other lands no mention make

[4] *ibid.*, pp. 3-4.

Of genius which did here awake;
Or deeds which heroes here have done
However meriting renown?
Much merit here of feeling heart
To make the breast heave, and tear start
Remains unsung; and valour's prize,
The golden hair and sky-blue eyes.
Hence I retract the wish, resign;
To Scotia give that harp of thine
To which all melodies are known
That harp has rung or pipe has blown;
Like thine own bard, thy Allan Bane
So full, so various is thy strain;
In torrent numbers, flood of sense
In bounds which judgement well restrains.

No fear of a short liv'd renown,
Or fading to thy ivy-crown;
For should some hidden fire or force
Of ocean in his changing course
Unfix Benledi from his stance,
Yet time at thee shall break his lance;
Or miss his aim and level wide
At thy more solid pyramid!
Go on; add lustre to an earth
So honoured by thy magick birth;
For not of mortal art thou born,
O darling son of orient morn!
Go on—and fill the rising gale
With Scotia's early lore and tale;
Make vocal and give life in turn
To every mountain, glen and burn;
As erst in Grecia did the god
Of poesy, his dear abode,
Attended by the sister choir,
That hymned the song or tuned the lyre;
For of Castalia ev'ry dream
Is found, in thy Loch Katrine theme;
And Pindus rises to our view

When that we think of Benvenue;
Or we forget all other song,
Thy inspiration pours so strong.[5]

Then he expressed his doubt as to the possibility of his praise ever reaching Scott:

Our praise is vain; what winds will bear
Encomium to a distant ear,
Or will it please, so little skill
Have we, however the good will?[6]

Before closing the "Epistle" he affirmed that he was impatiently awaiting Scott's latest poem, *The Vision of Don Roderick,* which, he said, had been announced but had not yet arrived.[7] Then after asking Scott to

Accept this distant homage given
To sounds that well deserve a heaven,

he closed with a modest but accurate estimate of his own lines:

But now no more; enough, enough,
Of these prosaick numbers rough:
We cease th' attempt, since it requires
A poet to tell, a poet's fires.[8]

This poem was published at once as a small pamphlet in Pittsburgh, and the next year it was included with an American edition of *The Vision of Don Roderick.*[9]

[5] *An Epistle to Walter Scott,* pp. 4-6.　　[6] *ibid.,* p. 7.
[7] *ibid.,* pp. 7-8.　　[8] *ibid.,* p. 8.
[9] On February 7, 14, 21, and 28, and March 13, 1812, the *Pittsburgh Gazette* printed the following advertisement for the Franklin Head Bookstore of Pittsburgh: "Have just received, a few copies of the Vision of Don Roderick, a poem. To which is added, An Epistle to the Author, by H. H. Brackenridge, Esq."

CHAPTER XXIV

THE AMERICANIZATION OF
BLACKSTONE

THE *Epistle to Walter Scott* was merely a literary interlude in the legal preoccupations which had claimed most of Brackenridge's attention since his appointment to the supreme court. After the *Epistle* was written he continued his juristic studies. In 1814 he published a collection of papers entitled *Law Miscellanies* which contains his most substantial contributions to American jurisprudence. The essays had been written at various times, and some of them cannot be dated. Those which had been previously published elsewhere have been utilized at the proper points in this study. Part of the book was printed by October 5, 1813,[1] and some of the topical material in the work can be assigned approximately to the year 1813.

The complete title, which gives an outline of the book, is as follows: *Law Miscellanies; Containing an Introduction to the Study of the Law; Notes on Blackstone's Commentaries; shewing the Variations of the Law of Pennsylvania from the Law of England, and what Acts of Assembly might require to be repealed or modified; Observations on Smith's edition of the Laws of Pennsylvania; Strictures on Decisions of the Supreme Court of the United States and on Certain Acts of Congress, with Some Law Cases and a Variety of other Matters, chiefly original.*

In two introductory notes Brackenridge explained his purpose in writing the studies. He had intended, he said, to prepare a "Pennsylvania Blackstone," by editing the English commentaries with notes indicating how Pennsylvania law differed from English law. After beginning this task he had found that it was too difficult for him; at least he feared that the learned in the law would not consider him competent for the work. "Not possessing any great

[1] *Law Miscellanies*, pp. 214-15.

celebrity on this head," he confessed, "it has not been fashionable to overrate the small talents which I may possess." Therefore he decided to publish only his "notes and observations," some of which he had worked up while instructing a pupil. He hoped, then, that his notes might be useful to other students. Also he thought that his observations should be "brought before the eye of the legislature of Pennsylvania with a view to supply, abrogate, or amend acts of assembly."[2]

Since Brackenridge intended the book to be useful to students, he included an introductory essay of advice to them, in which he emphasized the value of a classical education:

In order to qualify for the profession of the law, a *liberal education* is necessary. For, though there are instances of strong minds, that are but little indebted to a liberal education, making tolerable orators, and even lawyers; yet, it would have been of great advantage to them to have possessed this. For something like a universal knowledge of literary subjects, would be desirable; because, in proportion as we have a knowledge of subjects, the mind is enlarged. For there is scarcely a subject of human knowledge, but that when the mind is brought to bear upon a point of at least *moral discussion* it may not draw something from it to illustrate an argument or fortify a position. Not that I would have an orator to be able to support a thesis, in omni scibili et, de quolibet ente; but I would require some general information, on almost all subjects of science; especially that sphere of study which is fashionable, and I think useful, in our system of education. It is a question lately agitated whether the acquisition of what are called the learned languages, is useful. The perfect command of one's tongue, in which the advocate is to speak or write, is certainly necessary; not the command of words merely, but the delicate selection of words, and choice of terms. In order to have this, it is necessary to understand the precise meaning of words; and this is not to be collected from dictionaries; so well at least as from the roots of the words, which are found in those languages, from which our own is derived; and of which it is in a great measure made up, and composed. These are, of the ancient languages, the Latin and the Greek; of the modern, the French and the German. The farthest way about,

2 *ibid.,* pp. i-iv.

is said to be, oftentimes, the nearest way home; and in order to be master of the English language, I would think it the shortest course to endeavour to obtain a knowledge of these; and more especially of the Latin and Greek. . . .

But can anything contribute more to form a taste for style than the study of these models of language, where there is every ornament of grace and expression: strength, at the same time, which will depend in a great degree upon *conciseness and brevity*: perspicuity also, without which there is neither strength nor grace. For were I to lay down a rule of style, it would be to endeavour to obtain a *precise and clear idea* of what is to be said; and, to express it *with the utmost brevity*, and in the most *perspicuous phrase possible*. Where one is master of this, but which requires much previous discipline of the mind, a diction may be indulged with the *embellishments of figure*, and the *flowers of imagination*. But until this *rib and bone* of clear thought is obtained, all garniture but wearies. All this excellence of brevity, perspicuity, and grace, is distinguishable in the classical writings. Hence it is that the diction of a good classical scholar is distinguishable from that of one who has not had the advantage of this education, by a certain flavour, and, if I may so express it, *raciness* of diction that savours of the ancients. This, though not discernable in its cause in the hearer, is felt abundantly. There is a charm in such eloquence that is not equalled by him whose taste has not been so cultivated.[3]

Since much of the material in *Law Miscellanies* is concerned with technical legal points, only those parts of the book which express Brackenridge's philosophy of jurisprudence can be considered here. In this field as in politics he was liberal, as is shown by his numerous criticisms of unenlightened traditions and unjust legislation.

Early in the book he reveals his liberalism in his remarks on the judicial use of precedents:

It occurs to me to express a few thoughts on the respect due to prior decisions. Certain it is that the stare decisis is a salutary maxim, but it has appeared to me, that it has been carried sufficiently far in this country. In England there is such a thing as a departure from

[3] *Law Miscellanies*. pp. xii-xiii.

decided cases; and where there is not, we see nevertheless, in many instances, great dissatisfaction expressed with decisions. . . . With respect to our own courts in this country to which I bring my observations it would seem to me that we have been in the habit of paying more deference to English decisions than the most technical of the English themselves. They do sometimes by overhauling and distinguishing, make out to get clear of a case that seems to sanction what is unreasonable; but I do not know where that has been done in our courts. Be that as it may, I am not prepared to subscribe to our own decisions in all cases as conclusive authority. . . .

On a principle of tenure of real property, when an original and not a *derivative* title comes in question, it must be with great repugnance I can submit to a decision to which my judgment was opposed when at the bar, and which I cannot consider as having received the investigation of such a number of minds legally informed, so as to give satisfaction. I must acknowledge that I do not consider the principles of construction so far settled as to preclude examination. This I say not undervaluing the judgment of others, but as accounting for that freedom of thinking which I may indulge in some cases, and which is not founded as may be supposed in the vain ambition of being singular, or of being thought preeminent; but in the love of liberty, and repugnance to submission to what does not seem to be founded on reason, general convenience, or justice to individuals. I am willing to admit that much has been done towards building a system of jurisprudence in the state, but I am unwilling to apply the maxim of stare decisis to all that has been done.[4]

The passages in *Law Miscellanies* which give the most instructive examples of Brackenridge's dissent from English common law were written on issues connected with the War of 1812, which was in progress when the book was published. In these cases he attempted to show how the American version of English law must be freed from the feudal principles which still survived. The impressment of naturalized American citizens of British birth had brought to light the English conception that original allegiance could not be legally severed by emigration. From this feature of the common law Brackenridge dissented sharply. Commenting on a case which involved the right of expatriation he said:

[4] *ibid.,* pp. 54-5.

Speaking of the doctrine of natural allegiance the counsel in this case, represented it as a slavish principle not likely to prevail in these times, especially as it seemed to derogate from the principles of the revolution. This feeling was strengthened by a course of thinking on the one side, from our situation, and that of *emigrants,* in the revolutionary war and since. I had felt a predisposition before I undertook to throw out these hints, to be able to satisfy myself, that this principle of the *ne exuere,* might be found to rest on no good foundation. The fact is that I had become reconciled to a *resistance* to it; and there is no question with me as to the *right,* but the power, only. And I believe it is now brought to such a point that the *ultima ratio* must determine it.

It will not be understood, that I mean to say that the cause of the present war, or the continuance of it, is the naturalizing British subjects, though it may have led to it on the part of the enemy, and is the pretence for continuing it.[5]

With reference to Blackstone's dictum that the principle of natural allegiance is a universal law, Brackenridge said:

I did not wonder at that great man, the British commentator, laying it down to be the law of England, that the *natural born subject* cannot put off his allegiance; but that he should lay it down to be a principle of universal law, is the ground of my astonishment. But more astonishing still, is it that, even some in this country, the United States, seem to have been led away with something like the same sentiment. I can account for it only, in the case of intelligent men, on the ground of *political bias;* and this from not having a hand in the administration, or that party in the republic to whom they are attached, not having a hand in it. For I admit that when Jefferson in his inaugural address, said "we are all federalists, all republicans," he spoke the truth, with the exception of *a few* attached to foreign governments. But had he said, we are all *out,* all *in;* would this have been correct? I excuse the minority, on the ground of human passions. But the time in the nature of our government, cannot be remote when those who are *out,* will be *in;* and why suffer for a moment the messuage to be dilapidated, and a single stone of the building lost. I consider it, the losing a corner stone; the surrendering an essential right, if we admit for a moment the *degradation of our honour,* the lessening our privi-

5 *Law Miscellanies,* pp. 295-6.

lege as an independent people, that we cannot *receive all that come to us without questions asked, save so far as we chuse to put them.*[6]

In a note on Blackstone's exposition of the law of feudal tenures, Brackenridge made the following comment:

A legitimate principle of these tenures, was the doctrine of *unalienable and perpetual allegiance.* It was not necessary that the emigrants to these shores should carry *that principle* with them as applicable to their situation, having left, as will be admitted, this badge of servitude, the feudal system behind them. Those who give such a principle countenance, will deny that it is *peculiar* to this law, and will endeavour to give it a foundation, as Blackstone would wish to do, on the general grounds of *universal law.* . . .

How far this system has been broken down in England, and how far, what I consider to be the *root* of it, remains, this doctrine of *inextricable allegiance,* the student will investigate. I may say something of it in another place. But God forbid that I should consider it as introduced here. This vestige of the iron age, and vassalage of the *iron crown,* our republican institutions have put, and will put down.[7]

Besides discussing the points of English law that could not fit American conditions, Brackenridge treated other aspects of American legislation. His suggestions are marked by a thoroughgoing democracy. For instance, he favored extremely liberal naturalization laws, although much of the radicalism he had opposed a few years earlier was due to the immigrant population of Pennsylvania. On this point he said:

I am amongst those who carry my ideas in favour of the naturalization of foreigners, perhaps too far. I am for exercising the rights of hospitality to them, to all extent at once; making them citizens, and giving them the right of suffrage, and even office, the moment they set foot upon the shore. For I cannot see on what ground, we can justify a refusal. But I do not mean to discuss this point at present. I introduce it to show that I am liberal in my notions, with regard to the privileges of foreigners. But I admit that it takes some time to give them correct ideas of the limits of liberty. . . .

Digressing a little . . . I admit that emigrants come when they are likely to be in opposition to the existing government, or rather adminis-

---

[6] *ibid.,* pp. 403-5.   [7] *ibid.,* p. 422.

tration. This depends upon natural principles. The governments of Europe are most of them oppressive, and it is oppression that drives, in most instances, the inhabitants from amongst them. The poor or the most enterprising are those that emigrate. They have been in the habit of thinking of a reform, in the state of things in that country, from which they come; it is natural for them to think that a little touch of their hand may be still necessary here. . . .

Intemperance of mind, or manner in a foreigner, gives colour to the imputation, that all are incendiaries. It becomes, therefore, a matter of discretion, and just prudence on his part, to be cautious in coming forward to take a part in politics, until he has well examined the field of controversy. But because foreigners may abuse the privilege, I would not exclude them by a law, did the matter rest on first principles. . . . What right have we to exclude them? We are not born for ourselves; nor did we achieve the revolution for ourselves only. We fought the cause of all mankind; and the good and great of all mankind wished well to us in the contest. With what anxiety did we look to Europe, for assistance. We derived assistance even from the good will of nations. It is an advantage to have a popular cause in a war. Have we a right to shut ourselves up in our shell, and call the society we have formed, our own exclusively?[8]

In the conclusion of *Law Miscellanies* Brackenridge gave a brief account of his personal situation. Written in 1813 or 1814, it is the last autobiographical passage in his works.

This book has been written raptim, et captim; at snatches of time in the intervals of business; and these intervals have been short, never exceeding ten days at a time. For, though I have been two or three times in a year, near three weeks at home, yet the greater part of that interval has been taken up in making out statements of causes tried at nisi prius, for the sake of the court in Term. . . . But, still more, my time has been occupied, when at home, in considering cases *holden over under advisement* from the Term, and examining the authorities cited by the counsel in the argument. For it is only at the intervals of which I speak, from these occupations, that there can be leisure to make notes or observations upon collateral subjects and abstract matters of law. Nor would there be leisure for this, at these intervals, were it not that I abstract myself wholly from company, and neither

[8] *Law Miscellanies*, pp. 108-14.

visit, nor receive visits of ceremony, and, see no one, but upon business; except a literary character, or professional man, to whom I am always at home, and perpetually disengaged. Because from them I may derive something; information or instruction. Drawing near the end of my pilgrimage I consider all time lost that is not employed in leaving some memorandum of my existence, and that may be useful to men, either by contributing to mental enjoyment, or to instruct. I state this with a view to *exclude* the *conclusion* that this publication can be evidence of my having little to do, in my immediate official occupations. For, it is rather an argument to the contrary; and that I must have been industrious and attentive to the discharge of my trust, since the whole subject of the book, has a relation to the study and practice of the law.[9]

In this conclusion Brackenridge also stated his purpose in writing the book and expressed his view of the state of the Union:

I will acknowledge, as I have already hinted, that I have intended it [*Law Miscellanies*] a good deal, for the legislature, with a view to assist them in the amendment of the Pennsylvania code; and, this, by giving, as far as my understanding would lead me; a broad view of their law as improved, from that of England, or variant from it; or, how far still defective in our provisions by acts of assembly, or in the filling up, and completing our excellent judiciary establishment. It will be seen also, that I have given a glance at the encroachments of the national government, whether by acts of Congress, or judicial *construction,* upon state rights. Not that I mean, in the most distant degree, to shake the confidence of the state in the national government; on the contrary, my object is to preserve it by confining legislative acts, and construction to the constitutional orbit. "Esto perpetua," may it last forever, would be my wish. But this, in the nature of things, cannot be expected. I look for its dissolution, I am afraid at *no distant day.* The late symptoms of schism in the northern states, seem to bespeak an approaching catastrophe. I consider the opinion of the Massachusetts judges, in answer to the questions of governor Strong; together with the order from Martin Chittenden, governor of Vermont, to withdraw *the militia from under the command of the United States, as fraught with seeds of death, and destruction.*[10]

[9] *ibid.,* pp. 575-6.   [10] *ibid.,* p. 576.

CHAPTER XXV

"MODERN CHIVALRY": THE LAST ADDITIONS

I N 1815 the first collected edition of *Modern Chivalry* was published in four volumes. It contained not only the substance of all the editions from 1792 to 1805 but also a considerable amount of new matter. Of the fourth volume the publishers said: "The greater part of this volume is printed from scraps furnished by the author, from his portfolio, in consequence of our signifying an inclination to publish a new edition of this work."[1] This additional material did not grow out of a definite episode in Brackenridge's political career as the previous instalments had done, and is, therefore, even less unified than the other parts. It does, however, contain satire on various political and intellectual affairs of the years preceding its publication.

The most elaborate narrative in the new work is an account of a community in which horses and other animals vote, serve on juries, and otherwise perform the functions of civic life. An anonymous and extremely shadowy "visionary philosopher" appears now and then to encourage this humanization of the animals. Without a few comments on the narrative, which are casually introduced, the meaning of this section would not be apparent. After several chapters of the story, Brackenridge gives the necessary key for the interpretation of one aspect of it. With some surprise the reader learns from the following passage that he has been reading a satire on the property qualification of voters:

The preceding painting may be considered as extravagant; and exceeding all probability; the voting of beasts. But is it a new thing in the government that the right of suffrage should be made to depend upon property? No man shall be entitled to vote unless he is worth so much, say some of the constitutions. In this is it not his property

[1] *Modern Chivalry* (edition of 1815), Vol. IV, p. 44.

that votes? If this property consists in cattle, can it be said that his cattle do not vote? Ergo, a cow, or a horse, in some communities have the privilege of a vote in the enacting laws.[2]

In another passage it transpires that in this satire Erasmus Darwin's theory of evolution is strangely joined with property qualifications of voters. "The Governor," an indistinct character in the story, says:

And though I do not know that the Lord spoke all things to Moses that he is said to have spoken; for there may have been some mistakes in the translations from the Hebrew, as in other versions; yet there seems to me more probability in the cosmogony, of the Hebrew writer, than in the reveries of Darwin his Temple of Nature, or his Zoonomia. And even supposing the brutal to be capable of amelioration from one nature to another, until it reaches the human, it would seem to me, that its rights should keep pace only with the improvement of its forms; and that we should wait until the elephant comes to sit upon his one end, and ceases to go upon all-fours, before we think of introducing even the noblest of animals, in point of intellect, into a participation of civil institutions.[3]

In a brief characterization of the philosopher in the story Brackenridge indicates that his narrative had still another purpose: to satirize Dugald Stewart's doctrine of human perfectibility.

When I speak of the visionary philosopher, I do not mean him that had

"Read Alexander Ross over;"

but who had seen the Great Stewart, who delivered lectures in this country, on the perfectibility of man, and this student, or disciple, had been disposed to carry the matter still farther; and discuss the perfectibility of beasts.[4]

In this fantastic narrative Brackenridge had again exhibited his sturdy independence. He had attacked the recognition of class distinction in civic rights, and was to that extent still a good democrat; but he had also spoken sharply against the notions of perfectibility in man and animals, and in so doing he had again shown

---

[2] *ibid.*, Vol. IV, p. 101.   [3] *ibid.*, Vol. IV, p. 92.
[4] *ibid.*, Vol. IV, p. 91.

himself to be sceptical of ideas which were easily mingled with romantic democracy.

Another important section of the book pertains to the War of 1812, and gives Brackenridge's views of both the cause of the war and the American problems connected with its conduct. In war as in peace he found that common men were likely to be elevated to high place in a democracy, and he satirized the appointment of untrained men to high commands by making Teague O'Regan a popular military hero who almost became a general.[5] Another problem with which he had had previous experience was that of regional separatism. The affirmation by New England of the doctrine of State sovereignty recalled the earlier disintegrating tendencies in the West. To counteract this movement he recommended his history of the Whiskey Insurrection, which gave, he said, "a picture of a people broke loose from the restraints of government, and going *further than they had intended to go.*" "If that book," he wrote, "was republished at this time, and circulated in the *Eastern* States, it could not but contribute to show *the danger of even talking of a severance of the union, or an opposition to the laws.*"[6]

This passage must have been written during or after the Hartford Convention (December 1814-January 1815), as Brackenridge hinted at an intention to introduce a satirical account of that gathering.[7] The proposed satire was probably never written, since it does not appear in any of the editions of *Modern Chivalry*.

The causes of the War of 1812 had been touched upon in Brackenridge's legal writings. In the last part of *Modern Chivalry* he recurred to the subject, alluding to a topic which had stirred his wrath since the early period of American independence:

It was always a matter of astonishment to me to hear it suggested that this war in which we are engaged with Great Britain was *unjust.* The fabrication of a single scalping knife in their island, and sending it out for the inhuman purpose of Indian murder, and excoriation, was a just cause of war.[8]

[5] *Modern Chivalry*, Vol. III, pp. 144-51.   [6] *ibid.*, Vol. IV, p. 147.
[7] *ibid.*, Vol. IV, p. 147.   [8] *ibid.*, Vol. III, p. 178.

At the end of this volume Brackenridge included a "key" to the whole of *Modern Chivalry* in which he explained briefly how the various parts were related to "the history of the times and especially . . . of Pennsylvania." He also made large claims as to the corrective influence which his work had exerted. "Indeed," he said, "I flatter myself, that it is not a little owing to this book, published in portions, from time to time, that a very different state of things now exists." His first boast was that there had "not been a single bog-trotter . . . admitted by the *American Philosophical Society* for many years past." Then he explained how the political success of an uneducated opponent had induced him to make Teague O'Regan a politician, and why he had made Teague an exciseman in the Whiskey Insurrection. Passing on to the volumes of 1804-05, he said that the newspaper attacks on him after 1800 had suggested to him that Teague would make just such an editor as some of those who had written against him. He showed, too, how he had countered the popular agitation against law and learning, and how he had satirized the lawyers themselves for the long speeches which were a cause of the law's delay. He thought now that a wider circulation of *Modern Chivalry* might check the verbosity of members of congress. "Why is it," he inquired, "that congress do not buy up an edition of my book, and distribute it among the members? It would be of more use to them than the library of Monticello." Then he boasted of the popularity of the book:

The people of Pennsylvania are so sensible of the use that it has been in this state, that there is scarce a parlour window without a MODERN CHIVALRY. Five booksellers have made a fortune by it; for I have never asked a cent from any of them for the privilege of printing an edition.

Finally he showed that American political life offered material for still another continuation of his satire:

I have said that I do not know that I shall write more, though I have some transactions in my mind, that I should wish to chronicle; and characters that might be drawn. I know, that after the present war, which, in the nature of things, cannot last always, an ambassador will be sent to England; and Teague may be a candidate.[9]

Brackenridge did not live to chronicle the career of Teague in the post-war period. He did, however, revise the text of *Modern Chivalry*.[10]

Of Brackenridge's last days we have little information. He died at Carlisle on June 25, 1816.[11] "During his last illness," said Henry Marie Brackenridge, "he dictated his will, declaring that he left no accounts to settle, as he owed nothing and no person owed him, except the State for a quarter's salary."[12] He had not achieved the high ambitions of his youth; but long before he had critically reviewed his accomplishments and had become reconciled to the idea of holding only a modest place in the literature and history of his country.

[9] *Modern Chivalry*, Vol. IV, pp. 192-5.

[10] The revised edition was published in Pittsburgh in 1819, the copyright being taken out by Brackenridge's son, Alexander. The publisher's introductory note said: "This is the first edition of *Modern Chivalry*, published since the death of the author. Those which previously appeared were imperfect, particularly in typographical accuracy, as the judicial avocations of the author prevented that minute attention to the proof sheets which is always necessary in the publication of an original work. Hence almost every page had become disfigured with inaccuracies, which the publisher has been at great pains to expurge. The corrections and alterations made by the author since the former edition, have been introduced. Some chapters have been transposed, and a few excluded, as these were not intended to constitute a permanent portion of the work." Vol. I, p. iii.

[11] *Pittsburgh Gazette*, July 6, 1816.

[12] "Biographical Notice," p. 188.

CHAPTER XXVI

CONCLUSION

THE records of Hugh Henry Brackenridge's life reveal a personality which cannot be easily analyzed. His longing for fame, his independence in thought and action, his uncertain nerves, and his pride of intellect all combined to form a character which harmonized very imperfectly with the rough environment in which much of his life was passed.

Brackenridge's great passion was for learning and literature. He longed for fame in these pursuits, but he did not have sufficient talent to produce the great works of which he dreamed, nor did the communities in which he lived after the Revolution provide a social background suitable to the encouragement of literary production.

His writings are not completely satisfying if judged only from the literary point of view. His serious verse does not show a mastery of poetic form. It was, of course, written in his early years, but there is no reason to believe that he would ever have achieved a high degree of competence in poetic composition. His later Hudibrastic verse is too carelessly written even for that type, and is often obscure. His prose, at its best, is more satisfactory than his verse. It often has a colloquial ease not found in most American prose of the period. It is frequently careless, however, and sometimes lacks clearness. The lack of a national literary tradition and criticism no doubt accounts for these defects. Evidently Brackenridge did not often feel compelled to do his best. It is not only in the smaller units of phrase and sentence that his work is imperfect. None of his prose works are well organized. Even in *Modern Chivalry,* he seemed more eager to deliver his opinion on all topics of interest to him than to compose a unified narrative.

To yield its full value, his work must be considered historically. From the literary point of view, it is interesting to observe that he borrowed literary forms from Milton, Dryden, Swift, Butler,

Addison, and Burns for the treatment of American political and social life. Although he wrote under the influence of great English models, he did not produce vapid provincial imitations of them. His work is to be judged, then, by its content, historically considered. From this point of view his early writings appear as vigorous expressions of American patriotic feeling during the Revolution. His journalistic writings are sources of interesting data for the study of the frontier and of legal history. But *Modern Chivalry* is the book on which his reputation must rest. Certainly it deserves a high place among minor American classics. *Modern Chivalry* was," said Henry Adams, "not only written in good last-century [i.e. eighteenth century] English, none too refined for its subject, but more thoroughly American, than any book yet published, or to be published until the 'Letters of Major Jack Downing' and the 'Georgia Scenes' of forty years later."[1] Studied in its evolution and in relation to its background, it not only throws light on the beginnings of American democracy, but it also stands as a permanently valid commentary on persistent problems. It shows Brackenridge to have been steadfast in his allegiance to a thoroughly rational ideal. When the frontier democrats talked, acted, and voted foolishly, they became the butt of his satire. When the Federalists appeared to be serving the "moneyed interests," they were the objects of his criticism. Then again, when his own Republican party absorbed too much French and Irish radicalism, he directed his satire toward its follies. In a turbulent and critical period, in a crude environment, Brackenridge's vigorous good sense found authentic democracy in Plutarch and Thucydides rather than in Tom Paine and Godwin. This fact no doubt partially accounts for his lack of success on the frontier where democracy was a state of feeling rather than a conviction of intellect. As Professor Parrington says, "Federalist and Republican alike might lose their heads in unseemly clamor, but Brackenridge with good Scotch judgment refused to howl with the pack."[2]

[1] Henry Adams, *History of the United States*, Vol. I, pp. 124-25.
[2] V. L. Parrington, *Main Currents in American Thought*, Vol. I, p. 390.

A further cause of his political failure was his inability to subject his judgment to the control of an uneducated electorate. On the other hand, he was not able to make an heroic stand for an unpopular cause, partly, no doubt, because he was gifted with that fatal insight which sees too clearly the mixture of right and wrong on both sides of a controversy. Furthermore, he was inclined to indulge in pleasantry at inopportune moments, thereby offending literal-minded friends and foes alike. Being neither a good party man nor a fighter, he failed to reach a high place in political life.

He suffered too, socially as well as politically, from a certain psychological blindness—an inability to gauge the probable reactions of his associates toward lines of speech and conduct which, to him, seemed to be based on the purest and most unimpeachable logic. He worshipped Reason, but unfortunately he appeared to his contemporaries to have created his goddess in his own image, and he was therefore, without in the least understanding why, very often her only worshiper among a jeering and hostile crowd. The failures which his intellectual pride and egotism would not allow him to attribute to his own mistakes, led him to despise the blind and stubborn multitude who refused to be rational. Neither socially nor politically did he have any regard for the ignorant, no matter how highly they might be placed. For trivial people and trivial talk, he had no time, although there is no doubt that a judicious cultivation of both would have greatly increased his professional, political, and social success.

Considering his temperament and the disappointments of his career, it is certainly greatly to his credit that his satire was so good natured, so lacking in fundamental cynicism. He had, in fact, the true philosopher's touchstone: he was able to laugh at himself as well as at others, and, ultimately, to face with equanimity the realization of the modest character of his own abilities. Perhaps no greater praise can be spoken of any man of talent than that he has been able to face this knowledge without bitterness.

BIBLIOGRAPHY

PART I

General

A. BOOKS AND ARTICLES

Adams, Henry, *History of the United States,* 9 vols. New York, 1889-91.
———— *Life of Albert Gallatin.* Philadelphia, 1879.
Adams, John, *Works,* ed. Charles Francis Adams, 10 vols. Boston, 1850-56.
Addison, Alexander, *Reports of Cases in the County Courts of the Fifth Circuit and in the High Court of Errors and Appeals of the State of Pennsylvania. And Charges to the Grand Juries of those Counties.* Washington, Pennsylvania, 1800. Reprinted, Philadelphia, 1883.
Alsop, Richard, and Dwight, Theodore, *The Echo.* New York, 1807.

Binney, Charles Chauncey, *Life of Horace Binney.* Philadelphia, 1903.
Binney, Horace, *Reports of Cases Adjudged in the Supreme Court of Pennsylvania,* 6 vols. Philadelphia, 1809-15.
Birch, Christian, *Ludwig Philipp der Erste, König der Franzosen; Darstellung seines Lebens und Wirkens,* 3 vols. Third ed., Stuttgart, 1851.
Brackenridge, Henry Marie, "Biographical Notice of H. H. Brackenridge, Late of the Supreme Court of Pennsylvania." *Southern Literary Messenger,* Vol. VIII, pp. 1-19 (January 1842). Reprinted in *Modern Chivalry,* editions of 1847, 1856, etc.
———— *History of the Western Insurrection in Western Pennsylvania, Commonly Called the Whiskey Insurrection.* Pittsburgh, 1859.
———— *Recollections of Persons and Places in the West.* Philadelphia, 1834. Revised ed., Philadelphia, 1868.
———— *Sixty Years in the North and Twenty Years in the South.* Pittsburgh, 1865.

Brown, David Paul, *The Forum; or Forty Years Full Practice at the Philadelphia Bar*, 2 vols. Philadelphia, 1856.

Bruce, David, *Poems Chiefly in the Scottish Dialect, Originally Written under the Signature of the Scots-Irishman, by a Native of Scotland*. Washington, Pennsylvania, 1801.

The Cambridge History of American Literature, 4 vols. New York, 1917-21.

Channing, Edward, *A History of the United States*, 6 vols. New York, 1919-25.

———— *The Jeffersonian System*. New York, 1906.

Cobbett, William, *Porcupine's Works*, 12 vols. London, 1801.

Collins, Varnum Lansing, *President Witherspoon*, 2 vols. Princeton, 1925.

———— *Princeton*. New York, 1914.

Conner, Martha, "Hugh Henry Brackenridge at Princeton University, 1768-1771." *Western Pennsylvania Historical Magazine*, Vol. X, pp. 146-62 (July 1927).

Craig, Neville B., *Exposure of the Many Misstatements in H. M. Brackenridge's History of the Whiskey Insurrection*. Pittsburgh, 1859.

———— *The History of Pittsburgh*. Pittsburgh, 1851.

Crumrine, Boyd, *The Courts of Justice, Bench and Bar of Washington County, Pennsylvania*. Chicago, 1902.

Doddridge, Joseph, *Notes on the Settlement and Indian Wars of the Western Parts of Virginia and Pennsylvania, from the Year 1763 until the Year 1783 Inclusive*. Wellsburgh, Virginia, 1824.

Duyckinck, Evert A., and Duyckinck, George L., *Cyclopedia of American Literature*.

Eakin, Myrl I., "Hugh Henry Brackenridge—Lawyer." *Western Pennsylvania Historical Magazine*, Vol. X, pp. 163-75.

Eastman, Frank Marshall, *Courts and Lawyers of Pennsylvania*, 4 vols. Chicago, 1922.

Faÿ, Bernard, *L'Esprit Revolutionnaire en France et aux États-Unis à la Fin du XVIIIe Siècle*. Paris, 1924.

Findley, William, "An Autobiographical Letter." *Pennsylvania Magazine of History and Biography*, Vol. V, pp. 440-50.

Findley, William, *History of the Insurrection in the Four Western Counties of Pennsylvania*. Philadelphia, 1796.

Fithian, Philip Vickers, *Journal and Letters: 1764-1774*, ed. J. R. Williams. Princeton, 1900.

Forman, Samuel Eagle, *The Political Activities of Philip Freneau*. Johns Hopkins University Studies in Historical and Political Science, Baltimore, 1902.

Freneau, Philip, *Poems*, ed. Fred Lewis Pattee, 3 vols. Princeton, 1902-07.

Futhey, John Smith, *History of Chester County, Pennsylvania*. Philadelphia, 1881.

Gibson, John, *History of York County, Pennsylvania*. Chicago, 1886.

Hamilton, Alexander, *Works*, ed. Henry Cabot Lodge, 12 vols. New York, 1904.

Harding, Samuel B., "Party Struggles over the First Pennsylvania Constitution." *Annual Report, American Historical Association*, 1894, pp. 371-402.

Hazen, Charles Downer, *Contemporary American Opinion of the French Revolution*. Baltimore, 1897.

Heartman, Charles F., *A Bibliography of the Writings of Hugh Henry Brackenridge*. New York, 1917.

Hildreth, Richard, *History of the United States of America*, 6 vols. New York, 1856.

Jackson, M. Katherine, *Outlines of the Literary History of Colonial Pennsylvania*. Lancaster, 1906.

Journals of the House of Representatives of the Commonwealth of Pennsylvania. Lancaster, 1803-05.

Journals of the Senate of the Commonwealth of Pennsylvania. Lancaster, 1803-05.

Konkle, Burton Alva, *George Bryan and the Constitution of Pennsylvania*. Philadelphia, 1922.

———— *The Life and Times of Thomas Smith*. Philadelphia, 1904.

The Lee Papers. Collections of the New York Historical Society, Vols. IV-VII. New York, 1871-74.

Libby, Orin Grant, *The Geographical Distribution of the Vote of the Thirteen States on the Federal Constitution, 1787-1788.* Madison, Wisconsin, 1894.

Loshe, Lillie Deming, *The Early American Novel.* New York, 1907.

Loudon, Archibald, *A Selection of Some of the Most Interesting Narratives of Outrages Committed by the Indians in their Wars with the White People.* Carlisle, 1808. Reprinted, Harrisburg, 1888.

Loyd, William Henry, *Early Courts of Pennsylvania.* Boston, 1910.

McCandless, Wilson, *Ex-President John Quincy Adams in Pittsburgh in 1843. Address of Welcome, by Wilson McCandless, and Mr. Adams' Reply; together with a Letter from Mr. Adams Relative to Judge Brackenridge's "Modern Chivalry."* Pittsburgh, 1873.

Maclean, John, *History of the College of New Jersey, from its Origin in 1746 to the Commencement of 1854,* 2 vols. Philadelphia, 1877.

McMaster, John Bach, *A History of the People of the United States,* 8 vols. New York, 1883-1913.

McMaster, John Bach, and Stone, Fred D., *Pennsylvania and the Federal Constitution, 1787-1788.* Philadelphia, 1888.

Madison, James, *Writings,* ed. Gaillard Hunt, 9 vols. New York, 1900.

Martin, John Hill, *Bench and Bar of Philadelphia.* Philadelphia, 1883.

Meigs, Wm. M., "Pennsylvania Politics Early in this Century." *Pennsylvania Magazine of History and Biography,* Vol. XVII, pp. 462-90 (January 1894).

Minutes of the Eleventh General Assembly. Philadelphia, 1787.

Moore, Frank, *American Eloquence, a Collection of Speeches and Addresses by the Most Eminent Orators of America, with Biographical Sketches and Illustrative Notes,* 2 vols. Philadelphia, 1857.

Newlin, Claude M., "Dialects on the Pennsylvania Frontier." *American Speech,* Vol. IV, pp. 104-10 (December 1928).

———— "Henry Marie Brackenridge." *Dictionary of American Biography,* Vol. II.

———— "Hugh Henry Brackenridge." *Dictionary of American Biography,* Vol. II.

———— "The Writings of Hugh Henry Brackenridge." *Western Pennsylvania Historical Magazine,* Vol. X, pp. 224-56 (October 1927).

Oberholtzer, Ellis Paxson, *The Literary History of Philadelphia.* Philadelphia, 1906.

Paine, Thomas, *Writings,* ed. M. D. Conway, 4 vols. New York, 1894-96.
Paltsits, Victor Hugo, *A Bibliography of the Separate and Collected Works of Philip Freneau.* New York, 1903.

Papers of the Governors, ed. G. E. Reed. *Pennsylvania Archives,* Fourth Series, Vol. IV. Harrisburg, 1900.
Papers Relating to What Is Known as the Whiskey Insurrection in Western Pennsylvania, 1794, ed. J. B. Linn and W. H. Egle. *Pennsylvania Archives,* Second Series, Vol. II. Harrisburg, 1876.
Parrington, Vernon Louis, *Main Currents in American Thought,* 2 vols. New York, 1927.
Paulding, James Kirke, *Life of Washington,* 2 vols. New York, 1845.
Pope, John, *A Tour through the Southern and Western Territories of the United States of North America; the Spanish Dominions on the Mississippi, and the Floridas; and Many Uninhabited Parts.* Richmond, 1792.
Princeton University, General Catalogue, 1746-1906. Princeton, 1908.
Proceedings and Debates of the General Assembly of Pennsylvania. Philadelphia, 1787.
The Proceedings of the Executive of the United States Respecting the Insurgents, 1794. Philadelphia, 1795.

Quinn, Arthur Hobson, *A History of the American Drama from the Beginning to the Civil War.* New York, 1923.

Report of the Trial and Acquittal of Edward Shippen, Esquire, Chief Justice, and Jasper Yeates and Thomas Smith, Esquires, Assistant Justices, of the Supreme Court of Pennsylvania, on an Impeachment, before the Senate of the Commonwealth, January, 1805. Lancaster, 1805.
Robin, Claude C., *New Travels through North America.* Translated by Philip Freneau. Boston, 1784.
Roberts, Samuel, *Digest of Select British Statutes, Comprising those which, according to the Report of the Judges of the Supreme Court Made to the Legislature, Appear to Be in Force in Pennsylvania, with some Others.* Second ed., Philadelphia, 1847.

Sharpless, Isaac, *Two Centuries of Pennsylvania History.* Philadelphia, 1900.
Smith's Laws of the Commonwealth of Pennsylvania, 4 vols. Philadelphia, 1781-90.
Smith, W. Roy, "Sectionalism in Pennsylvania During the Revolution." *Political Science Quarterly,* Vol. XXIV, pp. 208-35.
Smyth, Albert H., *Philadelphia Magazines and their Contributors.* Philadelphia, 1892.

Trial of Alexander Addison, Esq., President of the Courts of Common-Pleas in the Circuit Court Consisting of the Counties of Westmoreland, Fayette, Washington and Allegheny, on an Impeachment, by the House of Representatives, before the Senate of the Commonwealth of Pennsylvania. Lancaster, 1803.
Tyler, Moses Coit, *The Literary History of the American Revolution,* 2 vols. New York, 1897.

Van Doren, Carl, *The American Novel.* New York, 1921.
Venable, W. H., *Beginnings of Literary Culture in the Ohio Valley.* Cincinnati, 1891.

Wagner, Pearl E., "Economic Conditions in Western Pennsylvania During the Whiskey Rebellion." *Western Pennsylvania Historical Magazine,* Vol. X, pp. 193-209 (October 1927).
Warfel, Harry R., "David Bruce, Federalist Poet of Western Pennsylvania." *Western Pennsylvania Historical Magazine,* Vol. VIII, pp. 175-89, 215-34 (July and October 1925).
Washington, George, *Diaries, 1748-1799,* ed. John C. Fitzpatrick, 4 vols. Boston and New York, 1925.
Watson, John Fanning, *Annals of Philadelphia and Pennsylvania,* 2 vols. Second ed., Philadelphia, 1856-57.
Wiley, Richard T., *Sim Greene and Tom the Tinker's Son.* Philadelphia, 1907.
Williams, Charles Richard, *The Cliosophic Society, Princeton University.* Princeton, 1916.
Williams, Mildred, "Hugh Henry Brackenridge as a Judge of the Supreme Court of Pennsylvania, 1799-1816." *Western Pennsylvania Historical Magazine,* Vol. X, pp. 210-23 (October 1927).
Witherspoon, John, *Works,* 4 vols. Philadelphia, 1802.
Woodbury, Margaret, *Public Opinion in Philadelphia, 1789-1801.* Smith College Studies in History, October 1919 and January 1920.

B. NEWSPAPERS

The Aurora (Philadelphia).
The Democratic Press (Philadelphia).
The Freeman's Journal (Philadelphia).
The National Gazette (Philadelphia).
The Pennsylvania Gazette (Philadelphia).
The Pennsylvania Packet (Philadelphia).
The Pittsburgh Gazette.
Poulson's Advertiser (Philadelphia).
The Tree of Liberty (Pittsburgh).

C. MANUSCRIPTS

Appearance Docket of Westmoreland County, Pennsylvania. In the office of the Prothonotary, Greensburg, Pennsylvania.
Deed Book B, Westmoreland County, Pennsylvania. In the office of the County Clerk, Greensburg, Pennsylvania.

PART II

A.

A Chronological List of the Published Writings of Hugh Henry Brackenridge

NOTE: Only short titles of books are given. Full titles will be found in Heartman's *Bibliography of the Writings of Hugh Henry Brackenridge*.

1772
A Poem on the Rising Glory of America. Philadelphia, 1772.

1774
A Poem on Divine Revelation. Philadelphia, 1774.

1776
The Battle of Bunkers-Hill. Philadelphia, 1776.

1777
The Death of General Montgomery, at the Siege of Quebec. Philadelphia, 1777.
The same. Norwich and Providence, 1777.

1778
Six Political Discourses founded on the Scripture. Lancaster, 1778.

1779
The United States Magazine: A Repository of History, Politics and Literature. Vol. I. Philadelphia, 1779.
An Eulogium of the Brave Men who have fallen in the contest with Great-Britain. Philadelphia, 1779.
Eine Lobrede auf diejenigen tapfern Männern, welche in dem Streit mit Gross-Brittanien gefallen. Philadelphia, 1779.

1783
"Narrative of a late Expedition against the Indians, with an Account of the barbarous execution of Col. Crawford and the wonderful escape of Dr. Knight and John Slover from Captivity in 1782." In the *Freeman's Journal, or North American Intelligencer*, April 30, May 7, May 14, May 21, May 28, 1783.
The same in pamphlet form. Philadelphia, 1783.

1786

"An Account of Pittsburgh." *Pittsburgh Gazette*, July 29, 1786. (This number of the *Gazette* is not extant. The article was reprinted in *Gazette Publications*, pp. 7-19.)

"Answer to a Challenge. By H. H. Brackenridge, Esquire." *Pittsburgh Gazette*, August 19, 1786.

"Observations on the Country at the Head of the Ohio River, with digressions on various objects." *Pittsburgh Gazette*, August 19 and September 2, 1786. (Earlier numbers of the series are not extant.)

"To the Electors of Westmoreland County." *Pittsburgh Gazette*, September 9, 1786. (Announcement of candidacy for State assembly.)

Letter, signed "Angus MacMore," criticising sentimental treatment of the Indians. *Pittsburgh Gazette*, September 30, 1786. (Reprinted in *Gazette Publications*, pp. 34 *ff.*)

1787

Letter from Philadelphia, dated December 16, 1786, reporting activities of the State assembly. *Pittsburgh Gazette*, January 6, 1787.

Letter defending vote on county bill in the assembly. *Pittsburgh Gazette*, March 17, 1787.

An answer to criticisms by William Findley. *Pittsburgh Gazette*, March 24, 1787.

"To the Inhabitants of the Western Country, by Hugh Henry Brackenridge." *Pittsburgh Gazette*, April 21, April 28, May 5, May 12, May 26, June 2, June 9, 1787.

"A Masque, Written at the Warm Springs, in Virginia, in the year 1784." *Pittsburgh Gazette*, June 16, 1787. (Reprinted in *Gazette Publications*, pp. 35-40.)

Defense of vote in the assembly on the Pittsburgh church bill. *Pittsburgh Gazette*, June 23, 1787.

A letter to the Rev. S. Barr. *Pittsburgh Gazette*, June 30, 1787.

"Notes on the Observations of William Findley. By Hugh H. Brackenridge." *Pittsburgh Gazette*, August 3, 1787.

"Narrative of the Transactions of the late Session of Assembly, so far as they respect the System of Confederate Government, proposed by the General Convention of the States at Philadelphia. By Hugh Henry Brackenridge." *Pittsburgh Gazette*, October 27, 1787. (Reprinted in *Gazette Publications*, pp. 53-7.)

"On the running away of the nineteen members of assembly from the house, when it was proposed to call a convention to consider the new system of congressional government; and on the apology made by them in their address. A Hudibrastic." *Pittsburgh Gazette*, November 3 and 10, 1787. (Reprinted in *Gazette Publications*, pp. 58-69.)

"On the Popularity of [William Findley]." *Pittsburgh Gazette*, December 1, 1787.

1788

"Address and reasons of dissent of the Minority of the Convention of the state of Pennsylvania to their constituents." *Pittsburgh Gazette*, January 26, 1788.

"Cursory Remarks on the Federal Constitution." *Pittsburgh Gazette*, March 1, and March 15, 1788. (The contribution of March 1 was reprinted in *Gazette Publications*, pp. 77-9.)

"Apology for the Dissentients in the State Convention." *Pittsburgh Gazette*, March 8, 1788.

A "sermon" in favor of the Federal Constitution. *Pittsburgh Gazette*, March 22, 1788.

A "sermon" in favor of the Federal Constitution. *Pittsburgh Gazette*, March 29, 1788.

A "sermon" in favor of the Federal Constitution. *Pittsburgh Gazette*, April 5, 1788.

A "sermon" in favor of the Federal Constitution. *Pittsburgh Gazette*, April 12, 1788.

"On the Road Bill." *Pittsburgh Gazette*, April 26, May 3, May 10, and May 17, 1788.

"To the Dissenting Assemblyman, by An Assenting Constituent." *Pittsburgh Gazette*, May 10, 1788.

Oration on the Federal Constitution. *Pittsburgh Gazette*, June 28, 1788. (Reprinted in *Gazette Publications*, pp. 271-3.)

1789

A "sermon" on village slander. *Pittsburgh Gazette*, March 29 and June 20, 1789. (Reprinted in *Gazette Publications*, pp. 86-93.)

"On the Subject of calling a Convention." *Pittsburgh Gazette*, May 23, 1789. (Reprinted in *Gazette Publications*, pp. 80 ff.)

1792

"Thoughts on the Present Indian War." *National Gazette*, February 2 and 6, 1792.

BIBLIOGRAPHY 319

"Thoughts on the EXCISE LAW, so far as it respects the Western Country." *National Gazette,* February 9, 1792.
Modern Chivalry: containing the Adventures of Captain John Farrago, and Teague O'Regan, his Servant. Vol. I. Philadelphia, 1792.
Modern Chivalry. Vol. II. Philadelphia, 1792.

1793
Modern Chivalry. Vol. III. Pittsburgh, 1793.
"Louis Capet Lost his Caput." *National Gazette,* April 20, 1793.
Open letter to President Washington criticising his neutrality proclamation. *National Gazette,* May 15, 1793.
Oration of July 4, 1793. *National Gazette,* July 27, 1793. (Reprinted in *A Political Miscellany,* New York, 1793; and *Gazette Publications,* pp. 121-4.)

1794
Discussion of the "proposition of Genet" and the President's attitude toward it. *Pittsburgh Gazette,* January 18, 1794. (Reprinted in *Gazette Publications,* pp. 273-6.)
Open letter to the militia pleading for justice to himself. *Pittsburgh Gazette,* November 8, 1794.

1795
Incidents of the Insurrection in the Western Parts of Pennsylvania, in the Year 1794. Philadelphia, 1795.

1796
Scots poems addressed to David Bruce. Printed in *Poems of the Scots-Irishman* (1801), and *Gazette Publications* (1806).

1797
Modern Chivalry. Vol. IV. Philadelphia, 1797.

1798
"Sketch of the ground of my opposition to the Election of John Woods as a Representative in Congress." *Pittsburgh Gazette,* September 29, 1798.
Political letter to the "Citizens of Greene, Washington, and Allegheny Counties." *Pittsburgh Gazette,* September 1, 1798.

1799
Article regarding a new newspaper in Pittsburgh. *Pittsburgh Gazette,* December 7, 1799.

1800

Open letter to Judge Alexander Addison. *Tree of Liberty*, November 15, 1800.
"On the Blackguard Writers in *Scull's Gazette* in the course of the Summer." *Tree of Liberty*, November 22, 1800.

1801

"Jefferson: In Imitation of Virgil's Pollio." *Tree of Liberty*, January 24, 1801.
"To the Scots-Irishman." *Tree of Liberty*, February 14, 1801.
"On the Means of Reconciling Parties." *Tree of Liberty*, June 20 and July 11, 1801. (Reprinted in *Gazette Publications*, pp. 224-7.)
"A dogrel said to be by Auld Brackie on the Scots-Irishman." *Tree of Liberty*, June 20, 1801.

1804-1805

Modern Chivalry. Philadelphia, Baltimore, Washington, Pittsburgh, and Norfolk, 1804. (Contains the material originally published in the two volumes of 1792.)
Modern Chivalry. Part II. Carlisle, 1804. (Issued in 1805.)
Modern Chivalry. Part II, Vol. II. Carlisle, 1805.
"The Standard of Liberty." *Freeman's Journal*, July 16, 17, 18 and 19, 1805.
"Ironical Reasons for a New Governor and Constitution." *Freeman's Journal*, July 29, 1805.
"Amicus Amicorum, or a Friend of the Friends of the People." *Freeman's Journal*, July 31 and August 1, 1805.
"An Address to the Federalists." *Freeman's Journal*, August 3 and 5, 1805.
The Standard of Liberty. Philadelphia, n.d. [1805].

1806

Gazette Publications. Carlisle, 1806.

1807

Modern Chivalry. Vol. II. Philadelphia and Richmond, 1807. (Contains the material originally published in the volumes of 1793 and 1797.)
Modern Chivalry. Part II, Vol. I. Philadelphia and Richmond, 1807. (A reprint of the volume printed at Carlisle in 1804.)
Modern Chivalry. Part II, Vol. II. Philadelphia and Richmond, 1807. (A reprint of the volume published at Carlisle in 1805.)

1808

Modern Chivalry. Vol. I. Philadelphia and Richmond, 1808. (Contains the material first published in the volumes of 1792, 1793, and 1797.)

"The Trial of Mamachtaga" and "The Lone Indian." (In Archibald Loudon's *Indian Narratives.* Carlisle, 1808.)

"On the Conclusiveness of a Foreign Court of Admiralty." *Poulson's Advertiser,* January 6, 1808. (Reprinted in *Law Miscellanies,* pp. 345 *ff.*)

1810

"The United States vs. Judge Peters." *Democratic Press,* March 15, 1810. (Reprinted in *Law Miscellanies,* pp. 362 ff.)

1811

An Epistle to Walter Scott. Written at Pittsburgh, during the sitting of the term, by H. H. Brackenridge, on reading "The Lady of the Lake"—Taken up by chance. Pittsburgh, 1811.

1814

Law Miscellanies. Philadelphia, 1814.

1815

Modern Chivalry. Vols. I, II, III, and IV. Philadelphia and Richmond, 1815. (Contains all the material previously published and a volume of new matter.)

Modern Chivalry. Vol. I. Wilmington, 1808. (Contains the material of the volumes of 1792, 1793, and 1797.)

1819

Modern Chivalry. Vols. I and II. Pittsburgh, 1819. (A revised edition containing all the parts previously published, with the exception of slight omissions.)

NOTE: The portion of *Modern Chivalry* which originally appeared in 1792, 1793, and 1797 has been frequently reprinted, e.g., in 1825 (Wilmington, Delaware), 1846 (Philadelphia), 1856 (Philadelphia), and 1926 (New York).

B.

Manuscripts Containing Writings by Hugh Henry Brackenridge

Autograph Collection of Simon Gratz. Historical Society of Pennsylvania, Manuscript Department.

Bradford Papers. Historical Society of Pennsylvania, Manuscript Department.

The Jefferson Papers, Vol. 109. Library of Congress.

Satires against the Tories and Father Bombo's Pilgrimage to Mecca.
Ms.Am. 0336. Historical Society of Pennsylvania, Manuscript
Department.

INDEX